PEACEWORK

Oral Histories of
Women Peace Activists

TWAYNE'S
ORAL HISTORY SERIES

Donald A. Ritchie, Series Editor

PREVIOUSLY PUBLISHED

Rosie the Riveter Revisited: Women, The War, and Social Change
Sherna Berger Gluck

Witnesses to the Holocaust: An Oral History
Rhoda Lewin

Hill Country Teacher: Oral Histories from the One-Room School and Beyond
Diane Manning

The Unknown Internment:
An Oral History of the Relocation of Italian Americans during World War II
Stephen Fox

FORTHCOMING TITLES

Life on the Homestead: Interviews with Women of Northwestern Colorado, 1890–1950
Julie Jones-Eddy

Between Management and Labor: Oral Histories of Arbitration
Clara H. Friedman

Grandmothers, Mothers, and Daughters:
Oral Histories of Three Generations of Ethnic-American Women
Corinne A. Krause

JUDITH PORTER ADAMS

PEACEWORK

Oral Histories of
Women Peace Activists

᠅

TWAYNE PUBLISHERS · BOSTON
A Division of G. K. Hall & Co.

Peacework: Oral Histories of Women Peace Activists
Judith Porter Adams

Twayne's Oral History Series No. 5

Copyright 1991 by G. K. Hall & Co.
All rights reserved.
Published by Twayne Publishers
A division of G. K. Hall & Co.
70 Lincoln Street
Boston, Massachusetts 02111

Copyediting supervised by Barbara Sutton.
Book design and production by Janet Z. Reynolds.
Typeset by Huron Valley Graphics, Inc., Ann Arbor, Michigan.

First published 1990.
10 9 8 7 6 5 4 3 2 1

The paper used in this publication meets the minimum requirements
of American National Standard for Information Sciences—Permanence
of Paper for Printed Library Materials, ANSI Z39.48-1984. ⊗™

Printed and bound in the United States of America.

Library of Congress Cataloging-in-Publication Data

Adams, Judith Porter.
    Peacework : oral histories of women peace activists / Judith
Porter Adams.
        p.   cm. — (Twayne's oral history series ; no. 5)
    Includes bibliographical references and index.
    ISBN 0-8057-9106-X
    1. Women and peace—History.   2. Peace movements—United States—
History.   3. Pacifists—United States—History.   4. Pacifists—
United States—Biography.   I. Title.   II. Series.
JX1965.A33   1990
327.1′72′082—dc20
    [B]   90-41683
                                                                   CIP

Contents

Foreword	vii
Acknowledgments	ix
INTRODUCTION	1

1. PROFILES OF PEACEMAKERS: OUR MOTHERS, SISTERS, SELVES

Ethel Barol Taylor	11
Jeanne Morin Buell	21
Esther Pollack Newill	31
Cora Weiss	37
Isobel Milton Cerney	47

2. TRIAL BY FIRE: WARTIME AWAKENING TO PEACE AND JUSTICE ISSUES

Helma Wilhemina Waldeck	59
Lisa Schmidt Kalvelage	67
Mariagnes Aya Uenishi Medrud	77
Marii Kyogoku Hasegawa	85

3. CIVIL RIGHTS AND PEACE

Mary Bess Owen Cameron	95
Erna Prather Harris	101
Enola Maxwell	107
Doris Cohen Jones	117

4. CONSCRIPTION AND CONSCIENCE:
   THE VIETNAM WAR

   Beth Robinson Coats   127
   Rose Rosenthal Dellamonica   133
   Lucy Whitaker Haessler   141
   Margaret Dawson Stein   149

5. VISION AND ACTION

   Madeline Taylor Duckles   159
   Louise Page Austin Wilson   167
   Rose Marciano Lucey   175
   Elise Hansen Boulding   185
   Dagmar Saerchinger Wilson   193
   Mary Buell Duffield   201

   CONCLUSION   209

   Bibliography   221
   Index   224

Foreword

Among the warriors and conventional politicians commemorated in marble and bronze in the U.S. Capitol stands the statue of a peacemaker, Jeannette Rankin, bearing the motto "I cannot vote for war." A pacifist, and the first woman to serve in Congress, Representative Rankin was the only member to vote against American entry into both world wars. In later years, while in her nineties, she protested against the Vietnam War. Along with many of the women who appear in *Peacework*, Jeannette Rankin was an active member of the Women's International League for Peace and Freedom, and like them her interests in peace and women's rights became interwoven and indivisible. While her story was told in headlines and cast in bronze, the oral histories recorded in this book are those of the rank and file of the peace movement. These women spoke out, lobbied, picketed, and risked imprisonment for their beliefs. In so taking their stand, they redefined themselves and women's role in society.

Oral history may well be the twentieth century's substitute for the written memoir. In exchange for the immediacy of diaries or correspondence, the retrospective interview offers a dialogue between the participant and the informed interviewer. Having prepared sufficient preliminary research, interviewers can direct the discussion into areas long since "forgotten," or no longer considered of consequence. "I haven't thought about that in years," is a common response, uttered just before an interviewee commences with a surprisingly detailed description of some past incident. The quality of the interview, its candidness and depth, generally will depend as much on the interviewer as the interviewee, and the confidence and rapport between the two adds a special dimension to the spoken memoir.

Interviewers represent a variety of disciplines and work either as part of a collective effort or individually. Regardless of their different interests or the variety of their subjects, all interviewers share a common imperative: to collect memories while they are still available. Most oral historians feel an additional responsibility to make their interviews accessible for use beyond their own research needs. Still, important collections of vital, vibrant interviews lie scattered in archives throughout every state, undiscovered or simply not used.

Twayne's Oral History Series seeks to identify those resources and to publish selections of the best materials. The series lets people speak for themselves, from their own unique perspectives on people, places, and events. But to be more than a babble of voices, each volume will organize its interviews around particular situations and events and tie them together with interpretive essays that place individuals into the larger historical context. The styles and format of individual volumes will vary with the material from which they are drawn, demonstrating again the diversity of oral history and its methodology.

Whenever oral historians gather in conference they enjoy retelling experiences about inspiring individuals they met, unexpected information they elicited, and unforgettable reminiscences that would otherwise have never been recorded. The result invariably reminds listeners of others who deserve to be interviewed, provides them with models of interviewing techniques, and inspires them to make their own contribution to the field. I trust that the oral historians in this series, as interviewers, editors, and interpreters, will have a similar effect on their readers.

DONALD A. RITCHIE
Series Editor, Senate Historical Office

Acknowledgments

In this decade-long project I have been assisted by many students, friends, and colleagues in the peace movement. I gratefully acknowledge all those who contributed their interviewing skills and those who contributed their stories to the project. Choosing among the almost five hundred hours of interviews was my hardest task because every interview is meaningful, important, and moving. I convey my particular thanks to the interviewers who contributed to this volume with me: Emily Breckenridge, Linda Shaw Cristofferson, Joan Drake, Jean Gore, Babs Glover, Leah Halper, Brenda Parnes, Christy Redman, Cary Robnett, and Stephanie Smith.

Photographers Renée Burgard and Helen Golden have contributed their considerable talents in capturing the images of these women as eloquently as the women's own words capture their spirit. Renée contributed black-and-white portraits and Helen contributed beautiful color slides. Barbara Jurin and Linda Long also assisted by making copy prints of historical photographs.

Thanks are due also to the Student Center for Innovation in Research and Education at Stanford, Stanford Workshops on Political and Social Issues, and the Women's Studies Program at San Jose State University where I taught the classes that formed the basis for this project and was able to involve the women and men who became part of the project. I also thank Linda Shaw Christofferson who worked with me to teach our first oral history classes at Stanford and who has contributed an interview to this volume. Thanks to Roxanne Nilan of the Stanford University Archives who believes in the value of oral history and has faith in women and in my work. I also thank Barbara Sawka of the Archive of Recorded Sound at Stanford for her advice and support. I appreciate the support of the Institute for Research on Women and Gender at Stanford, where I have been an affiliate scholar, for good afternoon discussions of feminist theory and work in progress. Thanks also to Alta of Shameless Hussy Press, Berkeley, California, for her interest in our work.

Many individuals too numerous to list have contributed financially. They have my thanks for their generosity and patience. The Money for Women Fund, in memory of Barbara Deming, contributed to our project, as did the Jane Addams Peace Association.

My special thanks go to members of the Women's International League for Peace and Freedom (WILPF), who adopted our project as part of their seventieth anniversary celebration, and to Women Strike for Peace (WSP), for their resources and dedication to peace, justice, freedom, and nonviolence. This volume is dedicated to the women who are no longer with us—they live on in their words, our memories, and our struggles.

The interviews with Elise Boulding, Beth Coats, Lucy Haessler, Doris Jones, Mariagnes Medrud, Esther Newill, and Louise Wilson are in the WILPF Oral History Collection in the Stanford University Archives and are used with permission. The interview with Bess Cameron is used with permission of the New York Metropolitan Branch of WILPF.

Finally, I thank my friends and family for their support and encouragement, especially Elizabeth Fischbach for late-night editing sessions and a sense of balance through it all and to Renée Burgard, who said one day, "Why don't we write a book about these wonderful women?"

The Women's Peace Oral History Project interviews will be deposited in the Swarthmore College Peace Library.

My final thanks to series editor Donald Ritchie for his gentle editing and example as an oral historian, and to editors Anne Jones, Barbara Sutton, and Janet Reynolds for their patience and perseverance as they nurtured this manuscript through to final copy.

What a foolish notion,
That war is called devotion,
when the greatest warriors
*are the ones who stand for peace.**

*"Foolish Notion" by Holly Near. © 1980 by Holly Near, Hereford Music. Used by permission. Photograph of the Women for Peace contingent of a march for "jobs, peace, and freedom," San Francisco, mid-1970s.

INTRODUCTION

THE WOMEN'S PEACE ORAL HISTORY PROJECT

The Women's Peace Oral History project began in 1979; as often happens, I got involved in it without knowing it would become a life's work. These women have become my friends, mentors, and models; we're in it together for the long road to peace.

I moved to California with my husband, Terry, in the early seventies. Terry had left the Air Force as a conscientious objector. He came to that decision without the benefit of a peace community, counsel, or really anything but his own thoughts, my support, that of a few friends, and the writers of the New Left whose works he read.

It would have seemed natural for us to seek the peace community when we came to California, but we became absorbed in finding a place to live and work. We went on with our lives, having that experience behind us, but in subtle ways it changed us. I had the chance through his questioning of authority to redefine my own sense of what was right and what was patriotic. As for so many of our generation, the Vietnam War became a crucible that changed us forever.

I became more actively involved in the women's movement following our divorce and through that I met some extraordinary older women active in women's rights and the peace movement. They helped me place Terry's decision to withdraw from the military in a historic context of pacifism. I had thought of myself as a supporter of his action; now I began to think through my own position and learn about the role of women in the peace movement and the links between it and justice and liberation movements. I wanted to continue working for peace, although by then the Vietnam War was over. What do peace activists do in time of peace? Many activists who came to the peace movement during the Vietnam War left when peace was declared; for those of us who stayed in the

1

movement, the focus shifted back to nuclear proliferation, conventional wars still being fought all over the globe, and related social justice issues still to be resolved. Activists in my community continued their nonviolent struggle against violence in our homes, in the streets, and among nations and warned of the effects of militarism on the economy and environment. They showed the way for lifelong activism and peaceful change.

I began to divide my time between issues in feminism and pacifism, joining the Women's International League for Peace and Freedom (WILPF), taking part in marches and rallies and supporting women's issues. The women of WILPF, mostly older than I was, encouraged me to find a level of involvement that fit my life. I came upon the idea of interviewing the women in the branch to preserve some of their experiences, as well as to learn from their stories. I could involve my students in the interview project and introduce them to some of the vital older women in our community, who had been politically active longer than most of us had been alive. What a surprise for them to learn that much of what they had studied in school wasn't the only "truth." What a surprise to meet women who had marched with their mothers in suffrage parades, who knew Martin Luther King, Jr., who integrated lunch counters, who were pioneer women in science, who combined home, family, work, and political activism, and who kept their sense of hope and humor through long struggles.

Some of the women we interviewed came to class to talk about their personal experiences as we read and discussed World War I, the Spanish Civil War, the depression, the Korean War, World War II, and Vietnam. History became so much more personal when linked to the lives of real women. College students, fresh with the assumption that the women's movement and civil rights began in the 1960s, learned about the deeper roots of protest in this country. We learned to examine "truth," testimony, and memory to broaden the base of our understanding of historical events.

The project began with an old tape recorder held on my lap in a noisy Peace Center office, constantly interrupted by the phone. We started to preserve the history of one branch of WILPF in Palo Alto, California; we have grown to a national project to record women peacemakers active in WILPF, Women Strike for Peace (WSP), Society of Friends (Quakers), Fellowship of Reconciliation (FOR), and other peace groups since most of the women were active in several peace and justice groups. We have interviewed over ninety women, and the project continues.

Our fundamental interest was in women's peace groups, primarily WILPF and WSP. We asked each branch to identify women over sixty who had been active in peace and justice work for a significant part of their lives—not necessarily the leaders, in this often leaderless movement, but the rank-and-file members, women whose energies held the organizations together. We developed an interview outline and sample questions: How did they become involved in peace and justice issues? Who were their models? How had world events affected their opinions? What was their first work for peace? How did they keep going? Did women have something unique to give to the peace movement?

We chose older women for our narrators because we wanted to talk to the women whose experiences spanned the longest period of involvement. What kept these women active and hopeful for so long? We also wanted to preserve their stories before it was too late. Human memory and life are fragile resources. The Women's Peace Oral History Project is a long-term one; I hope still to be at it when I'm old enough to be interviewed myself.

This book is not intended as a history of women's involvement in the American peace movement; rather, it presents a number of testimonies of individual women who for significant portions of their lives have been peace seekers and peacemakers. One should not make broad generalizations from these testimonies—the sample is too limited to do so; rather, they should be read as the moving witness to what some women have done for peace and how their lives have been shaped by a concern and struggle for peace. Their memories may not always be accurate about the dates of events, the size of demonstrations, or other facts. Other documents exist against which to compare their recollections. In some cases their memories of original motives and feelings may be altered by their present motives and feelings; that process of re-collecting the past and integrating it with the present is also of interest to the oral historian.

Each woman was interviewed for between two and five hours, and these published excerpts represent just a small part of their individual interviews and of the total sample. Although I have edited the selections, they remain primarily in each woman's own words. I can hear the cadence of their speech in these written pages because their voices echo from the tapes and from our conversations. I hope some of the flavor of the spoken word comes through to others.

Some of the interviews I have selected are of women of color and women with socioeconomic backgrounds different from the predominantly white, middle-class, college-educated women in our sample. They do not represent the actual percentage of women of color or of non–middle-class, non–college-educated women in the overall membership of either WSP or WILPF. These women are actually a relatively small proportion of the overall membership. As the groups evolved, they generally attracted women of the same class as the founders, despite concern about issues of race and class and efforts to recruit women of color or different socioeconomic levels. In part, this was because nonwhite women were often occupied by the more basic issues of day-to-day survival and did their primary activist work in civil rights or union organizing, and only secondarily worked for peace.

WOMEN'S WAYS TO PEACE

The decision to interview members of WILPF and WSP as a base for this collection seemed appropriate to me. The groups have overlapping membership in the San Francisco Bay area, where the project began. In addition, they provide an excellent organizational contrast: WILPF, founded in 1915, has a long productive history and a strong, traditional organizational structure. Jane Addams and Emily Greene Balch, both leaders of WILPF, each won the Nobel Prize (Addams in 1931 and Balch in 1946). WSP, founded in 1961, lacks those historical roots and chose to organize as loosely connected autonomous groups that sponsor separate peace actions and make decisions by consensus. Although Women's Action for Nuclear Disarmament (WAND) and other women's peace and disarmament groups have been active in the movement, WILPF and WSP are the two primary women's peace organizations still active in many communities. Their combined memberships total approximately forty-five thousand. WILPF has over twenty thousand members in international sections and fifteen thousand in the United States. WSP has approximately ten thousand members in the United States. The members of WILPF and WSP still active in the 1990s tend to be active or at least card-carrying members of a wide variety of organizations for social and political change, both secular and religious. But their primary peace organization for the most intense period of activity was either WILPF or WSP. They found the most support and sisterhood in the women's organizations, although most are firm believers in coalition work with other groups. Many of the women would not define themselves as feminists, but they are strong, active, independent women and effective spokeswomen for the right of women to enter the public sphere and influence national and international policy.

One reason for the appeal of WILPF has been its multi-issue approach to peace and its international presence as a nongovernmental organization (NGO) in the United Nations. It has combined community organizing on local issues with education and action on global concerns. Its members conduct thoughtful studies about issues and are active in education and lobbying; they are also out on the streets picketing, distributing leaflets, and demonstrating.

WSP was organized forty-six years after WILPF and for many of its members was their first involvement in political organizing, although the five founding members were active in SANE (Committee for a Sane

Nuclear Policy) in Washington, D.C. Despite its relative youth compared to WILPF, it has been an active and influential organization. At its peak, WSP involved over fifty thousand women in the United States in one-day actions in cities all over the country in protest of atmospheric atomic testing, and it has maintained a core of active members ever since, despite its penchant for a loose organizational style. Founding WSP members consciously chose a nonhierarchical, nonorganizational approach to planning their actions and initially rallied around a single issue—atmospheric atomic testing. They hoped they would succeed where other peace organizations had failed. The organization has continued, broadened its focus, and adopted a more traditional structure over time, with a national office and official membership. Some of the sharper differences between WSP's organizing (or nonorganizing) principles and WILPF's have lessened over the years, but WSP remains proud of its unique place in history.

Such diversity among organizations working for the same causes gave breadth to the movement and allowed individuals to find an appropriate niche for their activism. However, the same diversity had the potential to split the movement into competitive factions. The challenge to women's peace groups has been to retain their distinctive character without splitting the movement, already under pressure by exterior forces.

In order to be effective, some women's peace groups have sought to appeal to a broad base of women without diluting their force and energy and to meet specific needs without alienating other segments of the peace movement. WSP, however, had little historical consciousness of the past women's peace movement, and what it knew of earlier groups, it rejected for newer, nonhierarchical, more direct-action-oriented approaches. Something was lost in that lack of awareness and rejection. WSP never directly challenged the sex roles of women and men or raised gender issues in the political sphere.

The enduring irony of the women's peace movement is that now, as in the early days of WILPF, women are still subject to the double bind of the separate sphere argument. They are expected to embody the "womanly" virtues of peace and nurturance and practice them in the home. Yet when they attempt to bring these "private" values into the public sphere, they are attacked as unwomanly and naive because they have stepped down from their pedestals and challenged the status quo of institutionalized violence and male power structures. Women peacemakers wage a continuing battle against the limitations culture has placed on them as they fight the larger battle against war.

Women have constituted a significant part of the grass-roots movements for peace and justice. They continue to goad the world's conscience toward disarmament. There have been victories; that we are still here on this troubled globe is in part due to the dedication of these women to peace. Yet their stories often remain untold.

THE WOMEN INTERVIEWED

The roots and lifeblood of the peace movement are often found in older women much like those whose stories are contained in this book. Like most activists, they did a good deal of their work behind the scenes. They leave to us their groups' minutes and newsletters, posters and banners, photographs and other documentation of their lifelong struggle. They leave behind changed laws and institutions. They also leave a long list of things still to be accomplished. Beyond these legacies, they leave a fragile yet lasting gift: their words and stories resonate in our memory long after their passing and remind us of the personal costs and rewards in the struggle for peace and justice.

In many ways these women are not notable. They are daughters, sisters, workers, wives, mothers, grandmothers, neighbors, and friends. Some are well educated; others learned in the school of experience. They come from a variety of backgrounds and heard the call to peace work in different ways and at different times in their lives. They are not unusual except that they gave voice to and acted upon dreams of peace and justice many of us share but never actualize. They risked criticism and censure for their words and deeds. They looked through the complex web of national and international politics and did not lose heart. They decided to act and to act together because they could not ignore their individual sense of responsibility. They filled the generation gap with their experience, their convictions, and their faith in the future. They have left us with the richest legacies: faith that our single, common acts are significant, hope for change, and persistence in working for peace despite almost overwhelming odds.

Their individual acts may seem insignificant, but taken together they are the roots of a grass-roots movement. For example, one women we interviewed served on the telephone committee for fifteen years, keeping meticulous books of the membership names, telephone numbers, and issues that required action. Another woman staffed the local peace center for ten years, including the Vietnam War years when there were several bomb threats and one break in. Several were washed down the steps of the San Francisco City Hall with fire hoses during demonstrations outside the House Un-American Activities Committee hearings. One woman carried membership cards, peace literature, and a card table in her car so that she could set up an information table at a local fair, garage sale, or demonstration she might drive by. During the Vietnam years women's peace groups organized pickets every day at local induction centers, often committing civil disobedience. One WILPF branch's board meeting during the Vietnam War was conducted in jail where all the officers were being held after a civil disobedience action. They did informational picketing at local shopping centers. They protested ships transporting napalm during the Vietnam War. The small voice of conscience in the local paper was theirs. They had brothers, husbands, sons, and then grandsons of draft age. They led silent vigils protesting war. They were called "vicious bitch" and "Communist dupe" for standing up for peace and international communication. They hosted visiting Soviet women. Today, as then, they persist.

The organizational dynamics and goals of WILPF, WSP, and other peace organizations to which the women interviewed belong are important as a context for their peace work; however, the purpose of this collection is not to profile the organizations, but to present the women's stories—to tell how and why they became involved in peace and justice issues and what sustains them. Not all the women came to peace work early in their lives with supportive, activist families, nor do they all consider themselves pacifists. World War II was for many with families in Europe and in concentration camps a just war. But the atomic bomb changed the topography of war and international politics. Many of the women came to peace work as parents, working for a peaceful future for their children and grandchildren.

Most of the interviews share two common factors, however. First, nearly all the women expressed modesty about their own work. Many suggested someone else we should interview instead of them, someone who was more active or more articulate. Once they began speaking about their own peace work, however, they gave us a wealth of experience and insight. Second, although a few of the women had leisure time and financial resources to devote to peace work, most had to balance their responsibilities for a job and family with their conviction that they must work for peace. Where they could, they found time to make phone calls to organize a rally, combine dinner for the family with a potluck to discuss strategy with other activists, or write letters to their legislators while the laundry was in the washer. Like factory piecework, their peace work, done in bits during the busy days of "women's work," is all too often undervalued, even by the women themselves. Yet the cumulative effect of their efforts made considerable changes in local community attitudes, legislation, and the forward momentum of the peace movement.

The women came to activism by many paths; they defy categorization. Most were involved in multiple causes and recognized the interconnections between issues. Moreover, the selection of interviews in this book represents only part of one collection. Our hope is that these women's stories will stay in the readers' memories and move them to act as well as to remember.

I.

Profiles of Peacemakers:
Our Mothers, Sisters, Selves

Ethel Taylor, 1989.

ETHEL BAROL TAYLOR

A columnist once wrote a piece about me, and she called it "Rebel in White Gloves" because in the early days of Women Strike for Peace, women in the demonstrations, who were generally middle-class women, wore white gloves and hats. We used to do things like sit down and not move in the middle of the street, or whatever, but we would have our hats and white gloves on.

Ethel Barol Taylor was born in Philadelphia in 1916. Her primary peace affiliation has been with WSP, which is credited by many as having raised American consciousness and pushed Congress to enact the first test ban treaty in 1963. That WSP continues to exist today, having addressed nuclear disarmament, the Vietnam War, and other challenges to peace and freedom, is in large part due to the energies of women like Ethel. She says WSP is "more than an organization; it's a state of mind. I've never been part of a group . . . where there was such a feeling of sisterhood." She has been thinking for a long time of writing a book along the theme "Something Funny Happened on the Way to Disarmament: An Anecdotal Report on WSP's Struggle with the Bomb." She has a gift for starting branches and instigating activity and keeping her sense of humor.

She now finds time to sculpt—she wanted to go to art school as a young woman but her family couldn't afford the costs during the depression so she went to business school instead. She has made a figure of a woman tossing a baby into the air; it has become the joyous symbol of WSP, given each year to the Woman of the Year. She lives near Philadelphia.

I was catapulted into the peace movement with the dropping of the bomb on Hiroshima. I was pretty apolitical up to that point. I used to get up in the morning and start polishing the furniture until I was polishing the polish. I thought, "There must be more to life than this."

I had a daughter, who was a small child at the time of the bombing of Hiroshima. When I read that the blast was so hot that in some circumstances it incinerated people and left just a shadow against a stone wall, creating instant fossils, I was numbed. I realized there were wars and there were wars, but this kind of war must never happen again.

There were others who felt as I did, and a few of us got together and talked. We formed a little group of women to study issues. I think even then, even though I was not political, I had this feeling that because women are not in positions of power and they have no role in policy-making, that maybe what we had to do was to make policy outside of government and demand of government that it listen to us.

A columnist once wrote a piece about me, and she called it "Rebel in White Gloves" because in the early days of Women Strike for Peace, women in the demonstrations, who were generally middle-class women, wore white gloves and hats. We used to do things like sit down and not move in the middle of the street, or whatever, but we would have our hats and white gloves on. I always thought that was a real protection until once we had an action, and hundreds of people went to Washington as a symbolic takeover of Congress. We walked and we came to a narrow street. The police said, "Cross this street and you get arrested." Well, I realized then that, what could they do? They're not going to electrocute me. They're not going to shoot me. It was much easier to cross that street than not to cross that street, so I crossed that street. Then we sat on the ground and waited to be arrested. We sat down, but we decided we weren't going to be yanked by our armpits, we were going to walk like ladies to the police van. We did. We got to the jail, and they opened the back door of the van. I looked out, and there was a five-foot drop to the ground. I waited for the policeman to help me down. The policeman came around and said, "Jump, sister." So I jumped into an entirely new world.

I didn't realize when I first got involved, when our government dropped the bomb on Hiroshima and Nagasaki, that this was going to be a lifetime commitment. I think if I had realized it I might have thought twice, because it's a terrible business to be in.

I think most of the pressures were because of the issues, not just because I was a woman—although there were those pressures too. You can really go nuts working for something and never have a success, never see enough change. Camus said, and I'm paraphrasing, that just because a thing is hopeless doesn't mean you don't get involved. That sounds gloomy. We have had some successes, but when I first got in, there were two bombs and they were both ours. Now there are 50,000 in the world. Someone once said, "Ethel, that's going to look lousy on your resumé." I think I developed an early anger that leaders had such contempt for the people they were supposed to be leading. That anger really has sustained me.

My anger is directed towards leaders who threaten the lives of children now and those yet unborn with their inhumane policy of nuclear weapons. We started because of children, because the scientists and doctors said that the strontium 90 and iodine 131 from the atomic tests would poison our children's milk and cause cancer. When we first organized we sent out a call throughout the streets with leaflets saying, "Take your children off milk." We sent our children's baby teeth to a lab in St. Louis to determine if strontium 90 was present. We were concerned about an epidemic, like polio before vaccines, except that polio is viral and these were man-made epidemics. Those who were then children now have children themselves.

My work in Women Strike for Peace sustains me. Outside of my family and my friends, WSP to me is the most important entity. It started out as a one-day action. We would meet every week around my dining room table to plan our "strike." There was a sugar bowl in the middle of the table for contributions toward the action. Some women stopped going to the hairdresser and did their own hair and put the money in the bowl. Some put birthday checks in. In one remarkable case, a woman who had very little money would occasionally give blood to the Red Cross and put the five dollars in the bowl. There was a wonderful outpouring of feeling and sisterhood. We were the harbingers of the women's movement—our weekly round table discussions were certainly consciousness raising. It was really an amazing experience. We never pledged solidarity, but we really were solid.

It was like an electric current running through the country with these women who decided that this couldn't just be a one-day action; it would have to go on. That has been our strength and weakness, to try to make a permanent organization out of a one-day action. WSP is more than an organization; it's a state of mind. I've never been part of a group—and I've been in a lot of them—where there was such a feeling of sisterhood. That is not to say that we don't sometimes get furious at each other.

In 1962 some WSP members were brought before the House Un-American Activities Committee [HUAC]. In order to show solidarity, many of us wrote to the chair of the committee asking for an opportunity to testify. The hearing was in 1962. It was pure theater. There is a wonderful cartoon about the HUAC hearings and WSP. There are these two guys sitting up at the HUAC table, and one of them says, "What are we against, women or peace?" They were against both. When some of us walked in, the guards were standing out in the hall outside the hearing room minding baby carriages and babies. We all carried red roses, and each time a woman would step down from testifying, we would present her with a bouquet, and we would applaud. The committee kept threatening to clear the room. They were in real trouble! They couldn't get out of the sessions, and they became more and more permissive because we were all so good-natured. The committee was just ridiculed away. It was a tremendous victory against the hearings.

When Dagmar Wilson was asked if there were Communists in WSP, she responded very pleasantly by saying something like, "We welcome everyone as long as they are for disarmament." That was quite a statement to make. I can't really speak for the women who faced the committee, and what the effect was on their lives, but it wasn't like the early McCarthy days, when people informed on others because they feared for their jobs—or the brave ones who refused to buckle under were ruined professionally. Then there was the real unadulterated fear and panic, because once you were blacklisted, that was it. But these were middle-class women whose jobs did not depend on whether or not they were cleared by this committee. I'm sure the HUAC experience for the women questioned was pretty scary, but the great difference was the tremendous, enthusiastic support they received publicly. We had a clipping service of all of the newspapers that covered the hearings. It was all "hats off to the ladies," as I remember.

In 1975 President Ford appointed a commission on CIA activities within the United States. We learned things that amazed us. We learned that the CIA paid women, mostly housewives, one hundred dollars a week to infiltrate WSP. We suspected it at the time, but we didn't know. These women were instructed by the CIA to attend meetings, to show an interest in the purpose of the organization, and to make modest financial contributions, but not to exercise any leadership. It was a perfect cover; that describes half our membership—they don't want leadership roles, and they don't give too much money. The CIA also opened our mail. When we learned this we immediately instituted a suit against the CIA; we sued for surveillance, infiltration, and for mail opening. The first two charges were dropped, but they settled out of court for mail opening and gave us five thousand dollars. It wasn't so much money, but what a sweet moral victory! We used part of the money for our campaign to abolish the CIA.

During the Vietnam War three of us went to Hanoi to discuss the transmission of mail and packages between the prisoners of war and their families. It was the most exciting event in my life because up until that point very few letters were getting through. The Vietnamese didn't consider our soldiers prisoners of war under the Geneva Convention, since war had never been declared. They considered them war criminals. Others had gone before us, such as the Berrigan brothers, and a couple of prisoners had been brought home. The Vietnamese said they would not deal with the subject of prisoners with the government, but only with the peace movement.

A couple who lived in my neighborhood had a son who was shot down in 1964, and my trip was in 1969. They didn't know if he was alive or dead. When they heard I was going they asked me to try to find out about him, and they gave me a letter for him. They were active in the National Organization of Families of POWs [prisoners of war]. They notified their group that I was going to Vietnam, and I was flooded with letters for delivery from all over the country—letters for sons, husbands, and so on. We brought all these letters with us. While I was in Vietnam I asked the Vietnamese women about the status of my neighbors' son. One of the women left the room and later came back with a letter from him. His parents were at that time in Thailand on what they called a sentimental journey, so they could get as close as they could to where their son might be. I sent them a cable, "John is alive and well and I have a letter for you." Get this—it was Christmas. I came home with over thirty letters. My husband and I sat down, and we called families all over the country to tell them their son or husband was alive and that I was sending them his letter.

When I got back I was nearly deluged by the press. I was having a press conference in my living room when the phone rang. My husband answered it, and he came back and said, "It's a colonel from the Pentagon." I spoke to him. He said, "Mrs. Taylor, I want to tell you that you and the two other women have done a most marvelous job that no one else could do. I would like to send two of my men down just to discuss it with you." I said, "That won't be necessary. I'm glad you appreciate it." That night the television news anchor opened his broadcast by saying, "Local woman cited by the Pentagon." A couple weeks later the FBI warned the families not to accept any mail from our committee; they accused us of being a Communist group. Would you believe that one family wouldn't accept mail that we brought from their son?

After my trip to Vietnam I was invited to speak at many service clubs—the Optimists, the Lions, the Rotary. At one event I went through my talk, and in the back during the question period, they started chanting "Hanoi Hannah." They were very disruptive. While the chanting was going on the chair was in the process of presenting me with a plaque for distinguished service. When I left I met two of the men outside the room who I knew were opposed to the war. I said, "Why didn't you defend me?" They evidently were afraid to. So I wrote a letter to the membership chair who had invited me. I said, "There was a breath of fascism at that meeting. Reverend so-and-so and Mr. so-and-so were afraid to stand up and defend me even though they agreed with me when I spoke to them outside." I got a letter back from him that said, "I asked them and they said they never spoke to you."

I spoke at a church where as soon as I was introduced everybody got up and walked out. The minister had warned me when I came in. He said, "You are in John Birch Society territory." Another time I spoke on Worldwide Peace Day. The chairwoman had said, "After the program is over, Mrs. Taylor will go to the back where you can greet her and speak to her." By the time I got through speaking, I saw the backs of everybody moving out. She escorted me to the back, and a woman ran over to me, put something in my hand, and ran out. When I got outside I read the note. It said, "Please call me." I called her. She wanted to know something about WSP but was afraid to ask me. I shouldn't have been so naive. But they invited me, and I expected them at least to be courteous. I didn't realize how deep the hate was for me and what I stood for, because I was a very public person. I learned later, through my FBI files, that the federal attorney here in Philadelphia and the FBI communicated for a long time about whether I should be brought before the grand jury for sedition because of my activities in draft resistance.

During the Vietnam War, we had no choice but to lessen considerably our involvement in our original cause, atmospheric testing, and turn our attention towards the war. When we got back to our original concern after the war, it was evident that the government had not lessened its commitment to accelerating the arms race. The war economy had really multiplied. Our membership also suffered losses after the war; there was a drop, a lull. The women's movement also drew women away who decided to go back to school, to go out in the workplace, to have a career, and so on.

I think the situation today is so frightening because people seem to have forgotten the war in Vietnam, and they so glibly talk about Central America and the Persian Gulf. The war in Vietnam was a holocaust for the Vietnamese people. When I was in Hanoi a woman said to me, "The American people must put so little value on human life." I said, "You know, that's very funny, because that's what everybody says about Asians." She said she could not understand how Americans explain to their children why their fathers died nine thousand miles away from home.

Women have proven that they can be a tremendous power in their neighborhoods. Participatory democracy is alive and growing—mothers and fathers get together and block a street until the city provides a stop sign to save the lives of their children. We've got to make the antiwar issue that kind of issue so that people will get together, not only because the arms race is a threat to their children, but because of the tremendous displacement of funds for bombs instead of funds for people.

I made it very clear to my children, when they could understand it, that this was my decision to give my time and life to peace work. It wasn't my decision for them. But they were sympathetic. My husband was very supportive too; it was he who convinced me to go Hanoi. My son once said proudly to me, "You know, you're the only mother in the whole block who has ever gone to jail."

I'm tempted to say that women are more peace loving than men who are not in the movement, but then I think of women who have gained power, as of Prime Minister Thatcher, and the Falklands War in the 1980s, or I think of the screaming women who tried to prevent black children from entering a school in Arkansas during the civil rights movement, and the prolife women who scream, "Murderer!" outside family-planning clinics. I know it's a simplistic thing to say, but I think that women care; they have a very strong feeling for humanity. The bonds between women are stronger, perhaps, because women haven't gotten a fair shake; it unites women in a closer relationship than men, who generally are in power. At our meetings we dig into our experiences in order to create programs that might end war and bring peace and help our children. It seems like a womanly thing to do.

I think one of the amazing things about my own personal life is that on the day of that first protest, where we were challenged to cross the street, it was easier to do it than not to do it. The next time it was a natural thing to do. So many women in the movement did things that they never thought would be possible to do because of the deep feelings they had against war.

Here's a little story. I was appointed by President Carter to an International Year of the Woman conference. I was the only woman who represented a peace constituency—most of them were women's-issue-oriented. My job was to make peace a women's issue. After the conference the Carters had a reception for us at the White House in the East Room. WSP has bibs that we tied under our coats during protest marches; they say, "End the Arms Race, Not the Human Race." The other side says, "There is No Shelter from Nuclear War." I decided I was going to wear it under my coat and when Carter came to shake my hand, I'd reveal it.

To get to the reception we had to go through a subterranean passage. Everybody went through except me; when they came to me the security people said, "Just a moment." They got on the telephone, talking, talking. Then they said, "Okay, you can go too." I said, "Could you explain to me why everybody went through but when it came time for me to go through you had to make a telephone call?" He said, "There's a bad

Ethel Taylor out there. I made these calls, and they figured that if the president appointed you, you can't be the bad Ethel Taylor." Little did they know!

We got up on the dais, and the president came down the aisle and stepped up on the dais. The press was all there. He started to go to each woman shaking hands. He came to me, and I opened my coat and showed the bib with the message. His smile got caught in his teeth. He didn't shake my hand. He went right past me. As soon as it happened, the secretary of commerce, who was a woman, and a group of women, jumped in front of me and blocked me off from the media. Somebody said they looked over, and they saw me standing there and thought of Joan of Arc.

People have to align themselves with their elected representatives, and the elected representatives have to know that you're there watching. If a group of people set themselves up as watchdogs of a congressperson or a senator, I think it can have an effect. The letter writing which everybody is doing is a lifeline from the people to those who represent them.

I've survived by maintaining a sense of humor. It's better to laugh than to cry. I always got a tremendous amount of satisfaction and strength from the women with whom I worked. We can't always see immediate results from our work, but we have had an effect; we women have been dedicated and have made these issues ones that the government has to reckon with.

Jeanne Buell, 1988. Photograph © by Renée Burgard.

JEANNE MORIN BUELL

Christians through the centuries would pray that they would win
the war, as though it were possible that you could win a war.
When you wage a war and allow yourself to kill your enemy, how
could you hope to be heard in prayer?

Jeanne Morin Buell was born in 1916 in Crookston, Minnesota. In 1934 she joined the religious order of Sisters of Saint Joseph. She left the order in 1954, no longer able to live under the restrictions and repression it imposed. The Catholic Worker movement had a profound effect on her social conscience and inspired her to take a pragmatic approach to solving social and political ills. She married, worked with her husband in the civil rights movement, and joined in the protests against U.S. involvement in Vietnam. She is a long time member of the Fellowship of Reconciliation and is dedicated to change through nonviolence. She uses the legend of the Sabine women as an example of women and nonviolent action: the Romans raped and kidnapped the women, and when the Sabine men came to seek revenge on the Romans, the women stood between the men to stop the fighting. "Legendary as the story may be, it strikes a powerful blow at war and speaks loudly in praise of women as peacemakers." She now lives in Brookings Harbor, Oregon.

I remember very early in my life having a sense of fairness. When I was about three I came in the house with an angleworm and a caterpillar and demanded to know why one had "clothes" and the other did not.

My mother was outspoken when it came to the rights of others, and though there were no organizations for peace or justice as such in our town, she voiced her opinion on the rights of women and was very vocal in her criticism of the draft. She was years ahead of her time and saw the Catholic church as extremely patriarchal. So it was not without resistance that she let me go to the parish school when I reached second grade. Perhaps she feared I'd be propagandized, which I was.

My father was active in the clerk's union. He was very outspoken about the rights of the poor and the rights of people to organize. My father respected me as a person, and I can't remember that he ever said, "You can't do that," or "A woman just doesn't speak up." My parents were both involved in political campaigns and organizing, but they suffered war as something that couldn't be changed.

I liked the convent school I attended. A group of French nuns staffed the school with a considerable number of American women who had joined the order. Each day we had an hour of French and said all our prayers and sang hymns in English. Since I came from a bilingual home, it was easy sailing, and I was a source of pride to my parents and grand-parents when I spoke to them in what seemed like impeccable Parisian French.

Though boys were permitted to attend classes through the eighth, grade, the high school was exclusively for girls, not by the nuns' choice, but because of the bishop. The old codger looked upon women as tempt-ers of men, so he segregated the sexes from puberty on in school. But there were advantages: we girls concentrated on our studies and excelled in many ways, and we managed to meet with boys behind his back.

By the time I finished there I was completely convinced that being a nun was my calling in life. I saw my teachers as heroines dedicated to making the world a better place. Had there been alternatives like the Peace Corps then, I might not have chosen to join the order.

After three years of intense religious training in France, and hours of meditation and prayer, I returned to the academy as a kind of flunky working with the teachers.

I joined the Saint Joseph order in 1934. It was a small order and a poor order, so I got a taste of proverty. A lot of the children who came to us were poor. We ministered to the children of farmworkers at one time and did a lot of charity work. I got an education that way; we had a chance to mingle with the poor and minister to them. More than that we were poor ourselves. A lot of people say there's so much wealth in the Catholic church, but there's inequality and poverty there too.

My first ten years were spent in what I would call a sheltered convent because it was the training ground for the girls that came in. It was a boarding school, and there was very little contact with the outside. We were sort of a community within ourselves. So I didn't have much support from anywhere else. It was a closed world. Our lives were restricted in inconsistent ways. For example, we were not allowed to wear loafers because they were too casual, although they would have been comfortable. We were also not allowed to wear glasses with plastic frames because that was too "with it," so we had to wear gold or platinum frames. It was ridiculous for nuns who had made a vow of poverty to be wearing gold frame glasses.

In 1947 I met the superior general of our order from France. She was like the sun peering through rain clouds. I was struggling with what I saw as senseless repression of the nuns. She had the plastic framed glasses and said, "Aren't these the most practical things you could think of? I drop them, and my glasses don't break." She had visions of change. The long prayers should be shortened or scrapped to lessen the stress, she said; they had become a burden. When someone mentioned all the years she had spent teaching in Paris in secular clothes as a burden—the government had mandated that the habit be abandoned by teaching nuns—[the superior general] was amused. "Those were the best years of my life," she said. "The habit is a hindrance to our work. I grew closer to the students when I wore contemporary clothing." These were very revolutionary ideas at the time. She was really something, and she was not a young person. I think she was in her seventies at the time. But she had young ideas, and she knew what it was to be free. Here was someone after my own heart, and when I was called for my private interview with her, I found her seated on the floor like a guru. In France we had always knelt in the presence of a superior, and the custom continued in America. She asked me to sit, and I relaxed in her presence. I felt that my prayers had been answered. She drew me out. She told me that she would see to it that I attended college where I could develop my talents and acquire the credentials I needed to be a teacher.

I was sent to the College of Saint Catherine and was taught by another order of sisters, and there were a lot of lay professors. I got to thinking there might be another way to live. It's like there was a little hole in the dike and water was beginning to come through.

During the McCarthy era in the 1950s, I was in the nunnery and very little reading was allowed. It used to be read and digested for you to a great extent. It was considered a waste of your time. You were to read spiritual books. You were to read professional books. And if you were not teaching history or political science, you were not going to be concerned about McCarthyism. Before big elections came up, the social science teacher used to tell us who to vote for, and I resisted. I would listen to what was going on, and I would vote the way I wanted.

I'm ashamed to say that when I was in the order I didn't bat an eye when we dropped the bomb. People have asked me, "What were you doing the day the bomb was dropped?" I just say, "I was just absolutely oblivious of it." It seemed to be part of the war. Christians through the centuries would pray that they would win the war, as though it were possible that you could win a war. When you wage a war and allow yourself to kill your enemy, how could you hope to be heard in prayer? This is one of the worst things that could have ever been perpetrated, the idea of praying for victory. There's no way that praying to win a war could be a Christian thing. We began putting American flags in front of the church; in a Catholic church it meant putting the papal flag on one side and the American flag on the other, like these were our two loyalties, not to God, mind you, not our conscience, but the institution of the church and the country.

The greatest influence on me when I was a nun was probably the Catholic Worker movement, which was saying, "The teachings of the church have to be realized. They have to be brought about and lived." Here was Dorothy Day in the movement—and she was not even a born Roman Catholic. She joined the church after being a Communist—or when she was a Communist. She worked on the *Daily Worker.* I guess she became a Catholic because she discovered the gospel, and she saw in the gospel a liberation theology that needed to be lived and brought out: a concern for poor people, the rights of individuals and that sort of thing. Do you know that to her dying day she prayed that she would meet Marx in Heaven?

I taught school for seven years in Minneapolis in a parish with young parents who were about my age, and I saw that there were things that I could do and other kinds of work where I could possibly be better off than in orders and constrained as I was. I found that I did have some abilities to work out my own life. It is said that God never closes a door without opening another.

My motivation to resist came from the inside. We led a life that could enrich us in some ways, even though we were suppressed on the outside. On the inside, we had a prayer life that could lead to making us stronger, if we let it, because we had an hour of meditation each day, and that was a very personal type of prayer, where you could build yourself up. Now whether I got strength in that or whether my anger finally turned me around I'm not sure.

The priest who was director of the seminary became my friend; he was a psychologist. I spoke to him. I said, "I am at the end of my rope, and I can no longer tie a knot even and hang on, so I want to leave." He said,

"You've been here nineteen years, it just doesn't make sense." I said, "I became a nun because it seemed to me to be a good thing to do, and I don't give up easily. But I see now that I can't go on." I struggled a long time. They tried to keep me in there, for which I'm grateful, because I was worth saving.

So I left the order in 1954 after much soul-searching. I went to teach in public schools, and I enjoyed every moment of it. I didn't become involved right away in any kind of social work at all. I continued to be with the Catholic Worker movement. I met my husband; he, too, was disillusioned in a sense, not with the life he'd chosen, but with the hierarchy of the church. He found it lacking for not taking a public stand in numerous injustices like racism. He had gone to complain at the rectory about the racism he observed in the pastor. He wanted our bishops to speak out against militarism.

We were both ardent readers of the *Catholic Worker*, admirers of Dorothy Day, and enthusiasts of the social encyclicals. We got married and came out to California. It wasn't that easy because I had high expectations, having lived in a sheltered situation. I thought a husband would be like a knight in shining armor, but it wasn't that way. So we had a lot of adjusting to do. I had a lot of emotional baggage to leave behind me, but it was time to look ahead.

It wasn't until after our son was born and was probably about five years old that we became involved in farm workers' rights and the civil rights movement, through our church. From there we joined the Fellowship of Reconciliation [FOR]. Then came five years of resistance to our country's involvement in Vietnam. We stood in silent vigil with our friends on a corner in downtown in San Jose, California. We held signs declaring that we would be there every Thursday from twelve to one o'clock until the United States withdrew from the war. The Catholic Interracial Council didn't want to get involved in anti-Vietnam organizing. This later became our breaking point with our church because the priest there had told me that I should listen to President Johnson because he had been legally elected and knew what was best for our country. I came home, and I told my husband that, and he said, "I had a feeling that this was coming. Are we going to continue to go there and listen to this kind of thing and agree with it or are we going to pull out?" Well, you have to know what the Catholic church is like. It's not easy to stay and fight. There is just no place for dissent. We left the church like I left my order. We lived our Christianity in our own lives in our own house.

When we went into FOR I don't think we went in so much as Catholics, even as Christians, as we went in as aspiring pacifists. To be a pacifist is a full-time and a lifetime undertaking. I don't think that you become a pacifist overnight, because there's a resistance always, a tendency to violence in all of us. It's not easy to be a nonviolent resister. You constantly have to trim back your sharp edges and walk a thin line. You have to be both a strong person and offer peaceful resistance.

I feel that I am not afraid of anything. If I have done what my conscience thinks is right, I'm not afraid. If someone comes up to the door and says to me, "You're under arrest because you've spoken ill of your country," I will have to say, "Well, what did I say? I have nothing to hide." I don't feel threatened by things like that. If the day comes when we really are silenced, I suppose I would do it for reasons of expediency for the cause, but not to save my own skin. I find it really refreshing to see someone like Martin Luther King, Jr., who said, "If I must die, I must die." I like to think that I could do it. I don't find this foolhardy. I think if your cause is right, then you don't have to be afraid. If we do claim to have faith, then it has to be something that gives us strength and keeps us from being afraid. That's a message in Christianity; that's what the angel said, "Be not afraid."

Working for peace and justice is a source of stress for me, but you might as well be undergoing stress for something worthwhile than to be under stress because you can't get new carpets. Peace is worth being stressed about. My husband is a person with whom I could stand for peace. The more I have stood with him, the more he has loved me and the more he has stood beside me in what we're doing. I had a little card that was sent to me by one of the sisters in the mother house in France. It had a photograph of two calla lillies on it, and both of them are facing towards the sun, and it says on it, from Saint-Exupéry, "Love is two people looking together in the same direction."

We both know that we have a long way to go. My husband doesn't claim to be a pacifist. He says he's aspiring to be one, and heaven knows I haven't become a true pacifist yet, because I am very volatile. I don't really know how I would react if people started bombing us. Would I want retribution? I'm not sure. But you can always aspire to be a pacifist.

We picketed for fair housing, and we joined in a lot of movements and marches. We didn't go to Selma, Alabama, during the civil rights movement; we did our work right here in our own community. We came out, and we were counted. You'd be surprised how many people do not make connections between one issue and another. We brought up something concerning the farmworkers during the time the Catholic Interracial Council was involved in integration issues. The chair said, "This is not what we're about." Well you know, the farmworker situation is a racial one. They were using short-handled hoes because they were people of color.

When the farmworkers came, they came only in the summer to work in the beet fields, and there was always a special mass for them in the cathedral. It was said that it was a special—separate—mass because it was a Spanish service. But I also saw with my own eyes that many white people would not sit next to the Chicanos. Now we're finally like a little world; before we were just a ghetto. If the pastor has the guts the get up and say, "Finally we are catholic in this church and welcome all here as brothers and sisters," it will work. But leaders are afraid to do this because they might not get financial support from bigots. They would rather have the building and the money than the spirit of true religion.

As early as 1946 there was a movement within the Catholic church to bring racial rights to people; the Catholic church and all churches preached that all men are created equal, but they didn't live that way, because if they had, you wouldn't have a black Baptist church and you wouldn't have a black Methodist church. For instance, among the Catholic sisterhoods in this country, we had black sisterhoods, orders that had only black women in them. There was in the south what they called the black Crow Catholic church, and the Protestants had theirs. I don't think a priest would have stood at the door and said, "You can't come here because this is a white church," but when it came right down to the nitty-gritty, it happened in Minneapolis, which is certainly not the Deep South, when I was a nun.

When the priest saw Negroes moving into that parish, he said to me one day, "Look, do you know what's happening here?" and I said, "We should be getting more children in our school." And he said, "We won't." And I said "Why?" and he said, "These are Negroes; this is the kind of housing that will sell to black people. We will never pay off the parish debt if we integrate." I said, "You are prejudiced and dangerously un-Christian." The parents of many of the children I had taught banded together and took a petition to the archbishop demanding this pastor's resignation. He had refused to baptize a black baby and was forced to officiate. He fought the integration until the mid-sixties when it was integrated.

I went back years later, and it is all changed; there are blacks and a day-care center. I said, "This is karma in my own lifetime, to see a priest who is leading the women's movement to the extent that all the parishes refer to God as she, and even Gloria Steinem was asked to speak to the congregation. There are community masses where they sing together, and all the songs are projected on a huge screen." It has just swung around.

It's a battle for the human race. Until all of us are free, nobody will be. We should be there, wherever there is a group that is exploited. We're either what we preach in our lives or we're not; and if we're not, then it's not worth anything. Everyone can change. I have to believe that, and that's the thing that gives us hope. Some people just need a longer time. In my lifetime I've seen so much. I rode in a horse and buggy when I was a child and people are flying to the moon. Those are technological things. Other things take longer.

I'd like to think that I have made a difference on the planet and that I will be granted a few more years to help to save it. I am enough of a feminist to believe that women will have, or should have, the biggest role to play in making this world a safer and better place for everyone. It will be up to us to stand between our world and all that threatens to destroy us. If there has ever been any kind of movement for peace in any country or civilization, it has come from women. There were some outstanding conscientious objectors like A. J. Muste and Norman Thomas, but of course the media was with them. As soon as they made a statement everyone sat and listened because they were men. But who was saying, "We want to put an end to this. I don't want my son—anyone's son—going into battle." It was women. The actual protests on the streets and lying in front of napalm trucks and all that in our community, that was by women. Occasionally when they went to court they had a man for a lawyer because there were not that many women involved in law at that time. But the women were out there on the streets protesting.

Women have to learn that we all stand together or we all fall together. I think the women's movement has to be concerned with the mother, the homemaker, the working mother; all these people need their rights. You get the impression that the woman who has chosen to stay at home and take care of her family is not welcome in the women's movement, that she has nothing to contribute. It's the farthest from the truth because this woman can educate herself; she is right there where it is happening—she's taking care of a child or children, and she is seeing the community from its roots.

I believe that conflict should always be resolved peacefully, nonviolently, and that any kind of violence has to be the very last resort. There are boycotts and many things that you can do; it's pressure being brought to bear in a different way. Being a pacifist doesn't mean that we are passive. It's from another root, *pace* or *pax* in Latin, and it means peacemaker. It describes what we want to be. If we can't get along with each other, how do we expect nations to get along? I'd like to think that the faith and the hope and the love of many would be able to save the whole situation.

You can never tell who you have influenced. I've probably got miles to go, and I wish I did have years in which to do it, but we're all limited; we don't live forever. It's pretty hard to sit down and evaluate, to measure what we've accomplished. Our lives are like a weaving of some kind, and the top side makes sense. Finally in the end, people can make out a pattern, but it's not until it's complete that you see the whole pattern. If they look at the wrong side of it, there may be a lot of loose ends, but in the end it comes together.

Esther Newill, 1984. Photograph © by Renée Burgard.

ESTHER POLLACK NEWILL

*What is terribly important is how this struggle is
being waged, because how we treat each other and our
adversaries will shape what emerges from it.*

Esther Pollack Newill was born in Connecticut in 1911. Esther has
been a radical activist virtually all of her life, working to expose and
change social, economic, and political injustices. As a young woman,
she wrote several political plays, joined the Workers International
Relief in support of striking Kentucky coal miners, and worked in
New York City's Chinatown as the Works Progress Administration's
[WPA's] first teacher of English. She volunteered her time and professional skills in journalism to the antifascist movement from the
Spanish Civil War through World War II. Since the 1950s, Esther has
been active first with Women Strike for Peace and then with WILPF,
working for nuclear disarmament. In 1983, she and several other
WILPF "elders" joined over a thousand others in an act of civil
disobedience and spent sixteen days in jail for protesting the manufacture of nuclear weapons at Lawrence Livermore National Laboratories in California. She continues to agitate for change at the
Quaker retirement center where she lives in a community of other
activists in Santa Rosa, California.

On the night of Sacco's and Vanzetti's executions in 1927, I walked out of a church and I sat down on a step, crying, with my head in my hands. I had put years of my life into trying to keep them alive, and it was the end. Somebody went by and put a hand on my head and said, "We all feel that way, but we mustn't give way to this. We have to get up and go on and fight." Then he walked away. I never saw the person's face. But it was a night that I will never forget. It was the first overwhelming defeat. There were many to follow.

Knowing that these things happened to grown people when I was a child and knowing that people had commitments, such as my mother's, to fight against this kind of thing, I suppose whenever I came across any kind of injustice I reacted to it. I reacted to it on the premise that you could do something about it.

I was involved with the antifascist movement from its inception, but that was because I was involved with the radical movement itself before that, and I just flowed very naturally into the antifascist movement. I gave three years of my life to win the war in Spain, for the Republican side, and we lost. We tried everything. We raised money and solicited clothing. We solicited ads in support of our cause, and we wrote flyers. We wrote millions of letters to congressmen and senators and the president. Always the United States was helping the fascist side by sins of omission. The last was when they embargoed the sale of arms to both sides. Hitler and Mussolini were supplying the other side, so the U.S. embargo just strangled the Republicans. Our efforts to get the embargo lifted were defeated by a vote or two in Congress.

I was the publicity person for the first anti-Nazi organization to be formed in the United States after Hitler came to power in Germany. It was called the American Committee to Aid Victims of German Fascism. The first victims were not Jews; they were trade unionists, socialists, and Communists. But Hitler had to finance it; the way he financed it was by attacking the Jews. That was one of the techniques he took right from the Russian czar. In order to put himself on the map, Hitler turned people against the Jews. If they robbed the Jews, they had money to contribute to his cause.

Our antifascist committee had obtained photographs that were taken surreptitiously and smuggled out of the jails—that was before we used the words "concentration camps." I tell you, some of the photos were absolutely unbelievable. Some were of the backs of men who had been beaten with steel whips until their skin looked like raw meat. I took these photographs around, with stories that I wrote about them, to every newspaper in New York City. I saw the editor of every paper in the city and couldn't get anyone to print them. I remember one guy said, "I'm awfully sorry. I don't question this at all, but I can't print it." I brought documentation so he knew that it was authentic. But he couldn't—wouldn't—print it. It would mean his job. Only the left wing press would print them, because at that time everybody in the establishment was saying that you could do business with Hitler. It took a long time to realize that we couldn't.

I don't think the American people are stupid—brainwashed, yes, and misled. I know that one of the most important parts of this problem is that it's so hard to buck the establishment. When you present arguments to people that require that they buck the establishment, one of two things happens. Either they're the kind of people who say, "You're right—I've got to do something about it," or they're the kind of people who say inside themselves, "Well, I'm not going to buck the establishment," and they brainwash themselves. You accept the arguments of the establishment and believe them or convince yourself to believe them, because otherwise how can you look yourself straight in the eye in the mirror in the morning?

We have to have the courage to speak out in the face of opposition. When I was active with Women Strike for Peace in New York, there was a Catholic university I visited. The priest was very reactionary. He scared the hell out of everybody. They asked me to talk to him about the work we were doing. I said yes and went there wearing the clothes that I thought were going to impress him, my little white gloves and all that crap. As we talked I realized that he was very subtly trying to scare me by implying that what I was doing wasn't very patriotic and that there would be people who would be interested in knowing what we were doing. I'm very slow, but when I got the drift, I picked it up right away. So I said, "Well, you know, we're not exactly making a secret of our activities. In fact, the more publicity we get, the better we like it. If you want to contribute to it, that's fine." He realized that I was not scared and that I was answering him in kind. Just as subtly as he had become aggressive, that's how subtly he retreated.

The bulk of my activity before I came to California was with Women Strike for Peace. We had a very active nucleus of about seventy-five women. At one point we decided to have a milk strike—refuse to buy milk in Riverdale, New York. Now this was just one little suburban area. They were testing bombs in the atmosphere and the strontium 90 was getting into the food chain. We got dentists all over the country to save the first teeth of children. They were tested, and there was a lot strontium 90 in their teeth. We said, "You're poisoning our children. We're not going to feed them this milk." We wrote flyers and distributed them to all the grocers in the area telling them not to buy milk because we were calling a strike, and they would get stuck with the milk. Some of them believed us and some didn't. But when the local paper came out at the end of the week, they were hysterical because those who didn't pay any attention to us were stuck with a lot of milk. It was very successful. We got lots of media attention. We had public meetings and put pressure on the government. This was just one action of so very many.

Later, when I settled in California and got involved with WILPF, I took on the job of chairing the Disarmament Task Force. We worked hard for a test ban treaty and produced a booklet of articles that we wrote. We did a great deal of community education. But I can't be the chairperson of the committee anymore because I believe we've lost that battle. I don't believe anything can stop this war that's coming, except to have millions of people out on the streets in many countries saying to their governments, "We will not fight in another war." I don't see that happening. Short of that, the momentum for war is set, and it cannot be stopped. I don't know whether the use of atomic weapons can be prevented; I really don't know. We have seen wars since we've had the atomic weapons that have avoided their use, so one hopes.

People are protesting the arms race, worldwide, and being jailed for committing acts of civil disobedience. It took many, many years for me to put it all together and realize that jailing the opposition is a device of the powers-that-be to keep them off balance. They keep you so busy trying to take care of your own that you don't have enough time and energy and resources to fight the fight.

Being a dissenter in our society, being in opposition to the government, what does that mean? What happens when you are arrested? What goes on when you are in the power of your enemies? I finally came to the conclusion that there is only one way that you can possibly behave in that situation and maintain your integrity. You act just as you always did when you weren't under their power. You do not accept any of their premises for living or dying. They can kill you, but they cannot make you become a part of their value system. You have to accept, consciously accept, the fact that being a dissenter in any society is a very lonely business. You accept it as an occupational condition of life, in or out of their clutches.

It's good that there's a terminal point to life because humans can be just as inventive in their cruelty and injustice as they can be soaringly great and creative and beautiful. I have always had a great deal of righteous indignation about the terrible things we do to each other, so I think it's very good that there comes a time when you say, "That's enough. Let somebody else pick up the torch." But you can't give up until then.

The time I spent in jail for protesting the manufacture of nuclear weapons at Lawrence Livermore National Labs in California was an unforgettable experience. There were over five hundred of us in the women's jail. There were so many of us we were set up in a huge tent outside the jail, encircled by barbed wire. We had a ball. We organized ourselves into an active, exciting community. We had workshops on all aspects of the work at Livermore, on the arms race and its human costs, on the attrition of human services. We had exercise classes, from belly dancing to yoga. Small groups of women got together to rehearse for the shows that became a nightly feature, singing newly composed words to fit familiar songs, dancing, juggling, clowning, making costumes out of breastplates of Styrofoam cereal bowls and necklaces of toilet paper flowers and paper drinking cups. One group of women set themselves the task of making a thousand paper cranes, symbolizing peace, to send to Japan for Hiroshima Day. For about two dozen of us gray-haired old ladies—we were respectfully called "the elders"—a college instructor gave a virtual crash course in the feminist movement from the Abolitionist Period to the present.

Most important of all, we learned to manage among ourselves in order to maintain the solidarity that was our real strength. What is terribly important is how this struggle is being waged, because how we treat each other and our adversaries will shape what emerges from it. This takes learning. Day by day, of course, some of us had to leave the prison, for jobs, children, and other responsibilities. The arraignment meetings with the sheriff and his staff turned into an unforgettable ritual. When those who had to go responded to the call, we all rose, and those of us remaining formed two long lines, facing each other. With arms upraised, we made a tunnel for the departing women to pass through, as some wept and others sang until the last woman was on the waiting bus. Then the rest of us would surge forward and sing at the top of our voices, "Solidarity forever, solidarity forever, our union makes us strong!"

In time, the rest of us were taken to the main jail at Santa Rita and strip-searched, a most humiliating experience, given prison garb, and turned loose in the most depressing, dismal quarters imaginable. There we spent the next six days learning the true nature of our penal system— it is absolutely inhuman.

The nonviolent peace movement is moving forward in its own chosen direction, strongly and steadily. We are part of an ongoing process that goes back a long way and stretches ahead for as much time as it will take to win. It's not only my hope, but I really believe all the way down to the bottom of me that in the course of winning this struggle—and I know we're going to win it—we're going to change society.

Cora Weiss, 1990. Photograph by Anna Maria Fernandez-Gevaert.

CORA WEISS

I guess all my political activism has been characterized by feminism and an entrepreneurial spirit. We often didn't have options to choose from; we created our own. That's also wonderfully American. . . . We have taken what's best about our country and are using it. . . . There have been many other women's groups since the suffragist movement, but we were a group of women taking on our government and its ugly war.

Cora Weiss is one of those articulate, never-resting peace activists who leaves her distinctive stamp on the community. At the time of her interview she was the force behind Riverside Church's immensely successful peace education program in New York City. She was born in Harlem, New York in 1934. Her first political work was as a college student in Wisconsin, organizing against Senator Joseph McCarthy's red-baiting campaign. She studied law and social work and found herself in trouble with her supervisors for passing out birth control information to her clients. She and her husband hosted civil rights workers on "R & R" (rest and recreation) at their summer home to help them recover from the tensions of organizing. She was one of the founding members of Women Strike for Peace and, like many women in that organization, has a flair for the dramatic in peace actions. "We had no difficulty expressing outrage at the policy of our government. If you feel outraged, then you are prepared to do what might be considered outrageous things, which in retrospect seem perfectly reasonable because the most outrageous things are being done by governments who seem to care more about power than about life." She is currently the international representative of SANE/FREEZE: Campaign for Global Security, a member of the executive committee of Women for a Meaningful Summit, and a member of the Council on Foreign Relations.

I was born at Sydenham Hospital in Harlem because my mother had heard of its reputation for having the lowest infant mortality rate in New York City at that time. Sydenham, a small private hospital, subsequently suffered financial losses and was forced to close despite extraordinary efforts to keep it afloat, including public radio appeal by my father for support. It became a symbol of the inadequate resources that were placed at the disposal of the poor.

My mother came to America from Moscow and my father from Bialystock, then in Poland. He proposed to her on the Staten Island ferry, then still a nickel ride. We lived in the Bronx and eventually came to Westchester where I went to a WPA [Works Projects Administration] school. Occasionally I was stoned by the other children while walking to school, for being Jewish.

I first started political organizing as a student at the University of Wisconsin in 1952, the height of the McCarthy era. I spent as much time on the road as in class, helping run the "Joe Must Go" campaign begun by Leroy Gore, a Saulk City newspaperman who tried to have McCarthy recalled as U.S. Senator. I was often pelted with eggs, rotten tomatoes, and potatoes as we drove around the state collecting signatures. It later occurred to me that my car had New York State license plates. That was an important lesson in community organizing for an eighteen-year-old. The state officials, who probably owed their jobs to McCarthy, threw out many of the required signatures, alleging illegibility and invalidating the recall. It was my first experience in what is now called grass-roots organizing. We didn't have a name for it then.

At Wisconsin I chaired a student committee that wanted to invite the folk singer and activist Pete Seeger to sing. We were denied permission to use campus space—the long arm of McCarthy. Those were all politicizing experiences.

I was a fairly aware person, and I don't recall if I was frightened, but I do know that we were full of enthusiasm and determination and clear on what we were all about.

I chose Wisconsin in part because a professor at the law school there had helped write the United Nations' charter in 1945 and because of the legacy of the La Follette populist progressive tradition. I graduated in anthropology and then studied law. As I recall, in each of the three years of law school, out of a class of one hundred students, there was virtually one black, one Native American, and one woman. I learned all about tokenism. I thought we were called upon so out of proportion to our numbers that the other students didn't have to worry about being prepared. That experience planted the seeds of feminism.

I met the man who would become my husband, and the "Mrs." took precedence over an L.L.D. It was unthinkable that a woman would compete with her husband in the same field in those years. If you married a lawyer, you didn't become a lawyer.

We moved to New York City, where I went to the Hunter College School of Social Work, then called the Louis M. Rabinowitz School of Social Work. It was the first year of the now-established school's existence, so, in a sense, I was a pioneer. My classmates were all mature, many just back from Korea, going to school on the GI Bill of Rights. I majored in psychiatric social work and was first assigned to a welfare center in Yorkville and then to an outpatient mental health clinic on the lower east side of New York City. I remember handing out birth control information to women who were following their mother's pattern of bearing "out of wedlock" children. I felt the only way to liberate them was to show them a diaphragm. My supervisors, New York City employees and Catholic, didn't like that at all. I was severely reprimanded. Birth control education wasn't yet legal. Perhaps that was an example of being a bit ahead of the times. My determination hasn't diminished over the years.

I was rather active in the civil rights movement of the 1950s. My husband, Peter, and I helped bring the South north. That is, we used to offer R & R in our summer home to young people who had done a year of organizing in the field in Georgia or Mississippi and who were really brutalized by the experience. They would come up and spend a week or two with us on Martha's Vineyard. In doing so, we were also introducing blacks to a community where no blacks had ever lived before. There was plenty of civil rights work to do in the North, too. Rest was essential for these young SNCC [Student Non-Violent Coordinating Committee] workers. They were drained, abused, and hurt. They needed food and love and approval—everything a good Jewish mother is supposed to provide.

Peace and justice work fold very easily into each other. I consider myself an integrationist. Could you ever imagine really having justice and preparing for war, too? Your resources would have to be committed to the military, leaving little for human needs. One can't be concerned about racial discrimination and not also about the other threats to our security. Racism foments violence. Testing nuclear weapons is a threat to our security, and it is a contributing factor to the destruction of the ozone layer, a threat to our ecological security. Denying full freedom to the people of Namibia and providing military support to the Contras of Nicaragua or mercenary armies also threatens global security. And all the money voted for the military budget each year, in our country and around the world—that's a threat to our economic security and to our social programs so desperately in need. I believe we must look at security in a comprehensive way and work for global security.

When I was pregnant and had children in the late 1950s and early sixties, America was at the height of its nuclear testing program in Yucca Flats, Nevada. I joined Women Strike for Peace. We had many meetings, called study groups, in my living room. We studied strontium 90. We studied the science and technology of testing, and we studied lobbying. We approached newspaper editors, hoping they would give more publicity to the dangers of nuclear war. We marched in protest, wearing little sailor hats, in front of a navy ship that was to carry nuclear weapons.

I think it's fair to say that my generation of women were self-taught on these issues. I was a young mother; we were middle-class women who were trained in the professions. We were all taking care of our children at home. It was the "breast-feeding generation." I was forever with a baby on one hip, or both, going to meetings or demonstrations. I remember bringing boxes of crackers or bagels to keep the kids quiet, until they could join in and lick stamps, too. I was always racing away from meetings at three o'clock to pick them up from school. At my fiftieth birthday party our kids put on a skit and at one point my son said, "Had I known then what was keeping my mother, I wouldn't have minded waiting so long for her to pick us up." That makes a mom feel better. I must have kept them waiting often.

I organized a home and children. Women have a lot of organizing abilities. I believe there is a uniqueness to women's organizations, and creative genius is one of them. Women Strike for Peace did many things for the first time, ahead of the other peace groups. During the Vietnam War we were first to go to the Pentagon and take off our shoes and bang on the doors to let Robert McNamara, then secretary of Defense, know we wanted to see him. It was the first time in history that the Pentagon had closed its doors to the public. They must have been afraid of women.

We weren't afraid. We were outraged and had no difficulty expressing it. If you feel outraged, then you are prepared to do outrageous things, which in retrospect seem perfectly reasonable because the most outrageous things are being done by governments which seem to care more about power than about life.

To really involve women of color, it took a group of us in 1969 to found a new organization, the Jeannette Rankin Brigade, named after the first woman member of Congress, who was a pacifist. We recognized the link between poverty in this country and the obscene expenditure of funds to support the war in Vietnam. We joined hands with women from other organizations to build a march on Washington calling for an end to the Vietnam War and against racism and poverty at home. The war against Vietnam wasn't popular at home. Many considered it illegal, lacking proper congressional authority and using weapons and chemicals of mass destruction. Meanwhile, basic needs at home could have been met with the millions wasted killing people ten thousand miles away.

There were always questions about whether our activities were good for the children. For example, we worried if we'd be home at three o'clock. I could go anywhere, do anything as long as I was at home to welcome the children from school. Frequently reporters or neighbors asked if our husbands' reputations could withstand our peace and justice work. Would our political actions affect their businesses, their success? No one wondered whether a man's work was harmful to children or survival or [that it] affected his wife's success. I did not worry about the implications of my activities on my husband's career. And I have been careful. I've chosen not to be arrested (except once, when we were both arrested together). But I've always supported those who chose to be arrested as a matter of conscience. Our joint arrest was when the United States started bombing Cambodia, and under the constitutional right of redress of grievances we asked to see the speaker of the House, Carl Albert. When he refused to see us, we lay down in the entrance to the chamber. There were several hundred of us. At home, we have two pictures framed back to back of Peter and me being taken away in police cars. We were united in our arrest, protesting the bombing of Cambodia and the widening of the war.

I have been a strong proponent of teach-ins, of conferences, education and grass-roots organizing. I believe that an educated activist is the best citizen. Raising the consciousness of people to the dangers of war-making and to the possibilities of peace-making—to the real alternatives that are available—is important. One of the realities is that the press has escalated its requirements for making something newsworthy. A legitimate, democratic, well-done, and intelligent action, such as is done at Riverside Church in New York City by the disarmament program, will not get press. But if you spill blood or get run over by a train, it becomes news fit to print. As we won't fall into that trap, we risk not being covered by the media.

I guess all my political activism has been characterized by feminism and an entrepreneurial spirit. We often didn't have options to choose from; we created our own. That's also wonderfully American—expressing the ideals of rugged individualism, independence, creativity, and entrepreneurial skills. We have taken what's best about our country and are using it. We believe in the common good. There have been many other women's groups since the suffragist movement, but we were a group of women taking on our government and its ugly war.

Women Strike for Peace was important in the antiwar movement and to its leadership. Were it not for my role in WSP, I would not have been elected a national co-chair of the Mobilization for Survival and one of five—the only woman—in charge of the November 15, 1969, demonstration at the Washington Monument now referred to as the turning point in antiwar sentiment in this country. Women in WSP provided a fulcrum. We were anxious to participate in coalition activities. In the 1969 March on Washington, we insisted that if we were going to bring women and families to a national demonstration it would have to have certain characteristics. For example, we supported the presence of elected officials in the march and as speakers, which was opposed by certain antiwar groups. We insisted that marchers have the choice of doing or not doing civil disobedience. Had we not insisted and succeeded, we could not have assured a sense of protection to our members and the demonstration would not have been open to the public in as wide a way. We were a wedge, an opening, to a broader community, without compromising political goals.

Our high heels and gloves were a symbol with which many people could identify. It's not that we put the other demonstrators down. We marched with hippies and yippies. But we dressed as we did every day. We created entry levels for people into the peace movement. In every demonstration there was always a first; it was always a first demonstration for some of the women. It wasn't successful if it wasn't a first for lots of people.

One can't sit back and despair and suggest that we haven't accomplished anything. Every human being in this country knows how dangerous an atomic bomb is and [he or she] didn't learn it from the president of the United States or his science advisors. And remember how reluctant Americans are now to send troops abroad. After Vietnam we said no to U.S. troops in Angola and have continuously rejected presidential appeals to send troops to Central America. The peace movement is the conscience of the country. We wouldn't be a great democracy without one.

I keep at it because I have three children and I'd like to be a grandmother. I mean that both literally and symbolically. We've done too much good in this world, in this life, to see it blown away. War is the wrong word to use for nuclear weapons. Wars are won or lost. There is always a winner and a loser in a war. If there is a nuclear catastrophe, it will probably result from accident, and the chances of accident are high because of the number of weapons in the world. There would be no winners. I like to describe a band around the world. It is a "contraband" of outrageous violence. Wars of intervention and so-called conventional wars are all happening in the southern half of the world, the poorer half, the half with people of color. These wars must be stopped, too. We must call for deep cuts in conventional weapons while we call for the abolition of nuclear weapons. We must not allow the slow reduction of nuclear weapons to become the excuse for "modernization" of remaining weapons or as a trade-off for other weapons. We know we deserve better and we can do better. There is an alternative to dropping bombs and shooting guns. Nonviolent solutions to conflict cost lots less money.

The women in Women Strike for Peace linked arms with women from around the world. We never considered national boundaries as social or political barriers. We were up on the Canadian border on July 4, 1969, patriotically licking ice cream cones with Vietnamese women who were barred from entry to the United States, when our government wasn't letting us know what was really happening in Vietnam. We insisted on finding out for ourselves. We jumped into the lake, so to speak, of the Vietnam War, and it was a ten-year swim, often treading water. What was going on in the weapons research laboratories of Livermore, California, and Los Alamos, New Mexico, and [in labs] in Cambridge, Massachusetts, was the continued evolution in military technology and [the] buildup in arms. Vietnam provided a large live experimental laboratory for weapons development.

The Vietnamese women had just literally walked from the south of Vietnam to the north and then flew out to Canada. As a result of that meeting, I was invited to Vietnam. It was a citizen initiative, perhaps the first in citizen diplomacy. We started the Committee of Liaison with Families of Prisoners of War, which became the only reliable vehicle for certifying the names of those captured, and even improved the conditions under which prisoners were detained, by insisting they should receive more frequent letters and packages from home. Their mothers and wives and children were then able to send toilet articles, pens and pencils, checkers and cards, and aftershave lotion and books. The Pentagon and State Department people were beside themselves. They were embarrassed because there was a housewife from the Bronx and a committee of citizens from the antiwar movement who were putting one over on them. The families of the downed pilots were dependent on us for information. They weren't getting anything reliable from their government. The war department couldn't tell them if their son or husband was missing or captured, dead or alive, and the antiwar movement could. The government couldn't deliver their mail and we could.

We were investigated; we were followed; we were FBI'd and CIA'd. It was sometimes amusing and sometimes dreadful. We never did anything illegal. We were not trading with an enemy, we were not spying. We were not breaking any laws. In the end only peace movement people brought captured American pilots back alive before the end of the war. I personally flew to Vietnam during the heavy bombing raids of 1972 (one of five trips I made during the war years) with a delegation including David Dellinger, Rev. William Sloane Coffin, Professor Richard Falk of Princeton University, Peter Arnett of Associated Press, and two relatives—a wife and a mother—of pilots who were prisoners of war. We brought home three prisoners of war. Arnett, a Pulitzer Prize winner, now jokingly refers to the August 1972 trip as the "prisoner snatch." We didn't steal them. The Vietnamese gave them to us. Unfortunately, Henry Kissinger, who then made the "Peace Is at Hand" speech, supported bombing the daylights out of Haiphong harbor and Hanoi at Christmas 1972, which was a hell of a thank you for letting three POWs go. The POW release was an extraordinary peace gesture rare in wartime. Never in the history of war had mere mortal citizens done this kind of liaison effectively. We carried mail back and forth, packages and information on the conditions of people. We had hard data. "Yes, Jane," we could say, "your husband is alive in a North Vietnamese prison camp and we have seen him and he appears to be O.K. The conditions are obviously lousy because Vietnam is a very poor country, and we're bombing it. They're in danger from our own bombs. But he's alive, and here is his picture."

Riverside was the first church in the country to include a disarmament program in its ministry. Peacemaking should be integral to the mission of the church, said the minister, William Sloane Coffin. He called for a full-time paid staff, and I founded the program and directed it for ten years. What I did was to bring my long history of concern for and knowledge of the arms race to bear on the issues and used the organizing skills we had picked up during the Vietnam War. I started a two-track program there; one to educate and activate the congregation and community and then to see that whatever would work here we could put on the road and apply it nationally. We had a program called "Riverside on the Road." We were concerned about every dimension of the arms race—not just the nuclear arms race, but the conventional arms race and wars of intervention and with economic conversion. I sometimes got mail addressed to Reverend Weiss. What was a nice Jewish woman doing there? If it were not for the churches now, there would be practically nothing going on, because they have really provided so much of the space and the base for the Central American movement, the sanctuary movement, the disarmament movement, and the peace movement.

It's fair to say that the cold war is over and what we must do now is convert the cold war structures that remain and make the peace. The people who are most capable of making the peace are those who have been peace makers all these years—the women who have been active, who have come forward and demonstrated peacemaking in very concrete ways at every level of political office, in schools, in the community and in the world.

Isobel Cerney, 1984. Photograph © by Renée Burgard.

ISOBEL MILTON CERNEY

As a poet, I'm more of an ardent witness than anything else. But I've been glad to get in the middle of the fray and strike a few good blows for freedom myself. Women need a chance to tell our own stories.

Isobel Milton Cerney was born in 1912 in Chicago to a socialist mother and southern gentleman father. Her commitment to workers' education solidified with residency at Jane Addams's settlement house, known as Hull House. She also did summer work at Bryn Mawr Summer School for Women Workers in Industry and at the Hudson Shore Labor School.

She and her husband Edwin were fired from their public school jobs because of their refusal to sign the Loyalty Oath in California in the 1950s. In 1954 she ran for U.S. Senate as an Independent Progressive Party candidate advocating a ban on the H-bomb, fair employment practices, peace, and international trade and friendship. She has been active in the antiwar, disarmament, and civil rights movements and has been jailed many times for civil disobedience for those causes. She is a Quaker but not an absolute pacifist; she calls herself a revolutionary. Isobel currently makes her home at a Quaker retirement residence in northern California—but is far from retired from her lifelong work for peace and justice.

Jane Addams visited our youth group in Winnetka, Illinois, in 1927, at a time that the United States had a very small navy and no standing army at all. She had the most plain, glowing, warm way of speaking to people. She was determined to make clear to us that the way to peace was being led by women who had gotten together during a declared and terrible war, World War I, behind the lines and sought peace. She believed that the way into the future was through world government. She dramatized, in a wonderful way, that bread and peace are the important things. That made a great impression on me. Women seem to know a very great deal about real love, which means "to serve." Their "work is love made visible."

Some years after her visit, in 1937, I observed the Republic Steel strike with unarmed workers protesting/celebrating that they wanted recognition of the union in their plant. People were shot down around us, and we went to the hospital to try to help afterwards. I was weeping over the unneeded suffering that was going on there. A worker came along and said to me, "Just remember that no strike is ever lost, no struggle is ever lost. The stand that is being made here will go on and on, and this is all part of many things that have to happen." Later the newsreels suppressed the truth I had seen. The paper said the workers were carrying knives, guns. I knew they had on their best Sunday clothes and were carrying children on their shoulders. You have a whole different idea of what is going on if you're moving among the people and experiencing it and learning from them.

In 1934 when I read Lenin's *State and Revolution* and read him on imperialism, I realized that I couldn't be an absolute pacifist. I had to believe in the right of people to liberate themselves, in the right of revolution. It has always been the revolutionaries who spoke to my condition. I read Lenin with tremendous care and admiration, and I think I've been a changed human being ever since. In the preface he says, in effect, "It's been fascinating to write on this topic, but now I have to go out and lead the Revolution." I had been an academic socialist; then I became an activist.

Edwin and I left our classrooms in 1950, at the start of the Korean War because we wouldn't sign the Loyalty Oath in California. Some of our friends, fellow teachers, had been discussing the Loyalty Oath and saying they would never sign it, but they signed. They needed their jobs. We had gone cash and carry, and they had children and debt. So some of them came to our house and wept. We said, "Signing the oath is not the important thing. Are you opposed to it?" They said, "Yes." We told them, "Well then, sign it and then help those of us who won't sign by working to get the law changed."

We worked at odd jobs to keep ourselves going. We went to a Quaker friend in town and said, "Here we are, bag and baggage. May we sleep on your floor or your living room couch?" She laughed and said, "You say you're friends with a small "f," but I say you are a Friend, a Quaker; this is what they've done all through the ages, given shelter."

Whenever I went into the bank or the bakery or some place downtown on regular family errands, I would bump into people who had known us for years, and they would cut me dead. I had to keep saying to myself, "Remember nobody believes in a witch; they just don't want to be considered a witch or associated with a witch. So get off your broom." When you take a position, some people have to fall away from you because of fear or oppression, and it has nothing to do with you personally. Then new people come forward, and you have new friends.

In 1949 the first World Peace Council meeting was going to be held in Mexico City. I wanted to go but I didn't have the $100 to register. An old lady who was a friend of mine gave me $100. She said, "I've been saving this for my burial. I said to myself, 'What am I doing that for? I'm not dead yet, and why should money go to that anyway?' Let somebody else worry about my burial." She was a woman who all through the Korean War twice a week took the bus, wearing a lovely flowered hat and carrying a big tote bag. She would go through the bus leafletting the passengers on the war, talking to everyone. The day that the cease fire was signed she got on the bus, and they all started applauding. The bus driver said, "Missus, you've won the war; you've stopped it."

We were in Europe attending an emergency session of the World Peace Council in 1952. Local people had collected funds to get us there. We actually crossed the ocean without the funds to return, just leaving word, "If you want to see us again, you better have some money in general delivery so we can come back!" We had this vision of clasping hands with people from other countries. You move out on faith, exactly as the people did in the underground railroad in the nineteenth century. We were ministers without portfolio, citizen diplomats. We all feared the atom bomb was going to be used again.

We became friends with a Buddhist monk from Sri Lanka. At the end of the conference, he told us that people from twenty different countries in the Asian Pacific region had planned a peace congress in China to offset the danger of nuclear war in the Pacific. He asked us if we would consider being delegates to the peace congress. We looked at each other. Edwin said, "We have no money. We aren't even sure how we are going to get home. We couldn't possibly go." "Oh," he said, "the peace movement throughout the world will help to support your going, and you will be guests of the Chinese peace committee when you get there." Edwin then told him that as Chicago children we had done what all midwestern children do, started digging holes to China. We just never dreamed we would go there. Oh my, it was just the most exciting thing in the whole world.

The monk told us that Eleanor Roosevelt had been invited to this peace meeting, had applied to the State Department for a passport to go, and was turned down. The head of the Episcopal Peace Fellowship had applied, and other distinguished Americans, and they were turned down too. Because we were already out of the country, it would be easier. That's how we got there. We were such little fish that we could swim through holes in the net.

Edwin's old father, who was then in his eighties, a very simple working man who had never had to handle the press, had the press descend on him when we were in Peking. And so Pop did the perfect thing, I mean, he couldn't have had a public relations man who could have given him anything better to say. He said, "The children told me when they left home that they were going east to see the family." (Well, we had visited all of the Cerneys and Miltons in Chicago and the East Coast.) He said, "All I can say is, if they're in China, some big family!" That got on the front pages. Wasn't that just inspired?

The conference was called in the American press, if it was called anything at all, the "so-called Peace Congress." The first piece of peace-making we witnessed was in the plenary session in a great hall in Peking. Landlords from Pakistan were there in their ceremonial gowns and hats, three years after the liberation of China, which was getting rid of the whole rental and landlord system. One of them stepped forward and put his hat on the head of the mayor of Peking. The mayor of Peking put his arm around him. There were many other acts which cut across national sovereignty, class lines, ideologies.

We had read in the newspapers while we were coming home through Europe that the first people of the U.S. delegation who had come through immigration had lost their passports. When we got to New York we had a mass meeting set up for the next night for a report from the U.S. delegation. They snatched Edwin's passport away as soon as we entered the United States. They didn't even look up in his face but threw it in a drawer and slammed it shut. I held on to mine and sat down. In the glare of lights and passage of time and worrying about Edwin and the mass meeting later, I got tired of sitting there and surrendered my passport. I still don't have a passport. The passport cases were won late in the fifties and sixties. But by that time we were up to our ears in the liberation movement in the South and weren't interested in going any-where anyway. We were glad to get home to our little house.

When we left China Edwin said to me, "What is our main impression?" I said, "We have underestimated the human potential." He said, "Re-

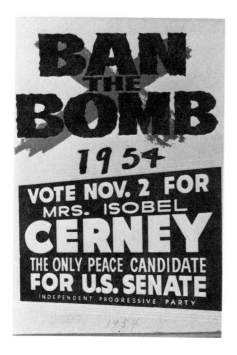

*1954 election campaign
poster, California.*

member when we went to the Grand Canyon—our idea of space and time was revolutionized? My idea of what human beings can be and do is revolutionized." Much of this progress has been pushed back now. However, people move forward like a great wave and recede and then go forward some more.

I campaigned for the U.S. Senate in 1954. Banning the H-bomb was very central to my campaign. I was the only candidate running for any office who brought out that nerve gas was being prepared and stored in Denver, endangering that whole area and of course the whole world. I had been nominated by the Progressive Party and cross-filed Republican and Democratic. The local paper ran a lead editorial saying that the Republican Party must be infiltrated with Communists since I had gotten so many votes. This was a statewide campaign for the Senate, but my part in the race was not generally considered newsworthy, although they would write up any dogcatcher candidate.

Once I was up in the mountains campaigning on Labor Day. Some kids were selling American Legion flags, so I stopped the car and went over to them and said, "Are you getting good sales?" They said, "Yes." I said, "Now listen, I've got something free that you can give away if you like it." It was my campaign literature. Pretty soon the kids were putting the flags aside and handing out my literature to the people instead. It was fun to be more popular than the American Legion.

I ran for Congress because it was an opportunity to teach on the hoof. I could go to everything that was free—all the League of Women Voters candidates' nights, and California Farm Grange meetings, and so on. I'd go to the door and say, "I'm a teacher and I'm for the same thing you are, raising things and making them grow." I would give them the pitch that we must not wage war and must stop wasting the earth. They thanked me for coming. I said as I was leaving, "You aren't even going to remember my name, but take a peace action in your own behalf now, even before you vote. Make your voices heard." What I was trying to do was fan the spark of hope in everyone and reduce the fears. Fear of job loss and blacklisting was everywhere in the era of Joe McCarthy.

The first time I went to jail in Atlanta during the civil rights movement in the sixties, I had gone down to the Baptist church to get some flowers for Soviet visitors coming to the Quaker guest house and I heard on the car radio on the way down that Dr. Martin Luther King, Jr., was calling us all downtown. So I parked and got in this six-block-long line of people going round and round a whole block of restaurants we were trying to integrate. The first thing I knew, cops were beating people over the head. So I thought, "I'm going to create a diversion." I guess I had always been impressed as a child about how a mother bird will trail an injured wing to protect its chicks. So I hurled myself against the doors of a restaurant. A whole bunch of people followed me, and the cops came tearing after them and stopped beating on the people in the line.

A black man I had never seen and never saw since—this was typical of the movement down there—elderly, so frail I could feel his bones, threw himself on top of me and covered my body so that nobody could beat me. Fortunately, he didn't get beaten either because some of the young got on top of him.

When I got in the jail I saw a matron whose face was a glory. She was listening to all of us singing, so I thought, "She's a friend." I walked up to her and said, "Please do not violate my religion. I have never been segregated in my life. Please don't segregate me in this jail. I'm here with my friends." She said, "Oh honey, I'd lose my job. I can't do that."

When I was in jail that time, the top security guard at the black college where I was teaching, who had served six years in the U.S. Army, was inspired to go all through the dormitories and poke out anybody who was in my classes who would like to come down and sing to me one night. So down they all came, about seventy of them, singing perfectly gloriously. Of course, they were all put in jail. We had some wonderful concerts.

Dick Gregory was in the jail with us. I could sometimes hear him holding forth on the floor above us. He was priceless. He said, "Now, we've got the only civilized and human place in Atlanta, if not in the whole United States. We have so many women and so many palefaces in here with us."

Another time I was in the same jail, but this time on charges of civil disobedience for an anti-Vietnam demonstration. One of the matrons sent for me. She had been puzzling over it since the first time I was in her jail. She said, "I am sincerely interested, as one woman to another, why, when everybody else is trying to stay out of jail, you all in the peace movement are trying to get into jail. I don't understand it." So I explained civil disobedience to her. She told me that many of her friends had young men in the war. "You seem to have hope that we can end this terrible Vietnam War," she said. I answered, "We have to end it, and the sooner we end it the fewer Vietnamese and Americans will be killed." She accepted that.

One of the most hilarious experiences I've ever had in my whole life was about saying that my religion was being violated in the jail because there was too much noise. Anyone who spends any time in jail at all suffers frightfully from the noise. I had not been aware of the kind of cultural garbage that was being poured over people all day long on television. Anyway, they turn the TV on at 6:45 in the morning to wake up the prisoners, and they run it top volume in a room about thirty-by-forty feet all day until 10:45 at night. I sent for the kindliest of the matrons. I said to her, "My religion is being violated." She said, "What do you mean?" I said, "We Friends worship in silence and there is no silence. Could you please put me in solitary?" She said, "Well, that's the first time in thirty-seven years that anyone has ever asked to be put in solitary." She took me down a corridor and right outside the solitary tank was a black woman ironing. She had her radio on low, not loud. The matron explained to her that I had to have silence in order to worship. So she put me in there and locked the cell. I was there for several hours. When the matron let me out the woman who was ironing turned to me and said, "Well, well, well. I never have heard a worship service like that." I said, "Heard?" She said, "You snored the whole time." I said, "I think God will forgive me." She said, "Oh yes, I think so."

I don't know anybody who has fallen by the wayside in this particular struggle. All the people I've ever known who were clear on what the nuclear danger is never forgot it, and they keep active in some way or another. You must be prepared to pay for it if you become an activist. But, despite the sacrifices, it's fun. You'd get bored if you weren't doing it. You have to do it without arrogance and dogmatism, and you have to take time to take care of your health, enjoy music, really see if the trees are blooming. You have to be prepared for a rhythm between success and failure. I used to do a dozen different things at the same time. Now I just do one thing. Maybe it succeeds.

I want us to get a satellite, the women of the world, with programs by women from various countries and different classes and ethnic groups and cultures. There is no choice now on our TV. Just think, twenty-four hours a day broadcasting songs and dances, children's stories and legends, angry women. Oh boy! They got a man on the moon. Fifty thousand people cooperated directly to make that happen. What a miracle of technology and cooperation! I thought we'd hear something like Walt Whitman from outer space, "The divine ship sails the divine sea," and what do we hear? "ROGER. OVER." Now, women won't do that from outer space, you know that. They'll put some lullabies out once in a while.

One of the black preachers in the southern liberation movement told me that he has a student in the theological seminary who is interested in electronics who dreams that some day they're going to "capture" earlier voices. You know the Native American saying, "be mindful that each song you sing goes on and on forever"? He hopes that we will hear the voice of Jesus giving the Sermon on the Mount, the voice of Mohammed, "There is no god but God," and all the rest, Galileo, Socrates, Sappho. . . . If I could hear the voices of women who worked with Sojourner Truth and who worked with Lucretia Mott, just ordinary people like myself, it would be very thrilling.

As a poet, I'm more of an ardent witness than anything else. But I've been glad to get in the middle of the fray and strike a few good blows for freedom myself. Women need a chance to tell our own stories.

Before I was a Quaker, I sold heaven knows how many war bonds for World War II at big meetings in Connecticut, where I was at that time teaching. I did all kinds of things to try to shorten the war and advance the war effort. I tried to get a job in a factory but failed the aptitude test abysmally. I'm not sorry that I supported the war because I firmly believe that Hitler would have simply taken over the world.

Actually I'm not a pacifist today, I'm a peacemaker. There is a difference, I think. I explained this very clearly to the Friends when I asked to be a member. Most Quakers have been reformers, and I'm not; I'm a revolutionary. I believe in the right of revolution, and I know that it's often true that there's no possible way of getting out of an absolutely intolerable situation except by revolution. I'm with the liberation forces. I believe that peace is strengthened wherever the profits are taken out of war and where the power and purpose are cooperatively shared among the people.

I am in the process of rethinking my life, how to do something fruitful that is my own, that if I didn't do it, it wouldn't get done. I've decided that I must have much more association with young children; that's what I'm trying to do, to find out who wants a storyteller. I think of myself as a catalyst and encourager. You never know when you drop a pebble into a pool how far the ripple will go.

It is a perfect nightmare to me to live at this time as well as a very great joy at the same instant. So I will just have to go through the world naked, the way I'm asking the world to become: naked, safe, disarmed.

2.

Trial by Fire: Wartime Awakening to Peace and Justice Issues

Helma Waldeck, 1985. Photograph © by Renée Burgard.

HELMA WILHEMINA WALDECK

*I've been a fighter for practically all my life. You shouldn't be
surprised that I'm still fighting forty-some years after liberation
from the war. I never dreamed that I had to fight against another
war. For me the most important thing is keeping the peace.*

Helma Wilhemina Waldeck was born in 1906 in Marburg, West
Germany. Her father was a Jew and a high-ranking officer in the
German army in World War I. He thought his status in the army
would save his family when the Nazis came to power; it didn't. Helma
was sought by the Gestapo and fled over the border to Holland. She
married a non-Jew and her religion was somehow not marked on her
papers, so she was able to work with the Resistance and help others
escape and go into hiding. She managed to get her parents out of
Germany after Kristallnacht, when the synagogues were burned.

She speaks with emotion and pride of February 25, 1941, when
the Dutch streetcar drivers went on strike to prevent a scheduled
mass deportation of Jews, assisted by a mass mobilization of Resistance workers. She was unable to save all of her family; her parents
and one sister died in Auschwitz. Helma's dedication to working for
peace is a lifetime commitment. "As for me, I only can say that as
long as there is a danger of war, I have to fight." She continues to
fight for peace, racial justice, and religious freedom, and to prevent
a second, and final, holocaust, a nuclear holocaust. Helma lives in
San Francisco, California.

My past experience of Hitler and fascism inspired me never to forget what led up to fascism and gave me the strength to fight for freedom and justice, wherever I am. I cannot refer to the present peace movement without giving a glimpse at the past. In the early days people were not aware of what fascism means. When I read Hitler's *Mein Kampf* I never thought he would realize, step for step, what he wrote. Many people thought this wouldn't happen, the same attitude people have to the danger of a nuclear holocaust.

Being a Jew married to a Dutch non-Jew helped save my life. I will never forget the invasion of Holland. Antitank guns woke us up. People were scared to death. The streets were deserted. At the time, Queen Wilhemina had already fled with important persons of the parliament to England.

It was not easy for a country of about 15 million to save Jews, political refugees, and students who were assembled for the war factories. There was strict discipline in the Resistance. At the meeting places, you waited no more than three minutes. If you carried a weapon you risked death. Famous artists helped us forge passports and were killed; streets were named after them after the war. One time I went to an address where the Gestapo had just left and where our friends had just been arrested to be killed later somewhere else—I never found out where. I was saved through the eye of a needle.

I am not a hero; I cried very often when I lost my best friends. But I learned not to get excited when some good man was shot before my eyes. If you showed any feelings, they knew you might have some connections to the Resistance.

I am against terrorism, and I believe in peaceful means. It takes a lot of peace workers to shake up a warmongering government and get the sympathy and understanding of all the people to prevent a horrible crime. In Holland there is now a museum where children can learn what happened during World War II. Our children here in America should be taught the same awareness as early as possible.

This anti-Semitic thing started at an early age in Germany. A sister of mine, the one who died in Auschwitz, was playing some kind of game in the street when she was a child. Her name was Ruth. Ruth and Jew rhyme—*Jude* in German—and so they called her "Ruth/Jude," you know. She came home crying. She barely knew she was a Jew. We did not live in a ghetto. In our family religion was never much talked about. My grandfather was religious, so I knew I was a Jew, but I cannot say that it was the main thing in our lives. We didn't go to the Jewish school.

In the First World War my father was a high officer in the German army. He was a leader in a hospital which was only for typhoid. Nobody wanted to lead that hospital because it was very dangerous. My father did it and even got a medal. He was the only Jew in all Germany to receive that medal. He thought later on that this medal would save his life. It didn't.

I remember in Cologne we had torches in the streets, and people came out of every corner for a big meeting in the biggest hall. That night the leader from the Communist party was supposed to speak, but he didn't arrive. The following day the Reichstag burned. From that moment on we did political work. I was betrayed because of my political work. I had given my key to people so they could come and go and have meetings in my apartment whenever they wanted to while I was at work. One day I got arrested in the office. The charge was that I was a left-winger. Some people with whom I worked were traitors and they talked.

I was sent to the prison in Cologne in the beginning of 1933. We were thrown in the cellar. We were not even given a mattress; we slept on the floor. I met one girl who was in a middle-of-the-road party. But that was enough for the Nazis to arrest her. The jail was not strict, however. A cousin of mine brought some cookies, and it was allowed. In fact, one day—it was not too long after I was arrested—the door opened, and they said, "You can all go home." I went back to the office. It was a Jewish firm, and they told me I'd better go away. "We'll pay you for a trip, wherever you want to go." I didn't accept it, but I could feel that the atmosphere wasn't the same. People I worked with turned away; they were afraid. After two or three months I received a call: "This is the Gestapo. We need some names from you. Could you come over to such and such an address?" I went to the boss and said, "I know you don't agree with me politically, but this call I got and I don't want to go. I'm not a traitor. I want to go away for good." They were awfully nice. They helped me go. I had no suitcase and I had some debts, but I left Germany.

My family lived in another city; they didn't know about my call from the Gestapo or my leaving. I had a boyfriend who brought me over the border to Holland. I had nothing with me. In the no-man's-land there was one street. We played like lovers so we wouldn't attract attention, and then I got over the border. I was without money. I was without clothes, except for the clothes I was wearing. I went to the Jewish Committee in Amsterdam. They helped me and put me in a boardinghouse. I thought my fight should be right there because we were not far from Germany— not knowing that Holland would be invaded later on.

I married a non-Jewish Dutch man I met in an organization. We had the same ideas. Then our task was to bring Jewish people, children, and political people—when I speak about political people I mean antifascists— over the border, to find someplace they could sleep, try to finance them. It was a very hard job. The reports we got from Germany were awful. In fact, I went back to Germany on a Dutch passport in 1936 to get my parents.

They lived in a German town close to the border. At that time you still could move about legally. They actually went to Holland more or less legally.

I was with them just after Kristallnacht when the synagogue burned. My mother heard about it in the early morning. She came in crying and said, "The synagogue is on fire." I said to my parents, "It's time you move." I took them with me to Holland. They had a hard time in the beginning; my father could not find work. You had no room to hide somebody, and you took somebody anyway, somebody you didn't know or who was sent to you. It is like a prison in your own house. But if you have to live in close quarters together to save a life, you do it.

In the meantime, Norway was already invaded, and then Czechoslovakia. We knew something might happen to us in Holland. We got addresses for people to hide. We were not interested if they were Jewish, Christian, or whatever. We didn't ask about their political party because all we were interested in was if a person was against fascism. Then there were the students who were being shipped to Germany for the war factories. At last we didn't have any more room to hide. People who were active like me at that time couldn't take anybody; we were more of a danger than a help. My own parents I couldn't take. It got very difficult.

One rich Jewish family, former Germans, became traitors. I didn't know. I had not read a brochure that the queen, who had escaped to England, had written; in that brochure that family was listed as traitors. I came to them for money and addresses for places for people to hide. They found all the Jewish families I had helped. The Jewish people who were arrested thought I was the traitor because I brought them there. They didn't know the details.

Then we heard that all the political people and all Jews would be arrested—all. I said to my former husband, "Let's go." We had an address in the country to hide, but he said, "Look here, if they want to arrest us, they can do it any day." One day I lifted the curtain and saw two guys putting their bikes against a pole outside. I said, "They're coming for us." We escaped to the roof, but they arrested us. They came through with guns. They found on the table a card from somebody from a concentration camp, who thanked us for what we had done. They said, "You have helped Jews." I went to prison. My husband did not.

I knew one girl in prison who had a brother who had destroyed a whole building where there was a file with the names of young men who should go to Germany in the factories. He destroyed the files. It was a big, big thing to do, the finest sabotage done. The brother was already in a concentration camp; there was no hope. They had an old mother in another town who was allowed once a week to visit her to pick up the dirty laundry. The poor woman was as old as I am now. There was an

Italian girl in the same cell, and the other girls gestured to me that she was a spy by drawing their hands across their mouths. We couldn't talk too much to each other on account of her. There was a German girl who had stolen cigarettes, and the other ones made the gesture that she too was a spy.

I got very sick, and they put me in another cell, and one of the prisoners took care of me. The one good guard smuggled some bread from the bakery because she knew we were hungry; we had only cabbage from morning to the night. I don't eat cabbage now. When we went to the prison people threw tomatoes and other food into the trucks for us; they knew we would have nothing to eat. From the houses around the yard where we went out for exercise, they threw food for us too.

Some people were executed; I could be glad that I only got beaten up. I had a feeling that they would let me out. I was sick, and the doctor was OK. My former husband went to his house and said, "Look here, she is naive." The doctor got me out; that's what we think. Afterwards, they told me I had to go to the Gestapo and talk to them. I didn't do it. If they had beaten me, I wouldn't have talked; I wouldn't have hurt anyone. They could have shot me. They could have tortured me to death. I know myself. I was prepared to die. For some reason, they didn't come for me. They decided to watch me all the time instead. I couldn't do anything for the Resistance because they were watching us. It was too dangerous for other people, not only for ourselves. I didn't do anything for half a year; then I brought more people in. In the meantime, nearly all my friends, they were caught and they were killed.

On February 25, 1941, Dutch streetcar drivers received notices to be on the street around five o'clock in the morning in order to work twelve hours this day. Many streetcar lines, which otherwise had different routes, were changed to the Jewish Theater, others to the main railroad station. Everyone understood that something unexpected was in the wind. The Resistance movement went to work at once. News spread that many Jews were to be deported the following day. The whole night, people worked in feverish anticipation, mimeographing leaflets, painting on the streets, on the squares, and on the walls, "HELP THE JEWS!" It was a hard job. Everything had to be done quickly and unseen. We were protected by the partisan watchguard. Earlier there had been some individual arrests of Jewish citizens. But never since the German fascists had occupied Holland had a real mass deportation taken place.

Many drivers belonged to the underground. They already had the leaflets in their pockets before they went to their various carbarns. The drivers refused to work their streetcars for this horrible purpose. They decided to go on strike. Women passed information to civilians, as well as to streetcar drivers, so everyone would be aware of what was to happen.

At six o'clock in the morning we took our bicycles and rode to the different carbarns. On our way, we met the first workers walking to their work with understanding smiles on their faces. Two of these men took red handkerchiefs from their pockets. All those little signs we understood. We ran out of leaflets, and printers offered their services to print more.

The news spread like fire over the entire city. After some hours the "master race" appeared, sitting on their panzer-wagens, rifles at ready. The atmosphere was loaded with unbearable tension. They called us "Judashelper," and with this curse on their lips, they opened fire. We had no munitions. Our weapons were ideas. For those who fell, others took their places. At last we had to give up for the time being. We made a vow that this would not be the last of the Resistance.

The printing machines were running full speed to publish the names of those who had been killed. The women put the posters on streetlamps and in other visible places. One woman was caught. Three bullets and there was nothing left. I never saw her before, but I felt as if she were my sister now. Nine civilians were killed, forty-five injured, and we lost count of the killed or arrested drivers. One printing plant was discovered, and all the workers in it were arrested. During the day, the city workers joined the strike. The strike also spread to other places in the northern part of Holland. Jews, in bitter grief at these killings, were proud at the same time. They had never known before that they could become the focus of such heroism. Many of the Jews and many others were finally deported to the concentration camps; but not according to the plans the fascists had laid for the 25th of February, 1941. My parents and one sister were taken away later and died in Auschwitz.

After the war, I came to the United States. I had to find a job and learn the language. I think it was not the women's movement, but the McCarthy era which gave me the push to get involved in social and political issues here. I got involved in civil rights. It takes a long time to fight. It takes many years to make a revolution. It was the same with the Jews as with all oppressed people. Look how long the women fought for women's rights, and Negroes for theirs. The hardest thing is when you are not successful. You get discouraged. I have to say for myself that I was often discouraged.

I've been a fighter for practically all my life. You shouldn't be surprised that I'm still fighting forty-some years after liberation from the war. I never dreamt that I had to fight against another war. For me the most important thing is keeping the peace. You can't get peace by praying for peace. If there is something wrong, the painting of a swastika on a synagogue or a bombing, I don't let it rest. I don't know all the answers, but I do not let it rest, and I see what I can do. I have seen what is going on. Because of what I have seen, I'm more sensitive. Now, if it is a Negro person or a Negro church that is harmed, I would protest because the racism is an organized thing. Peace people have much work to do, and each thing is important. Naturally the nuclear danger is most important, but we have to work against other wrongs too.

Some people would have thought me brave, but I've seen much braver ones. I was not the opposite from brave; you cannot go into the Resistance if you have no courage. You don't know your enemies. You have to have a lot of courage. I would say you have to have even hate. I am an admirer of Dr. Martin Luther King, Jr. He said you shouldn't hate people. It's very hard.

Some of my friends in Holland are still peace workers; I will be until I die. I cannot stop. If they call me up to do something for the jobless, I would do it. It's in a person, and I do not think you change much. At that time I was young, but I don't think I have changed in growing old. The only thing that is disappointing for me is that I still have to do it. I didn't dream that I would still have to. You don't know what a joy peace is unless you have suffered and lost your friends and family. During the liberation of Holland, you dance in the streets, you sing in the streets, you kiss every man. I don't know how many soldiers I have kissed.

It overwhelms me to think I have to be in a peace organization today, to my sorrow. As for me, I only can say that as long as there is a danger of war, I have to fight. I hope that a nuclear holocaust can be prevented. I wish people would learn that the highest priorities are freedom and justice. Now I am old and say to the young people, you will be the victims in the future, you can learn and act now to stop the most terrible holocaust that history and humanity will ever see. Much has to be done. We as peace workers want to see young people in the ranks. Memory is to think back, but also to think about the future I wanted. I still have hope as an old woman that the future generation, in spite of everything, will achieve world peace.

Lisa Kalvelage, 1984. Photograph © by Renée Burgard.

LISA SCHMIDT KALVELAGE

As Einstein said after the atomic bomb, everything
has changed but the way we think. Now we have to change
that, or we will drift into catastrophe.

Lisa Schmidt Kalvelage was born in Nuremberg, Germany, in 1923.
She was trained as a medical technologist and lived in Germany until
1946 when she married an American GI. As a young woman during
the Nuremberg war crimes trials, she learned, as did other Germans,
the extent of the Nazi campaign against Jews. She vowed never to be
silent or unaware when injustice was done by her government. She
was on the board of the ACLU and coordinator of the San Jose Peace
Center in the late sixties and early seventies. She committed civil
disobedience during the Vietnam War to protest the manufacture of
napalm and its storage in her community: "I was a respectable housewife with six children. . . . We were all very respectable, and we were
dressed very respectably. As a matter of fact, we had high heels on
and gloves with which we carried the picket signs. We wanted to
show the news that those women are 'peaceniks' and didn't fit the
radical image." She lives in San Jose, California.

During the Vietnam War a reporter came to the peace center to talk to some of us. He had flown over a storage area and said, "You should see the napalm bombs that are stored there. There must be thousands of them. You know, we have to get the spotlight on this." The area was closed to the public; he was willing to commit civil disobedience to expose it since you obviously couldn't go there legally.

Four of us decided to commit civil disobedience. We went there and climbed over a little rise and went through a fence. We came up to a barge where they were unloading napalm. The napalm bombs were filled up at another company, and every night they brought new drums down and stored them where we were. When they had enough, they would come at night with a long group of barges to take them up to the port to ship to Vietnam. It turned out there were thirty-six thousand bombs there; the man who owned the storage place testified at our trial that there were that many.

We sat down in front of the forklift operator. He was a very mean-looking young man. He told us to get out of there as fast as we could. We said, "No, we came here to protest this." When we told him that we wouldn't leave, he said, "I'm going to get my dogs." So he walked over to his car to get the dogs. We had only one support person there; he had noticed that things were moving fast so he went to the telephone and called the police and the newspaper. The police chief came at about the same time as this guy brought out his two vicious dogs. The police chief told him he would arrest him if he didn't put the dogs back because the dogs were snarling even at the police chief.

We were there for about an hour before we were arrested. The police chief bent over backwards to avoid arresting us. The man who owned the storage facility was practically pleading with us. He said he was a very good Catholic and a church-going man, and he didn't want it in the newspaper that he owned these storage places for the napalm. He was supposed to swear out the warrant for our arrest because of trespassing, and he wouldn't do it. Then they got some policewoman to talk to us woman to woman. But we were committed to the civil disobedience because we wanted publicity on the fact that napalm was stored in our community and publicity on the fact that not only students and hippies were against the war, but also respectable housewives.

I was a respectable housewife with six children. My husband was a businessman. One woman's husband was with IBM. The third woman's husband was a construction worker. We were all very respectable, and we were dressed very respectably. As a matter of fact, we had high heels on and gloves with which we carried the picket signs. We wanted to show the news that those women are "peaceniks" and didn't fit the radical image. That's exactly what happened.

When they realized that we weren't going to leave, they arrested us and took us to jail. It was about noontime, and they told us we could not be arraigned that day because the arraignment was for two o'clock and they couldn't get us down to the courthouse in time. However, they would be able to arrange minimum bail which would probably be $100 a person, if we would accept bail. We had decided in advance that we would not accept bail; they would have to jail us.

We accepted that we would have to stay overnight. We were called by the jail matron, and we showered and were shampooed with lice shampoo that made our hair bright red. We went in the recreation hall. Then the matron came in and told us that the judge was making an emergency arraignment for us. They took us out of the jail immediately, handcuffed. Our hair was red from the shampoo, and we were in these incredible huge jail dresses, sweaters, and tennis shoes. On the same day as we were arraigned, a man was arraigned who had shot another person; this guy appeared in court in a business suit. We were a mess. We were very angry. A friend of ours was able to call the newspapers so that there were TV cameras there. We were arraigned and released on our own recognizance. We went home, and the next day it was all over the papers, with wonderful pictures. That was exactly what we wanted because there were all kinds of reactions and letters to the editor about the secret napalm storage facility.

The trial lasted three and a half days. We were charged with a trespassing violation. The code is divided into two parts. The first part covers "regular" trespassing. That's like if you come into my backyard, and I tell you to leave. If you refuse to go out, I can have you arrested for trespassing. The second part of the ordinance covers trespassing with a purpose to stop lawful business or any lawful activity. We were charged with the second part of the ordinance. That was the luckiest thing because we were able to challenge the legality of the business of napalm storage under international law. If it wasn't a legal business, we were not guilty of trespassing on a legal business—and we could testify about the illegality of napalm manufacture, storage, and use. It all depended on whether the judge was open to such testimony under the code. He was.

We had an attorney who was an international lawyer. He called a witness who was an ex-Green Beret, gung ho in Vietnam, and who later changed his attitude and said, "Never again." He was a peace advocate. Napalm will burn people and causes a tremendous firestorm that cuts off all the oxygen. Even if you were on the periphery of the firestorm, because all the oxygen is sucked up, you would be asphyxiated. So in the villages even on the outskirts, people died because of the asphyxiation. The Kellogg-Briand Act after the First World War's gas warfare said that even in war there were limits to what could be allowed. Napalm violated these limits.

[My attorney] also felt that my testimony would be very important. I'm a native of Nuremberg, Germany. After I became a U.S. citizen I became involved in the peace movement because of my experience in Germany. After the Nuremberg trials I felt strongly that people had to say no and had to stand up against their government when it was doing wrong. We didn't want to put our hopes too high because we didn't know who the judge was going to be. We could get a judge who would throw the book at us and not listen to any testimony; it could be over in fifteen minutes.

Our witnesses cited the asphyxiation effects associated with napalm and that asphyxiation gases are outlawed in the chemical warfare pact and the Kellogg-Briand Act. On the next day we gave our testimony. The first woman, whose son had been in Vietnam, talked about her reasons for her disobedience. Everyone had a personal reason why they did what they did. I testified last and was on the witness stand for four hours. The judge asked me about my background and Nuremberg. I told him that I made up my mind that was not going to happen again to me, that somebody says, "Where were you? What did you do? Did you just step back and let it all happen? Didn't you know that you had an obligation?" If you see your government do evil, then you have to speak up.

I was in the fourth grade when Hitler came to power. I remember this really well. I had a male teacher for two years who was a member of the Nazi party. He would politicize in the classroom. I remember sitting right next to the window. He said to me, "You look out the window. Look across the street to the apartment building. When you see something happen, you call me to the window." I had no idea what was going to happen. All of a sudden the window opened, and someone hung a huge swastika flag out the window. I said, "Teacher, teacher, look." He went to the window, and he said, "All right children, I want everybody to stand. This is an historic moment. Right now Adolf Hitler was named chancellor of Germany, and from now on everything is going to be wonderful. Your fathers are going to have to work, and we are going to be a big country, and everybody will respect us."

I didn't personally know anybody in Germany against the war. The first time we really found out that something was happening was when some men in the military made an attempt on Hitler's life. It also became known that in Munich there were some students working in the underground. After the war I read books about military men who formed groups against Hitler but who were discovered before they could do anything. The government didn't want people to know that there were people opposed to Hitler. My mother had a lady friend whose husband was a Communist party functionary. In 1933, right after Hitler came to power, he got arrested for sabotaging the government. He was sent to a concentration camp, to Dachau. He later was released, and my parents visited him at Christmas. My father said to him, "You were in Dachau." He said, "Yes." My father said, "Is it really true that things are pretty grim there?" He looked my father in the eye and said, "I'm not telling you, but if you think about it, it doesn't take much to figure it out."

Yes, there was anti-Semitism. I think the German people knew that something was happening. Everyone knew some German people in the concentration camps, and we didn't want to jeopardize their safety. People would rationalize. That the Jews were deported was one thing; that the Jews were killed was another thing. The extermination camps were not in Germany. If people knew, they didn't talk. With a totalitarian government that controls communication, you get terrorized and frightened if you don't keep your mouth shut. A girlfriend told me the Jews wouldn't come back. How much of it was a rumor and how much was true, I didn't know. When I think back—of course I was very young—but I knew it was not right to take people out of their homes. I remember waiting at the streetcar, and there was an elderly Jewish couple hanging on to each other. They had those yellow stars of David on, and there were some rowdies who were yelling "Jews! Jews!" I remember this very well, and the feeling I had that something is wrong, that it shouldn't be happening to them.

I remember also on one Sunday morning my father and I were going someplace, and we were standing on the street waiting for the streetcar. It was the wintertime, and the bus was late. All of a sudden, three or four open trucks went by, and there were thirty to forty men on each truck. There were several people waiting for the streetcar. One man said, "Those are a bunch of Jews. They're all going to be taken back where they came from, namely, from Poland." People said, "Oh really."

The Nuremberg trials were in 1947, and I was twenty-four. We listened to the radio reports of the trial. Nuremberg was chosen because it was a kind of symbol for the Nazi party. Every year Hitler had this big fancy congress there for ten days, a big celebration. The American announcer reported every day what was going on at the trial. He would say, "You people out there, you don't have to be too smug sitting there. You are just as guilty. You knew what was going on. If I had my way you would all be on trial." It went on and on. I was fascinated by it because I wanted to know what was going on. As much as I hated it, something made sense. I thought, that's true, Ja, the German people were standing on the sidewalk yelling, "Heil! Heil! Heil!" They said yes to everything. The German people for years thought the war was beautiful and went forward to the bitter end until Europe was destroyed and all those people were dead. When the trial was at an end I knew people must take responsibility. How could the German people have followed a man like

Hitler? They have to face it, and they have to take responsibility that it doesn't happen again.

I was sixteen when the war was over. I probably would have been dead if I had questioned it then. But I will not be silent again.

When I was testifying several of the jurors were crying. The prosecutor said, "I know this is a very emotional thing, and the whole Vietnam thing is very emotional, but here we are not dealing with emotions, we are dealing with the law. This is a simple question. This is not an international court of law. This is a municipal court. OK, let them go. Anybody here work for Lockheed—many of your husbands? Tomorrow morning when you go to work, if they make a line across the freeway and say you are doing illegal business there, it's your responsibility. You're opening a Pandora's box. If you let them go they are going to be there again, tomorrow morning."

The jury was out for four hours. When they came in they said we were guilty. We expected it. We were prepared to go to jail, but among us we had twelve children of school age. We could receive a sentence of up to six months. What would we do if we were still in jail when school started? We accepted probation. We were put on probation with a ninety-day suspended sentence. For two years we couldn't get arrested. After one year we were notified that the charge had been cut down to one year and we could have it expunged. But we made the point and got the publicity. I acted on my conscience and responsibility.

After the trial, I was contacted by Pete Seeger, who wanted to use my testimony for a song. I said, "Of course." The song is called "My Name is Lisa Kalvelage." It is taken verbatim from part of my testimony:

> My name is Lisa Kalvelage
> I was born in Nuremberg
> And when the trials were held there nineteen years ago
> It seemed to me ridiculous to hold a nation all to blame
> For the horrors which the world had undergone.
> A short while later when I applied, for I was a GI bride,
>   an American consular official questioned me.
> He refused my exit permit, said my answers did not show
> I'd learned my lesson about responsibility.
> Thus suddenly I was forced
>   to start thinking on the scheme
>   and when later I was permitted to emigrate
> I must have been asked a hundred times where I was and
>   what I did in those years when Hitler ruled our state.
> I said I was a child, or at most a teenager,
>   but this always extended the questioning.

They'd ask me where were my parents, my father and my mother,
    and to this I could answer not a thing.
The seed planted there in Nuremberg in 1947
    started to sprout and to grow.
Gradually I understood what that verdict meant to me
    when there are crimes that I can see and I can know
    and now I also know what it is to be charged
    with mass guilt.
Once in a lifetime is enough for me.
No, I could not take it a second time,
    that is why I am here today.
The events of May 25, the day of our protest
    brought a small balance weight on the other side.
Hopefully some day my contribution to peace
    will help just a bit to turn the tide,
    and perhaps I can tell my children six,
    and later on, their own children
    at least in the future, they need not be silent
When they are asked, "Where was your mother when?"*

During the war in Vietnam it was a different constituency than we have now in the peace movement. Middle-class people were not concerned as a whole because their children didn't go to Vietnam. Their children had student deferments. So many middle-class people didn't support the peace movement. I remember I was picketing the draft board during lunch time. It's in a building with law and insurance offices and banks. A couple hundred people came down for lunch, and people would do their banking. There was extreme hostility by all those people. They would say, "Why don't you go home to your dishes? Don't you have anything else to do? Go back to where you came from." It took quite a while but eventually we got much better responses. People got fed up. There were fifty thousand dead. There was a slow recognition that it couldn't go on anymore.

I think the constituency that we are working with right now is totally different. You can say to them, "You cannot hide at your house if we have a nuclear holocaust. It will get you no matter where you are or who you are. If you don't die right away, you are going to die in the nuclear winter, or you or your children and grandchildren will die of horrible diseases."

As Einstein said after the atomic bomb, everything has changed but the way we think. Now we have to change that, or we will drift into catastrophe. I tell people that they count. There will always be the uncom-

*"My Name is Lisa Kalvelage." Words adapted and music by Pete Seeger. © 1966, 1967 by Sanga Music Inc. All rights reserved. Used by permission.

mitted people, always the ones who don't know what's going on. But we don't need 100 percent of the people; if we get 30 to 40 percent of the people to believe that we must stop it at this point or we will all be destroyed, we can change things. When I talk to people, they say, "I know, isn't it horrible? I don't want to think about it. I feel kind of hopeless that something is going to happen, and I've never done anything." I say, "Write some letters, make some phone calls." I think what we do has an impact.

Yes, there were some times when I felt really down, but I feel more hope now because I think there is a general awakening of the people to the danger. We have to educate people. Eisenhower said that someday the people would want peace so badly that they would push the government into it. I'm in there pushing.

Mariagnes Medrud, ca. 1988.

MARIAGNES AYA UENISHI MEDRUD

It was strange being in a camp and having to say a pledge of allegiance inside barbed-wire fences. I found that very difficult to accept. I finished high school there, and I remember the bitter feeling I had about wearing caps and gowns inside the confinement of camp.

Mariagnes Aya Uenishi Medrud was born in Malden, Washington, in 1926, the daughter of a working-class Japanese American family. Her grandparents worked doing laundry and cooking for the railroad in the West. Soon after Pearl Harbor the FBI picked up her father, who was taken to a relocation camp immediately. The rest of the family was interned later, after Executive Order 9066 was issued. Three years passed before the family was reunited in a camp in Idaho. "We never talked about the war. We never talked about our anger. We never talked about our frustration. We never talked about things like what we were going to do after we got out of camp, because . . . we didn't have any idea what was going to happen to us."

After her family left the camps at the end of the war, she went to Japan with the Army of Occupation, where she met her husband, a GI in a Tokyo weather station. Her experiences as a medical secretary, seeing the damaged young men from the Korean War, motivated her to work for peace. Her husband, who was a Lieutenant Colonel and a career military officer, left the service because of his opposition to the Vietnam War. She now lives in Boulder, Colorado, and continues to work against war and racism.

My grandfather came to America in 1898. He worked in a cannery in Alaska and finally found a job with the railroad running a restaurant for other railroad workers. He sent for his wife, and then both my grandfather and my grandmother worked together for the railroad. She cooked and did the laundry for all the railroad workers. Around 1906 they decided to bring my father and his other two brothers to the United States. Like migrant workers they would move from one place to the other with the railroad.

In 1923 or 1924 my father went back to Japan to find a wife. My grandparents wrote to relatives to get a matchmaker. They properly trotted out, I suppose, four or five women, and my father chose my mother. They were married in 1924 just before the immigration laws prohibited any more immigration from the Far East, so she got in just under the deadline.

My father did a variety of work. During the depression he sold encyclopedias door to door. He came home every night very, very discouraged. I cannot imagine anyone who would be so optimistic as to try to sell encyclopedias during the depression, when people were having a difficult enough time just keeping body and soul together. In many ways my father was not a very pragmatic person.

My mother, on the other hand, was a very highly motivated, reasonably aggressive women. The Japanese, even in the United States, did not prize aggressive women, but my mother kept pushing my dad to do something better. I don't suppose that caused a great deal of peace and tranquillity in the family.

One of the things that I remember about the day of the attack on Pearl Harbor was that it happened on a Sunday. I remember listening to the radio, and my father and mother being very, very distressed. My father kept saying, "This is very bad; in all probability we'll all be shipped back to Japan." The next day was the Feast of the Immaculate Conception, which is a holy day in the Catholic church and we're obligated to go to Mass. I was the only member of my family who had converted to Catholicism, so I got up by myself and walked to Mass on the day after Pearl Harbor, scared stiff, because by this time my father and my mother's fears were very much impressed on me. I didn't know whether I would get killed on the way to Mass. When I went up to receive holy communion I felt that everyone was staring at me.

We had moved to our house just before Pearl Harbor. My mother and dad had finally gotten enough money together that we had a new rug on the living room floor. My dad had bought a new car, a green 1940 Chevy. So we had some fairly nice material things accumulated by that time. Shortly after Pearl Harbor the FBI came to the house. They dumped everything out of the cupboards and dresser drawers. They yanked everything in the closet off the poles and dumped everything in the middle of the floor. They tore everything apart. I suppose they were looking for contraband. There was a list of things that you had to turn in. My father had to turn in his samurai sword. I suspect that one of the reasons why he was one of the early ones to be picked up was because he belonged to a fencing association, a Kendo-Kai which did demonstrations on the art of the sword.

My mother was hysterical with fear; she just knew that my dad would be picked up and that he would be killed, just be taken and shot. My father was very quiet. I can see him smoking his cigarette, sitting on the couch in the living room, not speaking to anyone. Then the FBI came in the middle of the night and took him away in his pajamas.

We didn't know where he was taken. We had a telephone, but he was not given the right to call home or call a lawyer. He was treated as an enemy national. From the time he was picked up in December 1941, until he was released in January of 1944, he went from camp to camp to camp. My father was considered an enemy alien, but he was a Japanese citizen because Japanese were not permitted to apply for citizenship. In fact, my mother and my father did not receive their American citizenship until 1956, when those who had lived in this country a sufficient number of years were given the permission to apply for citizenship.

I continued to go to school until April of 1942. There was no income; I don't know what we lived on. They froze all of his assets, so I don't know how and where the money came from, but we managed to survive until the Executive Order 9066 was issued by President Roosevelt, which required all of us to report to certain collection points. We were to be put in Army trucks and shipped to assembly centers, they were called. Ours was to be Puyallup County Fairgrounds for the Seattle area. We had been given about two weeks notice before we had to leave for the camps. We had to leave behind what we couldn't sell. We had hordes of people who came to buy our things: the car, the rug, the ironing board—everything. We left behind some of our Japanese children's festival dolls. In 1947, when I went back to Seattle, I went to the house to see if there was anything left. There was absolutely nothing there.

We were told we could take what we could carry. My mother, being a person who thought that what you could carry meant "suitcase," got a suitcase for each one of us kids, and we had to decide what we could take in our suitcase besides our clothes. The other Japanese families were much smarter; they took sheets or blankets and piled everything inside and made a great big huge bundle in which they could carry all their household stuff. I took three books: the missal for the Catholic Mass, the *Last of the Mohicans,* and Helen Hunt Jackson's *Ramona.* I find it interesting that they were both stories about Native Americans.

It was chaotic at the collection points, which were actually telephone poles on which a notice was nailed by the army that said we were required to report by such and such an hour—of course it was in military time, like 0800, which I didn't understand. But there were enough army GIs around to make sure that everyone came. We all piled into big army trucks and were carried to the assembly center.

It was a small county fairgrounds, so you could imagine what it was like with six thousand people. We stayed in stalls, which had no ceiling to the partitions and a dirt floor. You could hear all the noises; there was no privacy whatsoever. They slapped whitewash over the partitions. Lying in a canvas camp cot—which had a mattress stuffed with straw that I suppose was used for the horses in the fairgrounds, normally—I was picking at something on the whitewashed partition. I suddenly realized I was picking manure they had just painted over. The stalls were under the bleacher area, and there was no light except a naked light bulb they had hanging here and there.

I did a lot of daydreaming. I laid on my cot, and I just looked up at the ceiling. One of the reasons why I don't remember much about it is because there was not much to do. I didn't have many Japanese friends because I went to a Catholic girls' school, which was at that time all white—I was the only Asian there. When I started kindergarten I couldn't speak any English at all, only Japanese. There were no Japanese-speaking teachers; they couldn't find jobs. So, I was often a "loner."

We had no idea where my father was; we had no communication with him. Toward the end of our stay in the Puyallup assembly center we got our first letter from my father. I think he was in a camp in North Dakota. He was allowed one letter a month. All of his letters had great big gaping cutouts in them where they had been censored. What could a man who'd been put in a prisoner-of-war camp say in his letters that was of national security risk, that they would cut it out? I cannot imagine. He wrote, "Be strong." "Help your mother." "Take care of your sister." "Take care of your brother." "Work hard in school." That's all I remember from his letters.

Then the time came when we were told to bundle up our stuff, and we gathered at a central place in the camp. We stood around for a long time and then were put into army trucks again and taken to a railroad spur, where we were loaded on trains. No one knew where we were going to go. The train was completely blacked out. The shades were drawn and they were nailed down, so you could not even peek out. The train had wooden benches because this was wartime and the troops got the better trains. We were on the train for two nights. Finally we were told that we had arrived, and it was only then that we were allowed to pull the shade up. It was southeastern Idaho. It was nothing but tumbleweeds, dust, blowing sand, and sagebrush. We were dumped in this place and waited until some more army trucks came. Then we were trundled off and dumped into the camp. There were tar paper barracks buildings, just one after another. Black buildings, if you can imagine, in this desolate, dusty, sagebrush country.

The first meal we ate when we got off the train was Vienna sausages and sauerkraut. It was horrible. I got desperately sick and had to stand in line for the outhouses because the camp was not finished. We got a lot of Vienna sausages and sauerkraut at the camp. It was not until I was grown that it occurred to me why we got Vienna sausages and sauerkraut. It's German food they couldn't sell. To this day, when I see a can of Vienna sausage, I get nauseated.

There were four of us—my mother, my brother and my sister, and I. We were allocated a room that was about ten by fourteen feet. The cots were metal, without sheets at the beginning because of the shortages. We got there in September of 1942 and stayed there until January 1945. In January of '44 my father was sent to our camp, and we were finally reunited. When my father finally joined us, my mother hung a sheet across the room. It must have been very hard for my dad to come back to be with us in yet another camp.

Finally we had school after we'd been in camp about two months. More barracks buildings. The teachers had been teaching in Bureau of Indian Affairs schools so they treated the kids the same way they treated the Indian kids, with no respect. I hated it. I had been such a good student, and I absolutely hated every day that I had to go to school. They were more interested in getting us skilled in office work than college prep, and I was very much interested in going to college. In the beginning we had no proper school. We had slat benches and no desks. By the end of the first year, they began to get tables and chairs, traditional school-type furniture. We had no books. It was strange being in a camp and having to say a pledge of allegiance inside barbed-wire fences. I found that very difficult to accept. I finished high school there, and I remember the bitter feeling I had about wearing caps and gowns inside the confinement of camp. Our graduation ceremony was out in the dust. I got a bloody nose from all the dust.

The son of the camp director was killed in the South Pacific in a plane crash. He gathered everyone, all ten thousand people, in front of the administration building where the American flag was flying and told us, en masse, " 'Your' planes killed my son today." I was so angry because I could think of three or four women I knew in camp whose sons had been killed in the Italian campaign. He was treating us like the enemy!

One time I was walking by the fence around the camp; it was one of the few places you could walk in the camp and be by yourself. One of the

GIs who was on duty told me either to step back or I'd be shot. I was so startled by what he said that I stepped back immediately. We were treated like so much cattle.

We never talked about the war. We never talked about our anger. We never talked about our frustration. We never talked about things like what we were going to do after we got out of camp, because we were afraid to talk about it. We didn't have any idea what was going to happen to us. When we finally got out of camp we moved to New York. The only way you could leave camp, at that time, was to be sponsored, just like refugees are sponsored today. One of the priests who worked in the camp made arrangements for us. My father got a job as a custodian for an orphanage in upstate New York. While we were in New York I visited the Hawaiian Nisei soldiers who were sent to the Utica Army General Hospital. If you're eighteen years old and you haven't seen anything physically brutal, it's horrible to see young men with half the body blown away.

On VJ-Day I knew nothing about the fact that the atom bomb had been dropped, just that the war was over. There was a lot of celebrating going on in downtown Utica. I remember a woman turning around to look at me. She said, "Of all the nerve! What makes you think that you should be down here celebrating?" Before I could answer, she said, "Get the hell out of here!" I remember going home feeling pretty dreadful.

After the war I met a young man who said that they were soliciting people to sign up for civil service with the Army of Occupation in Japan. I got a position and went to Japan in 1947. I visited Hiroshima and Tokyo, which was still a very devastated city. As we came off the boat, there were a lot of men who came scurrying around to try to get our bags for us. How poor they were and what rags they were wearing and how many there were trying to pick up our bags to get some kind of a tip! I was stunned by what this meant. The Japanese as a race were absolutely, totally defeated. I don't know how to describe it, except that if you're defeated, there's a tremendous loss of self-worth, especially if you've been pumped up during the war years in Japan that you're the super race. The devastation in Hiroshima was incredible. It was only then that I realized the impact of the bomb.

I married in 1950. My husband was a U.S. Army officer working at the Tokyo Weather Central, which was a cooperative weather forecasting center with Japanese weather forecasters.

It was the Korean War that made the horrors of war most real to me. The Tokyo Army Hospital had so many litters and wounded that they simply put them in the hallways because there was no room. There were feet that were gone and arms that were gone and bodies that were just terribly mutilated with the bloodied bandages lying there. One of my jobs was to help process the patients so that they could be shipped back to the States. The others were kept to be repaired sufficiently so they could be sent back to the front lines. It was my first real understanding of what death was. I can still smell the stench of young bodies in their beds or stretchers. That's when I began to feel very torn by what I was doing, which was to help process these men, to be part of the "system."

All of these experiences led to my beginning to question what war was all about. Up until then, even during World War II, I hadn't really put it together. I began to think about what war really was, in the context of what death was. To my dying day I will not forget the Korean War experience. At that time I was pregnant with our first child. All I could think about were the brutal effects of war; this could very well be my own son some day.

During the time the Vietnam War was really beginning to heat up, my husband had reached a crossroads in his military career. By this time he was a lieutenant colonel, and he was invited to attend War College. The War College is where they train generals. It meant a commitment of another ten years. By this time he was at the Pentagon, and he was very uneasy about our military policy in Vietnam. He felt that the Vietnam War was unconscionable. He didn't oppose World War II, and even during the Korean War he felt that our U.S. policy was preserving democracy. But the Vietnam War was really quite different. So he resigned his commission.

I joined WILPF because it was a legitimate organization for women with a long-standing history; when you looked at all of the different peace movements and peace groups that came and went, WILPF was one of the few that continued to survive.

In various groups I've been irritated at being the token Asian. I have often felt marginalized because I'm the one who brings up racist issues. There have been times when I felt I was really butting my head against the wall. It's not to impugn the goodwill of these groups. It's just that they are, after all, members of this greater society, and so they have the same kinds of problems with sharing power as society as a whole.

I can remember a time when Japanese weren't hired in Seattle for any teaching jobs. They ran fruit stands, and they were farmers and farm laborers. And these are college graduates. The climate has changed, but we have not reached the ultimate potential we can have in terms of understanding. People still say to my face, "But Mariagnes, I never think of you that way"—that is, as an Asian. That denies the person that I am. And they're well-meaning people, which makes the job all the more frustrating and difficult. I know that great strides have been made, and real attempts have been made to involve women of color, but I don't think we've done enough yet. There will be tremendous changes in the next ten years and change doesn't always come easily.

Marii Hasegawa, 1985.

MARII KYOGOKU HASEGAWA

I had read about the firebombings in Dresden and the bombings in Tokyo and all that, but it had never actually penetrated. It was all just part of war. But the atomic bomb was different; I began to realize that if we were to go on the way we had, the world would be destroyed.

Marii Kyogoku Hasegawa was born in Hiroshima, Japan, in 1918. Her father was a Buddhist priest and teacher who brought his family to the United States in 1919 when he came to minister to the religious needs of the Japanese here. In 1942 the family was sent to Tanforan Relocation Center near San Francisco, where they were held in hastily "refurbished" horse stalls and then transfered to Topaz camp in Utah. "We did get assistance from the community," she says, "but it was only to ease our way to camp." Marii had an opportunity to become the American equivalent of Tokyo Rose—to prove her patriotism—but the plans for the broadcasts were canceled.

She joined WILPF in 1947 because it stood for peace and freedom and had protested the evacuation of the Japanese. She served as president of international WILPF. Her community of Richmond, Virginia, recently commemorated Hiroshima day by erecting a World War III Memorial Wall displaying the names of all the people in town taken from the phone book.

My father was a Buddhist priest who had majored in English at the university. He was asked to come to the United States by his church because they thought he would be the proper person to help meet the religious needs of the immigrant population that was increasing in California. So he brought my mother, my sister, and me in 1919. Asians were not allowed to become citizens in those days, until 1952 when the law was amended by the Walter-McKerron Act. After the law was passed, I did not immediately become a citizen because, for one thing, I was protesting the discrimination against places of origin of many people of color. I was also still very petrified of McCarthy and the HUAC hearings. I was afraid that if I started a citizenship application and went through all the investigation, that my ability to work for peace and justice issues would be nullified. Eventually it became very clear to me that even one vote might make a difference. So I became a citizen of the United States in 1984.

I grew up in California. It was a very insular kind of life; the Japanese community lived in practically a ghetto. Since my father was a priest, all of our organizations were Japanese American in character. But in junior high school and high school I began to break away and become more active in the larger community. I was quite unusual in those days because people were expected to stay with their own groups. But my father had always encouraged me to try to do everything I wanted to do. My sister and I went to the University of California. We could not find a place to stay in Berkeley. There were no rooming houses which would accept Japanese Americans or people of Japanese ancestry. We eventually rented a house in the Japanese section of Berkeley and later moved to the international house on campus, which was accepting people of all colors and races.

I had friends among all races. I wasn't particularly a part of the Japanese American group or anything like that. I have always been very interested in breaking down racial barriers. I was also in the YWCA, which was a very good experience. They were trying very hard to overcome discrimination.

After I graduated I wasn't able to find employment in my field. It was in the midst of the depression, and other people weren't finding jobs, but it was particularly difficult for Orientals. People didn't want to work with Japanese. I knew that. The Japanese Americans knew that when they went to college. Some people thought that it was a waste of time for us to go to college because we would never get the kind of jobs we were qualified for. In those days, we didn't think a great deal about career goals. We thought that if we got out of school and got a job, that was about it. So I didn't really go beyond trying to find a job. I think the first Japanese public school teacher hired in California wasn't until 1949. My sister couldn't find work after college either and had to do maid's work. My father thought it would be good if she went back to Japan and tried to use her education. So she went back to Japan to a women's college. I stayed here in the United States.

My politics were always on the liberal side. I was greatly influenced for instance by my English teacher who let us out of his class on November 11, when there was observation of Armistice Day. There was a ceremony of two minutes of silence. That started me thinking about the implications of war. I opposed the Japanese invasion of China, and yet all around me in the community there were people who were collecting things to send to Japan for the soldiers to use. I never participated. I boycotted Japanese silk by refusing to wear silk stockings. My political development was by little spurts. I didn't spend much time thinking, "This is the answer to everything." I read a lot of stuff about the war and about discrimination against the Jews under Hitler. But it was all an intellectual interest. It was not a real gut feeling that I should be doing something about it.

When the war broke out on Pearl Harbor day I could really not believe what I was hearing. It was like a science fiction story. It never occurred to me that it would have consequences for me because I knew that most of my relatives were in the United States and my father had always said to his students in Japanese language classes that their country is the United States. He told their parents that too: "You have to raise your children to be Americans. You must not expect them to ever be Japanese again."

First of all, there was an alien registration drive when the war in Europe broke out. All aliens had to be registered, Germans included, so we were registered. It turned out that things were much worse than I expected. I was a member of the Nisei Young Democratic Club. We testified against the decision to evacuate Japanese Americans from coastal areas. Later on, because we testified, members of that group were known as "reds." We were just using our rights of free speech; our name was the Democratic Club.

My parents and I were together during those last months before we were sent to camp, which was fortunate, because that meant that we went to the same place. We were given about six week's notice to report to the evacuation center. We were really pretty lucky; in some places they only got twenty-four hours notice and had to leave overnight. We were able to put all our things up for sale, but it netted us very little because people at that time knew that we had to get out. We tried to go to the interior part of the United States, rather than be sent to a camp, but few of us were equipped economically. Then the areas in the interior started saying that if California and Washington and Oregon didn't want us, they didn't want us either.

We did get assistance from the community, but it was only to ease our way to camp. The staff at the international house said we could use their basement for storing our things, which was very good, because my father had an extensive library. We left our car in a garage, thinking we might later come back for it. We gathered at the Berkeley Community Church on the morning we left on the buses. They helped us bring luggage from home to the church, although we were only allowed two pieces or whatever we could carry.

I felt very strongly that it was wrong, that we had not been given any opportunity to say what we thought, or anything. It seems ironic, but at that time the FBI was the only government agency that opposed our being sent to camp. They had already, on December 7, swooped down and taken up leaders of the Japanese community, members of the Japanese associations, and representatives of the Japanese army to separate camps. So the FBI thought that all danger was taken care of and there was no need to disrupt our lives. That was the only time the FBI was on my side. But at that time the Women's International League for Peace and Freedom was one of the few organizations that came out publicly against the evacuation, the concentration of the Japanese in camps. I had not known WILPF at all until then.

First we went to Tanforan Race Track. We were put in the stalls where the horses had been kept; they had been whitewashed so that people could live there. Barracks were hastily constructed in the center of the raceway so that people who could not be accommodated in the stables could live there. There were field kitchens equipped with coal-burning stoves. We were allowed to eat only in the mess hall. You couldn't even make tea at night because we were not supposed to bring any electrical appliances. There were communal bathrooms and toilets scattered here and there in the areas. The horse stalls we lived in only had partitions up three-quarters of the way. The tops were all open. My father and mother and I lived in this one little stall. We were issued cots, and we had to fill our mattresses with straw. We were not allowed to bring knives into the camp or anything that might be considered dangerous. But many people smuggled things in.

We stayed there from April until August. We were a very politically inert group, that's all I can say. We tried very hard to make sure that the children and the younger people did not get bored and get into trouble. We started classes. We had concerts and plays. Classes were Americanized, although there were groups that did Japanese singing. But the classes were an attempt to carry on what the students were missing while they were in camp. I was twenty-six. My parents were in their fifties.

Then we were transferred to Topaz camp in Utah. We stayed there for thirteen months. Conditions were much the same. In the communal kitchen seventy-two families ate together. Evacuees signed up to be cooks, and they prepared the meals. Families could eat separately if they wanted to. It was one of the causes of breaking up a lot of family closeness because the children, especially the teenagers, wanted to go with their peer group and not eat with their family.

It was really very difficult to have school in the camps because when we were talking about the pledge of allegiance to the flag, here we were in camp. Discussions would arise about the conditions, but we couldn't do much. About six months after our transfer to Topaz, relocation authorities decided to get us out of camp as soon as possible. We were no longer going to be there for the duration. One of the reasons was that there was a great manpower shortage. They needed our muscle. The farmers went out first on temporary leave to bring in the harvest. Later they could take more permanent leaves.

The rest of us had to answer a questionnaire about our loyalty to the United States. This is the first time that we had been able even to state what we felt about the country. They did that very badly. The questionnaire asked the infamous question 28: "Do you foreswear all loyalty to the Emperor of Japan?" It was like asking, "Have you stopped beating your wife?" You were implicated if you answered yes or no. Many people refused to sign it because they had had no loyalties to the Emperor. Others did not want to sign it because it would make them stateless persons, because they could not become citizens of the United States. Some of the Japanese in the camps were completely Japanese. They had exercises and saluted the Japanese flag. They were just preparing for the day they could go back. Families were split. Some young people left their families. We were also given another question about if we would do anything to harm the United States, which we were willing to sign.

My parents stayed in camp until the war was over. They wanted me to go. They felt that I would be wasting my time in camp. My father was still doing his pastoral work; he was doing a great deal of good.

I was beginning to formulate some ideas about how I felt. In fact, at that point I was supporting the United States wholeheartedly. I even tried to get into the armed forces because they were being opened up for Japanese Americans. But as an alien, I was refused. I could have been in what they called the intelligence service because I spoke Japanese and English. Then the defense people decided that maybe they could put me to use. Even if I didn't serve in the army, I could be the American equivalent of "Tokyo Rose." Tokyo Rose would broadcast over the radio to American GIs making them homesick, singing American songs. They wanted me to do the same to the Japanese soldiers, make news reports and so forth, to say, "Go home. You're losing." I don't know how I would have done, because it never came to pass. I had to make a recording and send it in. Then they wrote back and said they had decided it was a bad idea. It wasn't done. I missed my chance for fame.

My job in the camp was as a social worker because I spoke Japanese and English. Although I had no social service training, I was my father's daughter. I translated for people to see doctors and in schools and other situations. I also helped to run the camp newspaper and literary magazine. Most of the work in the camp was done by evacuees. The supervisors all came from outside the camp, and they lived in a section of the camp area in better apartments than we had. They were also paid more than we were.

We were able to leave camp if we had an outside job. That was very difficult, because you couldn't get a guarantee of a job unless you knew someone outside. I came out from camp eventually as a cook for the Baptist Home Mission Society, which had a hostel. Much later I got into my field of nutrition. I worked for the Women's Hospital in Cleveland, Ohio.

I was able to communicate with my family in Japan through the Red Cross and with my family in the camp by phone. My sister was in a town just outside Hiroshima, so she did not get the full impact of the blast. She had been ill during her stay in Japan, and friends and family cared for her. They were so good to her—in Japan, when you go to the hospital, your family brings you food and takes care of you and washes your clothes. They carried her in a wheelbarrow to the hospital in this small town outside of Hiroshima and looked after her there. So she was safe.

I was in Philadelphia working for an agricultural workers union when the news came of the bombing of Hiroshima. It was a shock. It was then that I started thinking of war in terms of what it meant as far as casualties. I had read about the firebombings in Dresden and the bombings in Tokyo and all that, but it had never actually penetrated. It was all just part of war. But the atomic bomb was different; I began to realize that if we were to go on the way we had, the world would be destroyed.

When the war was over and the cold war came, it all seemed to be going down the drain again. I believed that war was not the way to settle international disagreements. I started to look for an organization in which I might be active. I remembered that WILPF had been one of the groups that had protested the evacuation of the Japanese, so I joined in Philadelphia. I think I have been a member since 1947.

I met my husband-to-be in Philadelphia. He was involved in the resettlement of the Japanese Americans. He had also been in a camp, but he was helped by a Quaker group, the Student Relocation Committee. It gave people whose schooling was interrupted an opportunity to go to college in the East. Some of the recipients of aid from that committee have now formed a group which offers scholarships every year to students from Southeast Asia. So we feel the spirit has gone on.

In 1948 I worked for a union, organizing and picketing. We were trying to organize office workers at RCA. Our neighbors ostracized us because a black delegate to the founding convention stayed at our house.

Over the years, we've been under pressure for our peace and justice work. My oldest daughter and I once went to a demonstration in Washington, D.C. Somehow our names got in the paper as being among those who had been at the demonstration; we started getting these telephone calls, heavy breathing calls. I was really very worried because of the children. One time I got a huge box of envelopes billed to us. In the corner they had printed "Mary Red and Company."

I stayed with WILPF because it was the one organization where peace and freedom were linked, and I felt that was very important. The two issues are inseparable. I think that one of the things that women bring to the peace movement as a whole is their ability to work hard, and sometimes that is to the disadvantage of the woman. I've always felt, for instance, that so many movements just push women aside except for their ability to send out mailings and all that kind of work. When it comes to decision-making or even in public appearances they always turn to men.

How can we have more freedom? It's not one of those things that will be accomplished quickly. I'm concerned that there is a lessening of caring generally in the United States. There is a lot more apathy. It might be better if people were strongly against you than this apathy. One of the reasons for the apathy is the terrible insecurity of the times. The future is so indefinite. Many people are insecure in their jobs and in their families. People want to hide from things and not participate in anything because they are upset and feel they can do so little about everything. People don't even want to vote. They just say, "What's the use?"

Constitution day is my birthday, so I think a great deal about things then. People aren't really aware of what the Constitution means. They think it's a nice sounding document and all that, but many people are not even aware that the original Constitution didn't have a bill of rights. People had to struggle for those rights. I'm not so much interested in children being able to name the five Great Lakes; I'm more interested if they recognize the Bill of Rights and can say at least five of them. That is much more important. What does 1492 mean? I think that was the beginning of white oppression in this country. We don't teach ideas like that.

Recently on Hiroshima day we had an event: It was called the World War III Memorial Wall, and it displayed the names of all the people living here in Richmond, Virginia. We cut up the telephone book and pasted it on a big wall we constructed. It came in nine sections. It attracted a lot of attention and made a point.

What keeps me active is habit; it's a good habit. I just keep thinking of all that needs to be done and try not to get discouraged. I keep on trying, really trying to get young people involved; to see them drop out makes me feel that I failed. You have to look to the future and young people are the future. Unless we are willing to be active, there might not be a future.

3.

Civil Rights and Peace

Mary Bess Cameron, 1990. Photograph by Brenda Parnes.

MARY BESS OWEN CAMERON

I began to get very intense about race issues in the 1930s. It came as quite a shock to discover all of these things. My father had been a Ku Klux Klan member. I remember that my first political parade was in Detroit in the twenties, walking on Woodward Avenue beside my father carrying a Klan banner, very proud.

Mary Bess Cameron was born in Detroit, Michigan, in 1915 and survived the depression with an independent and headstrong nature inherited from her mother, who worked one summer being shot from a circus cannon. The first political march she participated in was a Ku Klux Klan rally, which she attended as a child with her father. Rejecting those roots, she later helped integrate Indiana University. She intended to be a doctor and visited the dean of admission to a medical school with her entrance application and letters of recommendation. He told her that the school policy was to admit one woman and one black every year and that they had already admitted a black woman, getting "both in one crack." Her sense of outrage and injustice has carried her through activities against racism, sexism, and war. She now lives in New York City.

My father was a building contractor, and I lived in possibly twenty different houses. As soon as he'd build a house and finish it, we'd live in it, and he would put it on the market to sell. When it sold, we'd move into another house. So I went to seven or eight schools during my first five years in school. In 1927 we moved more into the country on seven acres of land, which my father subdivided. We had a large old farmhouse and had fruit and vegetables and a very rural environment. My family was probably the richest one in the area except that we owed the most money too, and when the foreclosures came, we were on welfare along with the rest. Welfare at that point meant not that you got any money from the government, but you could get beans and peas and old shoes by going down and lining up for them. The situation was extremely miserable. If you had any medical problems, which my mother did, you had to get the township trustee's okay before you could get any medical treatment. Now sometimes the trustee was not around, and you didn't get the medical treatment. I've always been strongly involved in movements for Medicare since that time.

My entire high school had one hundred students in it; there were twenty-eight in my graduating class. All the students in my high school were on relief. My father had no income except for a temporary political appointment for about one hundred dollars a month. That didn't give us nearly enough to live on.

For a while I had the only job in the family. I was paid seven dollars a week for clerking in a drug store. I ate all that I wanted to on the side and it was quite a benefit. When the boss wasn't around I had lots of ice cream. I'd get milk once in a while, but mainly ice cream.

I had that firsthand experience of not having enough. My friends around me were having as bad or worse experiences. One of my best friend's father was a skilled mechanic who had invented a number of automobile parts. But they lived in a shack. I can tell you how to winterproof a shack out of cardboard. You get corrugated cardboard boxes, and you cut these open and put them under your linoleum on the floor, two or three deep, and fill the sides of the wall in with the cardboard and do the same thing with the ceiling and put the wallboard back on. Of course it wasn't very fireproof. That's how people tried to keep their shack warm.

Her father made a little money buying up crankcase oil drained from cars, and he filtered it through four or five filters and sold it for fifteen cents a quart. People were happy to get the fifteen-cent oil. He had a motor, a twelve-cylinder motor from a Packard. He didn't have the car, just the motor, out in the garage. He'd tinker with that motor. He knew I loved cars, and he'd say, "Stop in after school; I want you to hear the car." He collected enough money for gasoline so that he could get a few gallons to get his motor running. We would sit there and listen to it, "Purr . . . putt, putt." It was just beautiful to listen to it.

I always knew I was going to college. My mother was certain of that. I wasn't going to be an elementary school teacher either, the usual position for women. I was going to be a psychologist or a physician or a lawyer. It never occurred to me it would be a problem. My mother had been a little headstrong too. As a young woman, she had a job as a night telephone operator in the post office. One night, instead of being at work, she went out for a stroll with her boyfriend. The courthouse burned down while they were out in the park, not paying any attention to what was going on. She wasn't there to call any of the numbers she was supposed to call—the police, the fire department, etc. The next day she was fired. There was a circus visiting town that day. Mother was a rather small woman, and she decided to see about a job with the circus. They said they had a job if she wanted to be shot out of a cannon. My mother said, "Yes, fine. What else do I have to do?" They said, "Go up in a tethered balloon." She'd do that. So she got the job with the circus, being fired out of a cannon—of course, she wasn't actually fired out of a cannon; she was propelled by a rubber band, but a gun went off and smoke came out. She got caught in a net weighed and measured for her. She had that job for a summer. So I come from a line of determined, independent women.

I lived with an aunt to get into college free, as a resident of Indiana. At first I waited tables in the university cafeteria. At Indiana University there were a fair number of black students, but I was totally unaware of them. They just didn't enter my life until I had to get tutored in French. One gal from New Orleans had been educated in Paris. She came from a wealthy black family, but she wanted to earn some money. First of all, we couldn't eat in the same restaurants when I tried to study during lunch with her. I learned from her that blacks couldn't live in the dormitories, and the only time they could take swimming, which was required, was on Friday afternoon just before the pool was cleaned. I was the only white student who ever ate at the black fraternity house.

I began to get very intense about race issues in the 1930s. It came as quite a shock to discover all these things. My father had been a Ku Klux Klan member. I remember that my first political parade was in Detroit in the twenties, walking along Woodward Avenue beside my father carrying a Klan banner, very proud.

Although I was not old enough to vote, I was a socialist. I joined the Young Peoples Socialist League. A woman who at one time lived next door to me in Chicago was a very devoted Communist, and she distributed the *Daily Worker* on campus. I started reading it. I did not like its policies because it was all for the Spanish War. I was a pacifist. My mother was a suffragist and pacifist. In college, I had read and loved modern poetry that was mostly antiwar poetry. I was very ashamed of my father's association with the Klan. I saw the threat of fascism, Hitler, as another Klan. My father and I didn't get along well.

I was always a strong feminist. I got a lot of ribbing even in high school. I remember someone placed on our bulletin board a picture of a Soviet woman with a babushka driving a tractor. Below it they had printed, "Bess Owen." So I was considered a radical feminist even then. A woman can do anything men can do. I could strip a motor and fix a car as well as any man. I was very fond of baseball and played baseball in high school; I played on the boys' baseball team one year in high school because they didn't have enough boys. I could play outfield better than the boys could.

In college and graduate school I was trained as a sociologist, and most of my friends were in the field. We were horrified by the war. The only thing the Army said a sociologist was equipped to do was to be a chaplain's assistant. One of my best friends was in the first draft. He was a very, very nice, tender-hearted guy. He was put in graves registration, which meant that he had to locate the burial spots of everybody in his unit who died.

There was a woman who came to Indiana University who tried to recruit me into the officers' training program in the Navy. I said, "No way." I would have been a conscientious objector had I been a man. However, I didn't remain a pacifist through World War II.

During the prewar days and in the 1940s, I was involved in black civil rights. CORE (Congress of Racial Equality) people came to Indiana, and I, among other faculty and students, sat with them in the restaurants and did all kinds of direct action. We got the National Association for the Advancement of Colored People [NAACP] started there. It was tough getting the chapter started. With a total of roughly two hundred black students on campus, they sought white members too. They decided to engage the Count Basie orchestra to come down for a big dance. There had never been a dance black students could attend. We had the gym filled with something like twelve hundred couples, all the black students and huge numbers of white students. The NAACP invited Mordecai Johnson, who was the president of Howard University to speak; he was a terrific speaker, a real black orator.

We had this enormous growth of the NAACP, and it hit the headlines. By this time we had the HUAC interviewing everybody, and much to their surprise, they couldn't find a Communist no matter how much they looked. Some of the people from the state didn't like this kind of subversive political movement, and I got a long talking-to from the head of the department. I was untenured faculty, so I was in a risky position.

When the war came, the race issue on campus was pretty well solved in one year. All the dormitories had black students in them; the marching band had blacks and the basketball team. The pool and dining facilities were open to blacks. But we still had sit-ins at local restaurants. A faculty member named Marshall Sterns had a party to which he invited NAACP organizers. The local newspaper, Republican and terribly reactionary, said in the headline, "Marshall Sterns, friend of Marshall Tito and Marshall Stalin, Gives Bloomington Party Mixed in Race and Mixed in Sex." The town went berserk. I was married about this time, and both of us taught. Somebody dug out an obscure ruling that no family could have two members on the state payroll. So one of us had to resign. I resigned.

About this time Truman dropped the atomic bomb. Mordecai Johnson came to campus and said, "War is not the same as it used to be. When this war ends, it will not end with something you hear on the radio. The next time you hear anything it will be the sound of the elevator taking you down to hell or up to heaven." We had a guest in our house, a field secretary of the NAACP. None of the hotels would admit blacks, so he stayed at our house and had his dinners there. He said to me, "They did not do this to Germany. They would never have dropped the bomb on a white nation. The only reason they did it was that it was an oriental nation, darker people."

Erna Harris, 1989. Photograph © by Renée Burgard.

ERNA PRATHER HARRIS

*I was always an actionist. When I was about eight and Negro
people had just gotten to the point of being able to vote, I went all
around the neighborhood to the Negro people and said, "Are you
registered to vote?" And if they said, "No," I would say, "Well,
you have to vote. If you don't vote, what are the young
people, like me, going to do?"*

Erna Prather Harris was born in Kingfisher, Oklahoma, in 1908.
Her father was a Gandhian who celebrated his birthday on Independence Day by having the family read aloud the Declaration of Independence. Always an independent spirit, Miss Harris refused to go
to a segregated college and, after graduation in 1936, started her
own newspaper. It lasted for three and a half years until her position
on conscription caused her to lose advertisers. She has long worked
for civil rights and disarmament. A staunch supporter and founding
member of the cooperative market movement, Miss Harris refuses to
have a telephone, in protest of the phone tax that supports the
military budget. She lives in Berkeley, California.

My father was a Gandhian. He first heard about him when Gandhi was thrown in jail in South Africa. In those days, Gandhi was considered very odd. The *Daily Oklahoman,* which was the daily paper we received, referred to him as "that little man in diapers," and would say what a fool he was. One time the paper said Gandhi would find out that he had a lion by the tail, and my father said—I can remember it so clearly, I must have been about eight or nine—"Yes, he does have a lion by the tail and some time he's going to pop that tail like popping a whip and break that lion's neck."

I'm not sure why my father had such great confidence in this poor little man—that he'd be able to break the neck of the great empire on which the sun never set—but he did. We had pictures from the newspaper of Gandhi all over our house. We had wallpaper and, with a long straight pin, you could pin up things like that, so my father pinned pictures of Gandhi everywhere.

My father was born on the fourth of July, and the thing we used to do at breakfast to celebrate his birthday was to read the whole Declaration of Independence. Most people just know the first few lines. But one of the advantages of being primitive and semiliterate is that you don't understand that you just read a few lines. You're so proud that you can read that you read documents all the way through. There's great stuff in there that says, "If they don't do you right, knock them on the head with this document or the Constitution." So I guess you could say that I got a revolutionary start to begin with.

My mother was an addicted reader. In our house there were books about us Negroes. My folks were remarkable in that they made a big effort to find books for us. As a matter of fact, the library in that town was about as big as a medium-sized cloak room in the courthouse. No Negro could get into that room. And if a white person out of the goodness of his heart would lend a book which he or she had borrowed from the county library to a Negro, that person would lose his checkout privileges as well as the friendship and admiration of most of his friends in the town.

I was always an actionist. When I was about eight and Negro people had just gotten to the point of being able to vote, I went all around the neighborhood to the Negro people and said, "Are you registered to vote?" And if they said, "No," I would say, "Well, you have to vote. If you don't vote, what are the young people, like me, going to do?" My mother didn't realize what I was doing until I had about half of the town covered and someone called her and said, "Do you know what that young-un of yours is doing? She's going around telling everyone to vote."

Of course all the schools in the area were segregated. My friend Kate and I cried for three days when we realized that grownups—who didn't seem to understand a single thing—were going to send us to different schools although we lived across the street from each other.

When I was a junior in high school I was offered a scholarship to a state university, Langston University, which was segregated. And to my mother and father's horror, because not only were we poor, but times were bad then, I said I wasn't going to go. They couldn't understand it. But I told them that when I graduated from Frederick Douglass School I was never going to set foot in another segregated school in my whole life. I wasn't even going to visit one. Let it be said that when I did go away, it was to the University of Wichita, an integrated university, which is now Wichita State.

I graduated from the university in 1936. Because the president of our college class knew very well I was coming to the graduation, our class was the first class in that university that had a banquet to which all the kids were invited, whites and Negroes. The interesting thing is that the banquet was at a big hotel, and the rule was that Negroes went up in the freight elevator. Nobody had warned the poor man who ran the elevator that I was coming, and when I arrived with four classmates whom I had picked up in a taxi, the elevator man came up to me and said, "The elevator for you is right around the corner there." I said, "The elevator for me opens onto the lobby, and I'm in front of it now." So I got on and he said, "Well, I can't take you up." I said, "Well, I guess I'm just going to have to run it myself." The man who was running the elevator—you could see his eyes twinkle—he was intrigued by this "idiot" who didn't understand. But I understood the laws of the land. If they put us off, I would have sued them for two floors of that hotel because I knew there wasn't any law that said I couldn't ride on that elevator. So he carried us up to the banquet room.

On the 6th of June, 1936, I received my bachelor's degree. On the 3rd of July I started my first newspaper, which I ran for three and a half years. I couldn't get a job; it was during the depression. There were no jobs and I was determined not to take just any job. I wasn't going to work for the welfare department; I was not going to work in a job where I had to tell mothers with hungry children that they couldn't have ten dollars more.

The paper was called the *Kansas Journal*. Circulation was about four or five hundred. About two-thirds of the subscribers were Negroes, a third were white. The whites bought it because they could not believe it. But they were very proud because the University of Wichita was a school that was part of the city, and in spite of my "misfortune" of being born the color I was, I was their kid. But I understood there were a few bets around that the newspaper wouldn't last a year.

My paper collapsed because they started talking about the National

Training and Service Act, which was conscription, and I opposed it. Three weeks after I had run one of the best editorials I have ever written against it, I didn't have a single ad. So I had to give it up.

I knew about Women's International League for Peace and Freedom when I was in college in Wichita. There was a strong branch there. But the members all seemed so well turned-out and I was so poor that I thought it wasn't for me. Being me, I referred to them as the "sterling silver set." I came up to northern California from Los Angeles in 1952. When I came I was looking around for a gang that was a peace group, and I was invited to a meeting of the WILPF. There was something about them that was really different from the ladylike stance of the people I had known in Wichita and Los Angeles, so I joined. I was one of the few Negro members.

We opposed McCarthy and the House Un-American Activities Committee. We worked against nuclear armaments and conventional armaments. We were working against the so-called peace atom. We had a motto for a long time, "There's no such thing as a peace atom." Business people hated us for that. We fought the effort to make the War Department into a Defense Department. We said it would make it harder to get rid of arms because who can be opposed to defending yourself?

The most successful thing I have done is live a life. Art is the thing around here at this moment, and somebody said to me recently, "I was wondering, do you have any artistic hobbies?" I said, "I'm working on the most gorgeous tapestry. I'm sorry you haven't noticed it. You see, I'm living." That's the great art piece that I've been working on for a long, long time.

Enola Maxwell, 1984. Photograph © by Renée Burgard.

ENOLA MAXWELL

I value freedom and I value freedom more than anything else in the world. If the day comes when I can't speak for freedom and justice, I've lived long enough.

Enola Maxwell, born in 1919 in Baton Rouge, Louisiana, considers herself a graduate of "the class of '63"—part of the 1963 March on Washington during which Rev. Martin Luther King, Jr., gave his historic "I have a dream" speech. Her first full-time job was selling insurance for a black insurance company in Louisiana. When she came to San Francisco during World War II to follow family members who had found work in Bremerton, Washington, and San Francisco shipyards, she was denied her license because of race discrimination. She found work as a domestic and later, after Truman integrated the civil service, worked for the U.S. Post Office. Never willing to have a "poverty mentality," she put her children through school and bought her own home. She became a lay preacher in the Presbyterian Church in 1967 and eventually served as spiritual counsel for the Black Panthers, urging them to nonviolence. In the seventies she ran unsuccessfully for San Francisco county supervisor, hoping to bring politics out of the back room and into the public eye. In 1972 she became the director of a multicultural community center in San Francisco, a position she still holds.

I grew up in Baton Rouge, Lousiana, where black people were constantly out there fighting for their rights through the NAACP and the Baptist church. I grew up in the Baptist church. My earliest memories are of being in the church and the NAACP meetings. I began to have this awareness of the horrible injustices that were heaped on black people. The NAACP fought legal battles, and they keep fighting. Just before I left Louisiana they had achieved equal pay for black and white teachers. We fought for that for many years. When I was in Baton Rouge, a black man shot a police officer and didn't even go to jail. Now that was really a landmark in Louisiana.

My family was involved in these things. My grandmother was really a liberated woman. I was never so proud of anybody in my whole life as this woman. During the depression was the closest our family came to being on welfare. This woman from the welfare came in and went into the cupboard in the kitchen. In the bottom drawer my grandmother had a can of condensed milk and some coffee and a nickel's worth of sugar. This woman said, "Oh! You got sugar." Like it was a major luxury. My grandmother said, "What do you expect me to sweeten my coffee with? Get out! Get out!" She followed her right on out to the porch until she went out of sight. Three of us grandchildren were following right behind her. She had dignity and pride.

When I came to San Francisco I found that black people were looking for dignity and pride, but you know I had dignity and pride all my life; I grew up with it and always had it. My grandmother, this woman couldn't read and write her own name, but the pride and dignity she had! I didn't understand all this at the time, but later I did.

The closest I ever came to throwing anyone out like that was in Louisiana. There was this white man who was selling industrial insurance; I was selling industrial insurance for a black company, and he was selling for a white company. Well, he comes in, and he begins to tell me how much better his policy was than mine. I listened to him for a while, and I said, "Well, I don't take insurance from any company that I can't work for." He said, "That's the trouble with all of you. We should send you back to Africa." He went on and on about how the niggers were getting above ourselves. I had this pot of water boiling, so I said, "Would you please leave?" He wouldn't, so I said, "OK, stay there," and I went back into the kitchen and got this pot of water and came out with it. He ran out the front door as fast as he could.

It was at that point that I decided that I would get a different attitude. I could not live with that anger and hatred; it's just too much. I had to learn to love these people with Christianity. Christianity had to work for me. Some change had to be made if I was going to be a Christian. So I started working on that and getting some quietness of spirit and peace of mind.

Before we left Baton Rouge it was really a struggle keeping the freedom and keeping from this hate business. When my son was a little boy, every morning he'd get up very early, and when the milkman came, he was out on the porch and would say "Good morning" to the milkman. The milkman, who was white, would never speak to him. One day he says, "Mama, why doesn't the milkman speak to me?" So the next morning when the milkman came I told him, "When my son says good morning to you, you say good morning to him. If you do not say good morning to him, do not leave another bottle of milk on this porch." So then he started saying good morning to him.

But it wasn't easy. We had not ridden public transportation much because my son, when he was about four years old, couldn't sit where he wanted—you know, the back of the bus business. If Dr. King had done no more than bring us from the back of the bus, the man would have achieved true greatness. My son and I had gone downtown on a city bus. He was walking ahead of me and sat on the first seat he got to. A black woman got on the bus, put her money in, and said he should sit in the back. My God, I thought, here is how we start teaching inferiority. So we never rode public transportation ever again.

When we got to San Francisco I was about twenty-nine. I had sold insurance in Louisiana, and I was ready to sell insurance in San Francisco, so I took a training course. At the end of the classes we got a notice to come down to city hall to get our license. I went on down, believing there was no segregation, no discrimination, that everything was fine above the Mason-Dixon Line. I sat down with my notice. The man came out and took all the notices and looked at mine, looked at it good, put it down, and went back into the office. He came back again and looked at it good and took it in there with him. He came back again and said, "Well, there seems to be some mistake; I'll call you later and send you another notice. You'll be hearing from us soon." I haven't heard from them yet.

This was a white insurance company. They had only one black insurance company in this city. But I didn't know that to be a black insurance agent in San Francisco for a white insurance company—and a woman— was unheard of at that time. I sat around waiting for something to happen. That was my ignorance. It was a long time before I found that it never was going to happen. So I got a job as a housekeeper, doing domestic work like most black people were doing in this city, and work in a laundry.

Finally, I got a job at the post office, a good-paying job. This money stuff—lack of money—was another thing like Christianity. There was no way I would be poor. Things had to be different. I just needed to have all of my needs and some of my wants met. I was not going to live in poverty. I told the Lord that something else had to be done because I refused to say Jesus Christ and God is my father and He is rich in powers and in land and I'm living in poverty. So I decided not to be poor, not to have the poverty mentality.

Not knowing I was poor was really a great thing. My mother and I bought a house. We didn't know we weren't supposed to buy a house, that we were too poor to buy a house. I even went and borrowed money from the bank. I didn't know we couldn't borrow money from the bank; a domestic worker didn't know that. It was an advantage not to know what you weren't supposed to do. When I found out I wasn't supposed to do it, it had been done.

In 1967 I became a lay preacher and elder at the Olivette Presbyterian Church. I was the second black woman elder, and our church was the only church that had women elders, period. This was a conservative church that went along with it. I said to myself, "Was that so hard?" By that time the Presbyterians were quite involved in the civil rights movement. I was a member of our Church and Society Committee. I used to raise issues all the time about discrimination. We had another group in the church called the Urban Ministry. I was head of that committee. I think those Presbyterians put me in that position for punishment. I got in this preacher's business for punishment!

I was living in a Haight Ashbury neighborhood in San Francisco where a lot of the peace people were. We went on the march in Washington in 1963 with Dr. King. Then Dr. King made his anti-Vietnam speech. Our church considered Dr. King to be a moral leader of the church. The seminaries supported him and went to Montgomery and built the tents for the march. My church sponsored me to Montgomery.

Peace and civil rights were not always connected for me; most blacks got involved in civil rights way before peace work. In the South we didn't worry too much about peace because the Army was an employment agency for black people. It did break down a lot of barriers in discrimination, and it did provide better income and jobs.

But when I came to San Francisco I got involved in peace. In the seminary where I was going many of the young men were conscientious objectors. At that time I joined Women [Strike] for Peace and WILPF. We were doing the demonstrations against the Vietnam War and marches and leafletting. In my capacity as lay preacher I was doing draft counseling and counseling for conscientious objectors.

I've been fortunate. People allow me to do these things. I would make some of the most outrageous statements in the Presbyterian church, and

Enola Maxwell (right) with Rev. Percy Smith and Coretta Scott King, San Francisco, early 1980s.

I'm telling you now, they wouldn't have been taken from a lot of colored people. Well, they love me, and they support me in whatever I do.

I started work as the director of the Potrero Neighborhood House in 1972. Before that I was on the board of directors. Fifty-one percent of the board had to be Presbyterian, and I belonged to the Presbyterian church. It was very racist at first. Jews and blacks need not apply. But a young minister came and decided he'd try to get a few blacks on the board. We had two black people at the church. Gradually more blacks came on the board of directors and eventually I was hired.

Naturally when I first came to work here people were very reluctant because it was feared that if a black person was the director the community would burn the place down. Now this was the rumor. I was working at the Olivette church down here, and that church had been firebombed twice. I can understand the board of directors' reluctance to hire me because they worried what might happen if they hired a black woman. But, after a lot of community pressure, they decided to hire me.

The place was really broke, and everyone was wondering if we were going to close it down. Some conscientious objectors from the Vietnam War worked there, doing their community service, so we decided that we couldn't close the building down. We found funds here and there. We initiated a visually handicapped program, a youth program including arts, singing, and dancing. We also had a tutorial program. At the church we had a consumer's food co-op; that group and other groups meeting at the church moved up to the community center. We had a legal defense organization and a domestic concerns group that would hold hearings with various elected representatives on cutbacks. And we had our peace movement work, as they still do—we had almost every group you can name.

In 1975 I ran for San Francisco county supervisor. I really don't know if I thought I could actually win. I think I came in seventh—you know there are six supervisors. I was a constant visitor to the board of supervisors, and when I saw how they made decisions, it just burned me up. They sit there in public, and you know that the decisions are made in the back room. I wanted to get elected so that I could bring the decisions out of the back room, so I could tell the public what goes on in the back room. If I would have gotten elected I probably wouldn't have lasted long, with my idea of telling everybody what went on in the back room.

I've always been in groups that stood for nonviolence. I got elected as a spiritual advisor for the Black Panthers, and I thought that was really something. I was so proud of that that I didn't know what to do. I got up and announced it right in the church. Now that's what I mean about getting away with things. Everybody, of course, was scared of the Panthers. I was going to their meetings, and I was encouraging them not to use violence. You can't win with guns. I was a Martin Luther King person.

Let me say some things about women in peace groups. The women are so much different than men; they don't think like a lot of the men in groups. We run the show and let the men do little things on the side. I like the sisterhood. There is a problem, though. Some women feel that they have to resent the men, they have to be *against* the men to be *for* the women. I tell them that they are making a mistake; you cannot allow those men to be over there by themselves because they might get out of hand. It is our responsibility to free the men because they are "unfree." It is their "unfreedom" that causes them to act the way they do. We need to be there to teach them how to be free.

For instance, you know white women didn't know they weren't free until they got into the civil rights movement and said, "Well, wait here, we don't have any freedom ourselves." They decided to try to get freedom. And the gays, they didn't know what condition they were in until they came out of the closet. It was terrible in the closet, and they came out. Look at the Hispanics; these people are the "other whites." Everybody has decided on freedom but the white male. White males have not made any declaration of freedom. They have been brainwashed into believing that they are free people.

I don't want to leave white folks over there by themselves, because if I'm not with them, there's no telling what kind of decisions they might be making. I'm going to force them to make those decisions in front of my face. I want to stand up and state my case and give them another idea. I am not going to let them make any decisions out of ignorance. We sometimes think that white people are so knowledgeable because they propagandize this whole setup; they don't know everything.

The women I work with work well with other women and are supportive of men and the young people. So many times I see some young person trying to start some coalition or something, and they swear their ideas are new and have never been tried before. These women will just sit there and listen. I've learned a lot from them. They knew we tried that idea ten or fifteen years ago and it didn't work, but it may work this time. They patiently teach that you need coalitions and need to work on more than one issue. One issue leaves me cold. You cannot hope to work in any political arena with only one issue. If you don't try to find some other issue, you are dead.

If I were president, the first thing I would do would be to have a meeting with the Russians. Instead of talking about what weapons we were going to freeze, I'd freeze hatred and distrust and all this stupidity and the lies we try to teach our people about each other. I would ask them, "How did you come to this place where you are now, in education, in rights for women, and all?" I would try to see just what we could do to adopt some of those things. I'd also want them to learn some things about America, some of our freedoms. I'd say, "Let me tell you how we came to this place and how you could come to this place too; how people could be free and love their country and not hate other countries." These are the things I would do. I would continue these discussions and see what we could do to bring about the kind of world we'd all enjoy, the Communists in their way and we in our way, but so we could live and not destroy each other. I don't even want to discuss destroying each other. If their ideas work better than ours, we'll decide, since we're a free country. If our way works better than theirs, then let them decide.

I've suffered enough in my life. I have not seen much change. We've had some black people like Dr. King, and Medgar Evers and others. If it looks like they're going to make a difference, that things are going to change, that they have a voice and people are going to listen to them, well, they can't go on living. Even white people can't go on living; if you're going to make a difference, you can't go on living. Lincoln didn't live; the Kennedys aren't living. What it seems to me happens is that if you're going to change things, you're not going to live. San Francisco was so different when Mayor George Moscone was here and Supervisor Harvey Milk was here, I'll tell you, and those men could not go on living. They were shot down. It was not just a loss to the gay community when Harvey Milk was assassinated; he could speak for anybody. And people like Dr. King. Dr. King could speak for anyone; when he spoke, whatever your color, you felt that you had been spoken for. When Harvey Milk spoke, I had been spoken for.

I value freedom and I value freedom more than anything else in the world. If the day comes when I can't speak for freedom and justice, I've lived long enough. That's all there is to it. I have nothing else to do that's more important than speaking for justice and equality. You know, I don't want to live in this world if I cannot work for peace and justice and equality. I have to do that.

I'll tell you what is so dear to me about all these good women who work for peace: it is that they have been there all of these years. They're going to be there until they die. They never gave up. They never stopped. We lost a lot of women; they died and the peace movement didn't. The peace movement goes on and on. Nobody can say anything that has not been said by these women.

Doris Jones, 1984. Photograph © by Renée Burgard.

DORIS COHEN JONES

I always raised a terrific fuss. I heard that one owner
with a segregated apartment complex said it wasn't so much
the black people he objected to, but, "that goddamn woman
from the NAACP"—me!

When Doris Cohen Jones was honored in 1983 for her work with the Mid-Peninsula WILPF, the young draft resister who presented her award noted her special qualities: "I soon found out that she had almost *all* the relevant information, possessed seemingly boundless energy, kept hours as insanely late as we college students, and always had in her pocket a highly organized 'To Do' list." She was born in New York City in 1915 to Russian Jewish immigrants. She attended Hunter College in the thirties, majoring in math and minoring in physics (the physics major was not open to women). She worked as a mathematician at the agency that was the precursor of NASA at Langley Field in Virginia and helped integrate and unionize the aeronautics laboratory there. A committed activist, she also was an accomplished scientist. She and her husband designed a high-quality telescope. She tirelessly worked against race and gender discrimination at the workplace and in housing. She organized People against the Draft and counseled young conscientious objectors and resisters. Doris died in Menlo Park, California, in 1987, leaving a legacy of hardheaded inspiration to younger activists who knew her.

My parents had a small neighborhood store, a mom-and-pop store that sold stationery, school supplies, toys, cigarettes, and newspapers. Education was important to my father. He was born in Russia, in a shtetl where there was a very high premium on scholarship. He worked constantly. I hardly ever saw my father. He left early in the morning, stayed all day, and didn't come home until seven or so, had dinner, and then went to bed, certainly too tired to do much talking. My parents were not political activists, and we never talked about politics. My father read widely, and he undoubtedly had his opinions, but I never heard them.

The first six years of my life we lived in Harlem, down below the cliff on which Columbia University sits. My mother looked Irish, and we were always getting into buildings where the neighborhoods didn't permit Jews to live. They would just have fits when my father came and signed the lease. It happened three times. As we moved further uptown, there were more Jewish people. The last place we lived was a totally Jewish neighborhood.

It never occurred to me that I was going to be anything but a teacher. In that milieu, that was just about the highest thing a woman aspired to. A boy might be a doctor or a lawyer or a businessman. If a woman was a good student, she was expected to be a teacher, maybe a social worker. I prepared to teach. I took all the courses I had to, but when I got out of college in 1934, it was still the depression, so there were no teaching jobs. When they finally started giving teaching exams I took the written and the oral tests. I failed the interview. The man listened to me for half an hour and talked to me mostly about the research I was doing. He said I was temperamentally unsuited to teaching. He was right. He did me the greatest favor in the world. He found out in half an hour what I hadn't found out in a lifetime, and so far nobody else had.

Then I took the Civil Service exams; I didn't care what it might lead to, as long as I got a job. Among the exams I took was an exam for a junior scientific aide. Finally an offer came for a job in Virginia at the Langley Aeronautical Laboratory. This sounded pretty good to me. I was a very romantic person, and the idea of being at a laboratory appealed to me. But the job was not what I thought it would be. When I got there I was called into the administrative office and was told by the head of the administration that there was no place in research for women and that I wasn't to misinterpret this job. They never gave their women anything but routine work to do. I got furious right then. I didn't say a whole lot. I just said, "Well that's pretty hard on the women, isn't it?" and froze up rather than get violent. But I didn't forget it. Not only were all the women confined to routine work, they were confined to segregated offices. We had calculating machines on our desks, and we sat there reading columns and entering the results of calculations. By the time you got out to column forty-eight you were absolutely numb; and instead of multiplying column seven by column thirteen, your eye had shifted, and you were multiplying column eight by column fourteen, or something. It was just a dreadful job.

Well, the first day, all the women got up at lunchtime and went off, saying not a word to me. I trailed along after them and sat down and listened to them all lunch hour discussing whether they should ask their roommate to do their laundry or what they would have for dinner and how the ironing was going and things of that nature.

That evening I met some of the engineers out in the laboratory. So the next day when we came into the cafeteria for lunch, I simply peeled off from the women and sat down with the men and had lunch with them and had a good time. Well it turned out that this was just perfectly awful. I got called into the supervisor's office. I hadn't noticed it but one side of the cafeteria was for men and the other was for the women, and I had gone across the line.

Eventually I was put into a more challenging computing pool. I worked with this man who had taught himself to be an aeronautical engineer. He got a job at Langley Field without having a degree. He was undoubtedly a great aircraft designer, but he really wasn't much of a mathematician, so I was able to whip his stuff into shape. We were a good combination. It was pretty absurd that he would have to come down every day to the pool and give me his figures, so he prevailed on the laboratory to have me transferred into his office. This was in the nature of a revolution, to have a woman working in his lab.

When our first report was ready to go we had another battle. They said it was out of the question for two scientific aides to publish. After waiting for a while to resolve this problem, we finally decided to submit the article to a professional journal, where it was about to be published. The journal had to clear it with the agency, and they blew up. However, they eventually published it. On another report, after we were married, I used my family name, because I had established myself pretty well in the profession. As far as they were concerned, it was not possible that I should put out a report using my maiden name. They brought us into the office. All day long they said in different ways that we were contributing to the breakdown of the American family and how would our children feel? I said the children thought it was great. Well, it was finally published under my maiden name.

There was more trouble. Some of us had the idea of joining up with what was then the American Association of Scientific Workers, a union. It was a liberal group of scientific workers who thought that scientists should concern themselves with public questions and issues and what was being done with the results of their work. This seemed like a really good idea to me. I had not been politically active, but I had a sensitivity to that sort of thing. So we tried to organize a branch of AASW in the laboratory. We tried to end the conditions I was describing, which were very detrimental to research; anybody with a spark of ingenuity or inspiration was promptly squashed. We really had no terribly radical ideas. We were simply trying to improve the climate of research in the laboratory. Nonetheless, apparently the parent organization was highly suspect. And there may have been some people at the laboratory who were in fact attempting to get scientific secrets to the Russians. I can recall now some mysterious approaches that were made to me. I was very naive and didn't see that at all. The laboratory did eventually improve, partly because of our efforts.

We came to California in 1946. In 1950 we were brought up for Loyalty Oath hearings, as were many of our friends from the old lab. Eventually everybody involved with that union, all our friends, were charged and fired. We were the only ones who weren't fired. Who in the aeronautics industry was going to hire somebody who was declared a security risk? I think part of why I worked so hard in the peace movement was to compensate for not having quit our jobs or for refusing to testify at the hearings. I always felt that we let our friends down by continuing to work for the laboratory. Some of the charges against us, in addition to our union organizing, were that a neighbor had heard records in a foreign language, believed to be Russian, being played in our home. (They were operas!) They asked about my Russian background. They were very concerned that I might still have some relatives in Russia and that I might be vulnerable because of that. They assumed I might have some sympathy with the Russian government because both my parents were Russian. So I simply talked about the fact that they had left during the czarist regime and under very hostile circumstances, and we would hardly feel loyalty to Russia.

Our other activities involved "integrating" the lab [at Langley]. The lab was located in a small southern town. Some of us would go to the black quarters to hear music and go to little jazz clubs. This wasn't very popular in the town. I didn't start out to be involved in race issues, or union organizing. It wasn't my objective at all. But gradually you just can't take any more of what's going on. Once we found a means of doing something, I got involved.

The Roosevelt administration set up the Fair Employment Practices Commission. During the war the Civil Service Commission was ordered to remove the photographs from Civil Service applications so that nobody could tell whether the applicants were black or white. One black engineer got hired; he was a student at Case Institute in aeronautical engineering. They were happy to have him until they saw he was black.

120

Suddenly this totally segregated laboratory found itself with a black em-
ployee, other than the gardeners, laborers, and the black female "com-
puters." A whole new set of signs were drummed up. The section to
which he was assigned suddenly developed a separate bathroom with a
sign "COLORED MEN." There was a good deal of commotion about
that. My section supervisor took his screwdriver and removed the sign.

The next day when the man turned up, we all went to lunch together.
There was one large table with a sign "COLORED" on it. We sat down at
that table, and I picked up the sign and put it in my purse because I was
the only one who had a purse—there are certain advantages to being
female. We had lunch together and left. The next day we came down,
and the table had a different sign on it. It said, "RESERVED." It was
reserved for only him. Eventually they gave up on the signs in the cafeteria, but so did our black engineer. He started bringing his lunch and
eating in his office.

But I saw people change their attitudes. Once the problem was
brought to their attention, they changed. Now what that did for me, you
see, was to persuade me that there was a way to change things. If we
could bring people into a situation in which they got to know one another, a lot could be accomplished. Once I could see that there was a way
to work on the racial problem, then I became involved. That's my whole
approach to life anyway. If there's a problem, you try to do something
about it or go on to something that you can do something about. There's
no point in standing around and wringing your hands and complaining.
I'm a very practical person, you see. And a problem solver.

Up until then I was aware of race issues but didn't think about doing
much about them. In New York if I came into the subway and there was a
seat next to a black family or person, that's the seat I would take. Even as
a teenager I was conscious of the problem to that extent. But that's about
all I ever did. Let me tell you a story. The first time I became truly aware
of the race situation was when I was on my way down to Virginia for the
job at Langley Field. I had all my worldly possessions in this one suitcase
in the rack over my head. It was an overnight train. I was seated with a
woman, somewhat older than I. We were having a great conversation,
and I wasn't about to sleep on such an exciting occasion. Up in front of
the car there was a whole bunch of people who seemed to be in a church
group. They were all singing beautifully. They had picnic suppers, and
they were having a wonderful time. I was enjoying every minute of it.

Then suddenly there appeared the conductor. He came up to me, and
he said, "You'll have to leave. Move now." I said, "Why should I move?"
He said, "Well, we just passed the Mason-Dixon Line, and this here is the
colored car and you're going to have to get out." I looked around and
sure enough everybody else in the car but me was black. I protested as

much as I could, but he had already grabbed my suitcase and carried it off. There was nothing for me to do but follow the suitcase. At least I didn't see anything else to do at the moment. It was just a dreadful situation. I was miserable all the rest of the way down to Virginia. That was my introduction to the South. At first I felt completely helpless to do anything about it.

I got involved in integrated housing issues when we moved to California. I felt that if we could integrate housing we perhaps wouldn't have the problems we had, so I chaired an ACLU housing committee in the mid-fifties. The first thing I did was infiltrate the real estate business. The problem then was largely with blacks who couldn't buy homes and were crowded into small, designated areas. My idea was that I would find where houses were for sale, and I would see to it that people looking for homes would have the opportunity to see the homes. If they wanted to buy it, I would buy it and "front" for them, as it were, and we could transfer the ownership. One or two of the agents believed in what we were doing—or were at least willing to make money by selling houses to us. But it didn't work, unfortunately. The people for whom I was looking didn't have the courage or weren't ready to go ahead with the deals. There was always someone in the family who worried about how the children would get along in school. In the end I would buy the houses and rent them out to blacks. It changed everything. The demand was a completely different one. I had some success in renting my houses to our black friends and even more success in persuading other people to do the same.

About that time the Monroe Civil Rights Act was enacted in California that said that no business could refuse to serve people because of race, and from my point of view, a real estate office was a business. We picketed the agencies or apartment houses that were most flagrant in their refusal to rent or sell to blacks. I did worry occasionally about being attacked by the property owners. I got a couple threatening phone calls late at night.

I would find out roughly what people wanted, and we'd pick out a certain number of apartments to investigate. We would have a white person go out and look at them first. Then we would have the black people come immediately after we had ascertained that the apartment was available. If they were unable to rent the apartment, then the white person would go back and rent it. Then we would file a complaint with the government. The manager or the owner would get a call from the housing authorities demanding to know why they were doing this. We had to take one or two to court, but we absolutely never lost a case.

This was probably the most exciting time of my life. Some of the strangest things happened. In one instance after the white person went and then the black person was told that the apartments were no longer available, the white person went back. She found the manager busily putting little nameplates on the doors and the mailbox slots. He said to her that he couldn't talk right now because the NAACP was coming back and he had told them that the apartments were all rented. He said he'd stayed up till midnight writing up fake leases. He told our checker all of this. He was in for a surprise! I always raised a terrific fuss. I heard that one owner of a segregated apartment complex said it wasn't so much the black people he objected to, but "that goddamn woman from the NAACP"—me!

I got involved in antidraft organizing when my son had to register. The first thing I did was to find out something about conscientious objectors. The leading draft counselor in this area gave me a talk on the issues. I was furious that these people on the draft board could demand an explanation of any young man's refusal to kill people. I felt very strongly that they should not be able to inquire about—or question—a person's religious beliefs. I'd been a member of the ACLU for a very long time. I had a strong capacity for righteous indignation.

I saw the young men going in like lambs for slaughter with no idea at all what they were signing up for. And I thought, this is where we should be, never mind the induction centers. We should be talking to the kids before they ever sign up, before they ever register. So I organized People against the Draft. We gave out little wallet-sized cards listing all the draft counseling centers and a list of dos and don'ts. We would start at eight in the morning when the draft board opened. I would put a carton of literature on the trunk of the car, and I would give out literature. We were there for two and a half years. We never missed a shift. We got a lot of respect and cooperation.

We've got to turn the thinking of this country around. There is such a readiness to resort to military action. What's the matter with people? Can't they understand what the next war is going to be like? War is unthinkable, and yet they're willing to risk it. You know, it's a simplistic reaction, just as if they personally had been slapped and reach out immediately to hit back. It's the only thing they seem able to think of to do. Anything else is so much more difficult. We can't afford to hit back—or land the first blow. It's just too dangerous. If all the intelligence, experience, ingenuity, hard work, and resources that go into creating implements of war were used to come up with solutions to the world's international problems, I'm sure solutions could be found.

I think it has to be done from scratch. Little children have to be taught. And who's going to teach them? We have to keep on educating and challenging people who think violence is the answer. I'm convinced that the only solution is to start with the littlest children at the nurseries and day care centers. Smash the TV sets. It's no use once they're adults and conditioned to admire the wrong things. The kids who used to show me flowers in the yard at five and six years old are now working to ban the bomb. We need to educate parents to have more courage to teach their kids nonviolence. My son would no more shoot someone than jump into a roaring fire. He conciliates, compromises; his role in the neighborhood was to settle arguments. Even in chess he worried about people who didn't win. And he's not a wimp. Boys can be brought up that way and not be weak and ineffective.

I was a typically "ivory tower" scientist. I have to be terribly worked up about something, and then I have to be convinced that I can change things—this same old business of looking for solutions. I felt when I leafletted the draft board it was not just a protest, but I was trying to save those kids, inform them. I was doing something concrete for which I could see an immediate result. It's a temperamental thing for me. I absolutely have to see concrete results before I can lay myself on the line. I do things that have some hope for success; this is the essence of math, to work on concrete things and get results you can check. There are no ambiguities. Working for peace and justice is a lifetime's work. This is why I hate housework because there's no end of it. You wash the dishes one day, and the next day the sink is full of dishes again. You run a vacuum cleaner over the house, and you think you've got it clean, and the next day the dust starts accumulating. Well, here we are in the world with exactly the same type of problems. It's depressing. As an old friend of mine said to me, "So you've given twenty years of your life to nothing." In a way, she was right. Well, you work on specific wrongs. But once in a while you win.

4.

Conscription and Conscience: The Vietnam War

Beth Coats, 1984. Photograph © by Renée Burgard.

BETH ROBINSON COATS

There was a big project in the whole San Francisco Bay area of people going to jail for sitting in front of induction centers. We went too. There was a big WILPF group that went to jail. In fact, our branch president was one of them, and she said that they could have a board meeting there, since most of the board was in jail.

Beth Robinson Coats was born in Long Beach, California, in 1916 and lived on her family's Sacramento Valley farm until they moved to Berkeley, where she attended college. She and her geologist husband lived in Fairbanks, Alaska, in the late twenties and thirties and moved to Washington, D.C., during World War II. She was active in PTA, Girl Scouts, Cub Scouts, and other similar organizations. In 1958 she became involved in the peace movement, first as chair of her local Unitarian Church World Concerns Committee and then through WILPF. The catalyst for her involvement came during a debate on the development of nuclear weapons. "I felt as if I'd been hit on the head. . . . I felt I could hardly walk. . . . What can I do? I figured that every day I would do something for peace." She has remained true to that resolve. Two of her sons became conscientious objectors during the Vietnam War, and a third son a war resister. The family was given emotional support by the Quaker community. In addition to her work for peace and justice, Beth has been a keen advocate of solar energy. She designed her own home, which uses solar energy for its heat. Asked what keeps her going, she says, "I have five grandchildren. I'm determined to do everything I can to make the world safe for them." She lives in Aptos, California.

As a child I was given the feeling that people all over the world were friends of mine. I remember that mother got me books about twins; oh, there were the Swiss twins and the Indian twins, and so on. I was learning about the home life of children in other parts of the world. That gave me a feeling of interest in the world. My mother had a humanistic point of view. She conveyed to us the feeling that we should understand people and help them.

As far as political activity, I didn't get started until very late. My family was very conservative. When World War II came along, I thought it was necessary. We were told to save fat because we needed it for armaments. So I saved every little bit of fat, which is quite a lot of work to do. You have to clarify it and all of that. I would save this fat, and somehow or another I never did get it turned in. I'd save it and save it, and then I'd set it out on the back porch, and dogs would come and get it or something. All the time I kept saving it because I felt I had to. But I didn't turn any of it in. As soon as the war was over, we were told to go on saving fat because it was needed for soap in Europe. From that time on I turned all the fat in. That made me realize that subconsciously I was a pacifist, but I hadn't admitted it to myself. I simply couldn't turn it in for armaments. But it wasn't until about 1958 that I actually became interested in politics and in making changes and began to really understand what changes were needed.

I had four children, and when the first two were in grammar school, I was active in the PTA. They didn't have any kind of United Nations committee or any kind of world policy committee, and I felt it was really important for us to support the United Nations. So I remember getting up and saying that we should have a U.N. committee. I was very shy and hated to talk in public, so for me it was a very brave thing to do. But it was necessary that I do this because of a conversation I'd had with my child that day. He had asked me, "Are we going to get killed in a war?" He had been hearing on television about bombs. This was after the war, in the late forties. There was a lot of talk about atomic bombs. I said, "No, I don't think we will, because there are people working to make sure we don't have another war. They're working in the U.N. and trying to bring peace around the world." And then he said, "What are you doing, Mommy?" That really hit me on the head. So I went to the PTA meeting that night and told them the story. They set up a U.N. committee, and it became fairly active.

Aside from a few things like that, it wasn't until the late fifties that what amounted to a religious conversion happened to me. I hadn't taken much interest in politics up to that time. I went to a meeting on the Nuclear Test Ban Treaty. At that time I didn't know whether we should have one or not; I was certainly not in the peace movement or even acquainted with it. Oh, I was interested in the subject; I was concerned about it. But I wasn't at all sure that we didn't need to test bombs. I just knew that it was a very dangerous thing and was worried about it. At this meeting they had two very good speakers, one of whom was a scientist from the Lawrence Livermore Labs, who was very knowledgeable about our weapons and a very honest man. He was completely convinced that we had to build up our weapons as fast as we could. He told us exactly what the weapons situation was—what the Russians had and why he thought we had to keep building more. Well, that was so scary. I hadn't really faced it before, and it terrified me.

Then a man from the American Friends Service Committee in San Francisco got up and said, "Well, obviously that way is madness. The only thing we can do is turn around and go in the opposite direction." And I felt as if I'd been hit on the head. I just realized that, well, he's right. That's all you can do; there's no alternative. Well, at the end of the meeting I felt as if I had the flu, it had affected me so strongly. I felt I could hardly walk; I was very weak. It was just like a religious conversion—that powerful. So I went home and thought to myself, "What can I do?" I figured that every day I would do something for peace. Every day I'll think about it and see if I can think of one thing I can do. The first day I wrote a letter to the president saying how much I thought we ought to have a test ban treaty, and after a few days, each day I could think of a few more things. About the end of the first week, I volunteered to be the chair of the World Concern Committee at the Unitarian church. Like I say, I just made a complete change.

About a month after that, I joined the Women's International League for Peace and Freedom. I told them at the time that I was busy with other committees and that it would be about a year before I could be active. I asked them not to urge me because I had all that I could handle. I had four kids. So they were all very nice about it. They didn't urge me for a year. Then at the end of the year they asked me if I'd be president. It was ridiculous because I'd had no experience with the WILPF, and it was simply because they were desperate for a president and didn't know who to ask. They'd tried everybody they could think of. But I accepted in the end because at that time in the WILPF almost all the women were very old. It seemed to me that the organization was a very worthwhile one, and if someone didn't do something quickly, it was going to die out. So I decided that I didn't have anything to offer except being younger than most of them, but I figured maybe that would help. They were all boasting about their brown-haired president!

Many of the women in WILPF had been active for their whole lifetimes, working for peace just years and years before I was born. It was a marvelous experience to get acquainted with these women and learn about what they'd done and how they felt about things. We were concerned, for example, about the Vietnam War before most people knew there was anything going on out there. Kennedy was sending so-called advisors over there. We were trying to alert people at that early time that there was danger. The country got into the war, of course, and the WILPF worked against it by counseling war resisters.

My son was a war resister. I have three sons. The oldest one became a conscientious objector before we really went into the Vietnam War. I had never talked to him about conscientious objector status. He did it on his own initiative. The second son became a C.O. during the Vietnam War; he knew very well that he wasn't going to fight that war. He was against war; it was the most logical position for him. Our third son during the early seventies decided that rather than being a C.O. he'd be a resister. He asked the Quaker meeting in Palo Alto if they would accept his draft card and send it to the district attorney for him. The Friends had a meeting to support him, which was a very marvelous thing, so helpful to my husband and me because we didn't want him to go to prison. He was young, and we felt it would really mar his life. We wanted very much for him to be a C.O. instead. But he felt that he couldn't do that. To see all the community support for him was very helpful to us, to help us accept it. We hadn't fought it, but we certainly hadn't felt comfortable with it until then. After that, I felt comfortable with it, and my husband accepted it. Then I started helping draft resisters.

We had an organization called Draft Refuser Support here in this area. Groups started here and in San Francisco and Berkeley. We had potlucks, and we'd invite all the draft refusers to come to dinner and conversation. Then we helped them to get jobs and homes and that sort of thing, and we worked with those in prison. Around this time, there was a big project in the whole San Francisco Bay area of people going to jail for sitting in front of induction centers. We went too. There was a big WILPF group that went to jail. In fact, our branch president was one of them, and she said that they could have a board meeting there, since most of the board was in jail. They were in for ten days.

My daughter Kitty was in junior high school then, I think. My son Tom sat in, too, as a resister. Kitty wanted to, but I urged her not to since she was underage. So she didn't. We sat in at the induction center just before Christmas and were in jail over Christmas, which was quite an experience. I was very glad I did it. We had twenty-one days in jail. I haven't gone to jail in protest since then. I may do it again. A number of times, I've wanted to join the farmworkers, but something comes up each time, and I haven't been able to.

The Vietnam War ended a month after my son Tom was killed in a canoeing accident. He was training in Philadelphia to be an activist in the

Movement for a New Society. He'd had one year of training, and he was going to have one more, and then he was going to come out here and form a branch in this area. I heard about his death on a day when I was on a march for the farm workers union. It was a beautiful march, a beautiful day, a large crowd. It was a very short time after that that the war ended. I was numb at the time, and I felt very sorry that Tom couldn't know that the war had ended. He worked so hard. Of course it was a tremendous relief that the war ended.

I wasn't really politically active again until about 1978, when I got involved in working for solar energy. Curiously, right after I heard about Tom, my feeling was that I wasn't going to let this make me stop; I'm going to work all the harder. I thought, I'm going to work twice as hard because Tom was a peace activist, and I'll have to do his part as well as mine. That was my feeling.

Right after we heard he'd died, I went to the Social Concerns Committee of the church—I was chairman of it—and I went on and conducted the meeting as if nothing had happened. I guess I was really just suffering shock and didn't know it. I just felt that I was going to keep right on doing things, but it didn't work that way right after his death. For a few weeks I went into a state of nothingness. Then I started talking art classes. That's what finally took me out of the house. It was something I'd wanted to do all my life and never had time for. Later I got involved in my WILPF committees again, like with the Energy Task Force, but for a while I just took art classes.

When you're suddenly confronted with a death that way, it gives you a very clear understanding of your own mortality. You realize that you don't have forever in this world. Anything you're going to do, you'd better darn do it.

Rose Dellamonica in the 1970s.

ROSE ROSENTHAL DELLAMONICA

It was triumph at the end of Vietnam, and the triumph was that the war in Vietnam was not ended by the president. It was not ended by Congress. It was ended by people going out in the streets in increasing numbers.

Rose Rosenthal Dellamonica was born in 1911 and raised in Syracuse, New York. She was a nurse and teacher. She first became involved in peace work when her children were small. During the Eisenhower presidency her grade-school children were going through bomb drills in school, and one child asked if it would be safer to hide under their desk or in the basement when a bomb dropped. She realized there was no safe place and her family and all people were at risk.

Her commitment to working for peace and social justice grew through her involvement with Women Strike for Peace, and the sense of community, purpose, and hope it provided. Her involvement deepened during the Vietnam War, when both of her sons were of draft age. While she was on a trip to Canada with her older son to explore his possible immigration to avoid the draft, her younger son enlisted in the service and was subsequently sent to Vietnam. While providing him emotional support through letters and packages, she immersed herself in antiwar work. She was a firm believer in the power of the collective anger and voice of the people to turn around governmental policy. Rose died in Oakland, California, in 1986.

My first involvement in peace activities was a memorial service for Hiroshima in the early 1960s. There was a reading from John Hersey's *Hiroshima* and then an hour's silent vigil. I had not anticipated that so many reporters and media people would be showing up. I was a teacher and felt that there was a very real possibility that on Monday I might be told that my services were no longer required because I had taken part in a political meeting.

I had been very concerned about atmospheric atomic testing because of my two boys. Radiation fallout was appearing in cows' milk, and I knew that it might be getting to my children and other people's children. I realized that something was happening in the world that needed to be brought under control even though it meant that we might have to make sacrifices to do it. It was a life or death issue.

During that hour I thought not only about Hiroshima, I also thought about the connection between the people in Japan and all over the world and my family. I came to the conclusion that the health of my children outweighed all other considerations. We were all at risk. I began to attend Women [Strike] for Peace meetings, and I became active on the committees. Our being together as a group of women with the same concerns gave us strength and unity. So this was a period in my life when I became very much aware that the entire future of the world was at stake. It went beyond patriotism and loyalty to your country. Your own personal safety was involved, and to allow decisions of this magnitude to be left in the hands of a few people in Washington was unrealistic.

To understand the significance of what is happening, you have to go beyond the commercial media. Most papers and TV programs do not go into depth on the significance of nuclear weapons and how they affect our future. And the schools need to go beyond conventional wisdom. There may be some gifted teachers along the way who say it's very important to learn to think independently, but it's not really something that you can count on. The biggest emphasis is on conformity, proving that you are loyal, patriotic, and that America comes before everything else. So many people simply assume that the people in Washington know much more of what's going on than we do and let them make the decisions. In WSP it was not an atmosphere of weeping, wailing, and gnashing of teeth, which would be pretty hopeless, but the feeling that working together we can change things. We were joining forces to make changes.

In 1972 I retired from nursing, and I had more time available and got more heavily involved in East Bay Women [Strike] for Peace. I was also involved with a group known as Jobs for Older Women and the Gray Panthers. I relayed peace information to Gray Panther membership through our newsletter. It's like a pebble being thrown into the water and the ripples spreading out indefinitely. We all stimulate each other and find ways to work together.

You will find quite a number of older people in the peace movement for the simple reason that they can remember a time when there was no Social Security, there was no unemployment insurance, there was no Medicare or other health benefits. People in trouble had to plead for charity, for handouts. They remember this as a very humiliating time. So they get involved in peace and justice issues because they are all linked; declining services for human needs are linked to increasing military budgets.

We learned to struggle for things and changes that needed to be made. We have that memory with us always, that nobody handed us anything on a silver platter. We had to demonstrate, we had to march, we had to write letters in order to make any kind of change at all. It was because of the protests that were going on that many of the reforms did take place, that Social Security and unemployment insurance did come about. A lot of those people are in the peace movement. They're not going to hold still for cuts and ignoring of people's needs. They are articulate people. They are going to speak up, they are going to protest, they are going to contact their congresspeople and talk to them when they are in recess and make their wishes known. These are the older people, but because of the Free Speech Movement and the war in Vietnam, there are more young people who are not willing to accept conventional wisdom, who do ask questions, who do not take things for granted, who feel that each one of us has a responsibility to make sure that the benefits that we've gained over the years are not lost.

The time when I became most directly concerned was during the period when our children were young and I was concerned about their safety, their health, and not just as an abstraction, but something that had to be gotten under control *now* before serious damage was done.

I have two sons. During the war in Vietnam they were both in school. I was extremely concerned. Our older son had a high number in the selective service draw and would probably not be called. He thought the whole war was absolutely stupid, and he had no intention of serving. He said that under no circumstances would he go there and that he would like to go to Canada. So he and I took a trip to Canada where we met with draft consultants who told him exactly how he would go about making these arrangements. It turned out that he was able to stay in school all during the war in Vietnam, and he wasn't called up.

The younger son was not clear in his thinking; he was in turmoil, not sure of what he wanted to do. He got a very low number in the draw. He spent a year in school, and he decided that was not really what he wanted to do. He wanted to make a change in his life. He knew he was going to be drafted because of his low number, so while I was in Canada with my other son, exploring his options, he talked to a recruiter who promised him he wouldn't have to go to Vietnam. He was barely eighteen at the time. When we got back to town it was all done. He enlisted. He was sent to Ft. Lewis, and I went up there to see him. He had lost about twenty pounds, his head was shaved, and I almost pushed his sleeves up to see if he had a stamp on his arm like somebody in a concentration camp. It was a devastating experience for me.

My husband and both of my brothers served during World War II, and we had accepted it as a necessary sacrifice. We never questioned their going overseas. We felt that this was something we all needed to do for our security, with Japan and Germany threatening our hope for any kind of future. There was a totally, totally different attitude then. There were sacrifices that we all made. When they all came home we were proud of them.

It was a totally different situation than in Vietnam. However, I was aware that my son was in a very disorganized state of mind where he didn't know what he wanted to do next, and he was just drifting along with the tide, so to speak. At the same time he wanted to be very grownup and independent. I recognized that, and at the time I never argued with him about any decision that he made. We were profoundly affected by his decision, but at the same time we felt it was a matter of life and death that we give him our emotional support. We never argued with him once we told him we did not agree with his decision. We never mentioned it or referred to it again.

Of course, he was sent to Vietnam. Anything that he wrote for, we sent. I wrote to him at least every other day, even if it was only a postcard, and our reward was that he came home intact.

Well, the peace movement was a great outlet for my energy at that time. I had days of despair. I watched the newspapers very carefully. I saw that the whole thing was so stupid, so self-defeating. I felt tremendous frustration, but at the same time knew that he had become enmeshed in a mistake that our whole society made. Society accepted the statements that kept coming from the Pentagon that there was "light at the end of the tunnel"—all we needed to do was to send more supplies and more men. But more men were being destroyed, and more men were coming back in plastic bags.

Finally society got the message that there were no victories in this situation and there was no hope that what we had set out to do could be accomplished. It was a lie. It was just as Lincoln said: "You may fool all of the people some of the time; you can even fool some of the people all of the time; but you can't fool all of the people all of the time." When the bodies came home, over 50,000 of them, people began to get the message that a terrible, terrible mistake had been made, a very costly mistake. The most costly kind of mistake is to lose members of your family, to lose people that you know, not just somebody out there in the newspaper. The saddest part of all was that the whole thing was a total waste.

I didn't do draft counseling. I didn't feel myself emotionally qualified. It would get too enmeshed with feelings about my son. My most effective work was in speaking, in making contact with other groups, in planning, in helping with the newsletter for Women [Strike] for Peace, which I did every month for about two years.

Whether people got involved in the peace movement during Vietnam depended a great deal on how it affected them in their personal lives, in their jobs and relationships. There were many people in our society who didn't feel that the peace movement had any special meaning for them. They began to feel it more when their sons, predominantly young black men, came back in boxes and in plastic bags. Then they realized that their sons were being cannon fodder. There was a great feeling of anger about it.

Although people might not be ready to question or to take the time to analyze very deeply, ways had to be found to bring these issues to their attention. I spent a lot of time leafletting. We would go out with fliers and stand in front of stores, city halls, hospitals. We went to different places, wherever people would be, taking fliers where people from the community who ordinarily would not go to a peace meeting would be, and we would hand out informational fliers. We must have passed out over ten thousand.

It *was* triumph at the end of Vietnam, and the triumph was that the war in Vietnam was not ended by the president. It was not ended by Congress. It was ended by people going out in the streets in increasing numbers. At the beginning there were a few hundred, and then in a few months there would be a thousand, and then a few months later there would be several thousand. The week before Lyndon Johnson announced that he was not going to run for a second term, sixty thousand people showed up at a demonstration against Vietnam in a stadium in San Francisco. It was not only packed to the top with people sitting around the rim, but you could look over the sides where thousands of people were milling around outside. That's what ended the war in Vietnam.

It was a triumph. It was the people of this country who made that decision. There is a recognition on the part of all of us that as long as there are nuclear weapons stockpiled in the United States and the Soviet Union and elsewhere the job doesn't end and the responsibility doesn't end. I know perfectly well that probably I will have a sense of responsibility until the end of my life.

I never thought there was anything in my background that led to my peace work. But there probably is, and I didn't realize it fully until I saw a film called *Fiddler on the Roof*. It is about a small village in Russia under the czar, where people were trying very hard to eke out a living. Whenever there was a depression or a famine, whenever things looked very bleak for people in Russia, then the Jews became scapegoats, the excuse why things were bad. Beating up on the Jews was a way of taking care of a problem, at least giving the illusion of taking care of a problem.

My father was drafted into the czar's army in the very early 1900s and was abused as a Jew. He made his way to the Finnish border, crossed the border at night, and went by way of Finland down to Denmark. Then he went from Denmark to England where a relative was living. He finally immigrated to the United States. Eventually other members of the family were able to get out and come to America. When I saw this film I had a picture right there before me on the screen of what it was that pushed them out.

The times that I have felt most rewarded personally in being involved in the peace movement have been when I was working closely with other people who shared my understanding, my feelings. It gave a sense of unity and a tremendous feeling of strength and hope. There were times when situations looked hopeless, and yet there was never, as I said before, weeping, wailing, and gnashing of teeth. It was instead a challenge: How are we going to deal with this? And so it was always a positive expression in response to whatever the challenge might be.

I think that there was a great deal of anger in what got us involved. Some of the things that happened were so outrageous; we felt that they were obscene, indecent—they threatened the lives of hundreds and thousands of people and were a total waste. We had a sense of outrage about the Vietnam War; there was a great deal of anger that gave us this energy. Instead of using our anger in hostile or revengeful or destructive ways, we used our minds to try to find other ways of doing things. Since our government couldn't set an example of what moral values should be, we had to do a great deal of soul-searching to create moral models ourselves.

As a teacher, one essential thing I could do is to start with children's daily lives: being fair with each other, helping them understand that positive kinds of behavior add to our own happiness and our ability to enjoy other people. Hostile kinds of activities only lead to unhappiness. This is how young children experience peace. The school has a responsibility to supervise, to watch what is going on, and to intervene when things start happening that are not good learning experiences. It can be done in a nonpunitive kind of way. This is the teacher's function, to redirect negative kinds of behavior.

It's quite a challenge to have a government that plays on every negative emotion that people might have, especially fearful, insecure people who are constantly looking for more outside security, more police, more soldiers, more weapons. They have the illusion that more weapons are going to make them safe. Realistically, this is not true. I can remember a time when we were at the beginning of nuclear development, and we didn't have these huge arsenals and nuclear bases all over the world. I can tell you personally that I felt much more secure at that time than I do now. Now I don't dare to let down my sense of responsibility for peace because if enough of us were to stay home worrying about peace and letting the government take care of us then our chances of destruction would be much greater. So it depends upon your definition of security. For me, security is peace and justice and destruction of all weapons arsenals. Security is peaceful understanding of all peoples. And each of us can do our bit.

Lucy Haessler in the 1970s. Photograph by Sam Vestal.

LUCY WHITAKER HAESSLER

*Later on in the Vietnam War—living in Detroit, we were right on
the border of Canada—I was one of a handful of women who
ferried draft resisters over to Canada. . . . I felt a very great
sadness that young men had to leave their families, their lives,
their jobs, their futures as Americans, and go to another country
because they opposed the war.*

Lucy Whitaker Haessler, born in 1909 in Brookfield, Massachusetts,
traces her involvement in peace and social justice issues back to the
early days of the suffrage movement when she joined her mother in
marches, leafletting, and other activities. A tradition of social change
and activism has been handed down from mother to daughter in
Lucy's family for four generations—her daughters and granddaughters are WILPF members. Active in establishing child care for working mothers in the forties, union organizing, the civil rights movement, and the peace movement, Lucy also drove draft resisters to
Canada during the height of the Vietnam conflict. Never one to give
up the fight, Lucy remains active in her "retirement" in Santa Cruz,
California, going to marches when she can and firing off letters of
protest.

My mother was very much involved in the suffrage movement. She had been chair of the program committee of the Women's Club in the little suburban town where we lived in New Jersey and created quite a stir, back in 1910, when she became very active and set up programs on the women's suffrage movement.

In 1914 we moved to Washington, D.C., where my father had been transferred. Washington was the place to be. Around Easter vacation that spring there was going to be a big parade including a section of suffragettes marching from the White House to the Capitol to present a petition. My mother, of course, was going to go, and I said I wanted to go. She said, "You're too young." I said, "Oh, please let me go. I want to be like you when I grow up, and I want to be able to vote when I grow up." Finally, she gave in.

From that time on I went with my mother, sometimes after school, sometimes on Saturdays, up to the Women's Party headquarters on Capitol Hill and helped get out mailings. There were vigils. There were pickets at the White House. There were petitions. I got to know people like Jeannette Rankin and Alice Paul, who was really the founder of the Equal Rights Amendment way back then. That experience has stayed with me all my life.

I don't think my parents belonged to any political party. They were just liberals. But I remember that when the Russian Revolution reached its final stages with the successful October Revolution in 1917, both my parents were tremendously excited. It was the beginning of a whole new world. A whole new society. Lincoln Steffens came back from Russia and said, "I have seen the future and it works."

One of the things I read at that time was that the Russian women were cutting their hair because it was a sign of liberation. I had a mane of heavy, long hair that I wanted to cut, but my mother said, "No." But one day, when I was fourteen, I went upstairs and took my mother's dressmaking shears and chopped my hair off all the way around as best I could. When I came down my mother had hysterics, but my father said, "That's my girl!" The next morning he took me to his club and marched me into the barber shop and said, "I want you to cut my daughter's hair." The barber said, "I don't cut women's hair." My father said, "You're going to cut this girl's hair." So he cut my hair after a fashion, and I went to school and was sent home. My father went to school and raised Cain, saying he would sue the school if they wouldn't re-admit me. So I got back into school, and the next week some other girls cut their hair, so we had our own kind of revolution.

I have four granddaughters. When they went into the long hair stage—which to them was a symbol of revolution or liberation or rebellion—I told them this story about *my* revolution for short hair. They were astounded. I said, "You know, that's the way history is."

In Chicago in 1927 there was a massive movement to try to save Sacco and Vanzetti. It was obvious that these two men, who were accused of murdering a plant guard, had been framed in an atmosphere of persecution. What I remember most vividly is that the night they were executed in 1927, there was a mass meeting in Ashland Auditorium in Chicago. I went to it with my friends. It was a very somber, well-behaved meeting because we knew the men were going to be executed that night. They had an open phone line to Boston, and when the word came in at about eleven that they were indeed executed, there was a lot of weeping and the meeting disbanded. We went out into the street to wait for street cars and buses. We had noticed when we went into the hall that the police squad cars were surrounding the place. We didn't worry about it because we were nonviolent and weren't going to create any kind of disturbance. So I was standing with my friends waiting for the bus to go into town when we were just simply attacked by the police. I was knocked into the gutter, and a tear gas cannister went off in my face. I was blinded temporarily. I couldn't find my friends. I don't remember how I got home.

In 1977 the governor of Massachusetts [Michael Dukakis] issued a proclamation declaring that Sacco and Vanzetti were indeed innocent and that the review of the case proved it. I wrote to him and thanked him for it. At that time I got a call from a reporter at the *Detroit Free Press* who was writing an article about it. He did an interview over the phone with me. It was a fitting windup.

During World War II, through my connection with the Women's Auxiliary of the CIO [Congress of Industrial Organizations] union, I was asked to be on a Civilian Defense Committee, which was set up to establish day care for children whose mothers worked in the war production plants. Funds had been appropriated under a federal act for day-care centers, and our job was to set them up. It was very hard to get the day-care centers established. The schools didn't want to do it. The churches didn't want to do it. The plants didn't want to do it. The situation was unbelievable. Here were women with husbands overseas, who had flocked to Detroit with young children to help the war effort by working in factories. They were locking their children in furnished rooms all day, locking them in cars while they worked night shifts. That's when children became known as "latchkey children," children who wore keys around their neck on a chain so they could get into the house while their mothers were at work.

That was the beginning of my consciousness that we were becoming a country that didn't value its children, that didn't look upon its children as its future. When I went to the Soviet Union in 1963 I saw how beautifully children were cared for there—not that life was easy. We haven't been willing to do that in this country. They do it in England and in the Scandinavian countries. But we haven't made day care available for women who work.

The era of which I am most proud and the time I look back on with the most poignant memories was the Vietnam era because I gave every ounce of time and energy and money and love that I could possibly muster to let people know how ghastly the war was. We are still paying the bills for that time; we're paying them not only in money and budget deficits, but we're paying them in ruined lives and broken homes and crime, drug addiction, alcoholism, all of which have increased since Vietnam.

I did very practical things. I spoke at meetings. I helped organize the student movement on the campus at Wayne State University in Detroit where I was living. I went—and took people with me—to every one of the major demonstrations in Washington from 1965 to 1971. The first time I went, there were just a handful of us on the flight from Detroit to Washington. The next time I booked fifty seats and filled them. By the time we went to the last demonstration, which was called the Spring Offensive, in April 1971, I had chartered two planes. My husband almost had a heart attack when I signed a contract for five thousand dollars' worth of airline tickets on two different airlines. But I sold every seat. It was wonderful. And I think we can take some credit in the women's movement for finally ending the war.

I went to Moscow in 1963. It was at that meeting that the French women wept with us and held our hands and said, "We know what you're going to go through in Vietnam. We went through it. And it's going to be worse for you." And it was worse for us. Much worse. At that conference we met with Vietnamese women leaders of the peace movement, all from the Vietnamese Women's Union. They were from both the north and the south of Vietnam, which they, of course, regarded as one country. There must have been six or eight women. They came with great difficulty, and they were uneasy about going back to Vietnam. They knew their reentry would be difficult. They had details as to the use of defoliants. How many acres of land had been cleared for airplane strips. How much weaponry was coming into the country. How many advisors were there. They talked about their struggle; their attempts to have elections that were promised under the Geneva accords in 1954, which were never held, and which the United States kept from being held. They talked about what they were going through. What was happening to their families, their land. There was only one issue, and that was that it was their country and they wanted everyone to get out so they could run it themselves.

Later on in the Vietnam War—living in Detroit, we were right on the border of Canada—I was one of a handful of women who ferried draft resisters over to Canada. I never got caught. In the early years of the war, men simply went over to Canada and stayed there. There were organizations that took care of them and got them jobs. Then unemployment began to be a factor in Canada, and they had to—rather reluctantly, I think—have some restrictions. To get into Canada, you had to come in as a landed immigrant, which was quite a complicated procedure. In order for the men who were already in Canada to qualify as landed immigrants, they had to be brought out secretly and then reenter with funds and a job.

I would get a call in the late afternoon or around dinner time which simply said, "We have somebody who needs a ride." I would go over to Windsor, Canada, through the tunnel. I would make a note of which entrance I used because there were two or three gates that you could go through, and I couldn't use the same gate again that night. I'd drive to a house near the other end of the tunnel, and there I'd pick up a man whose name I never knew. I would be given an envelope, which I'd lock in the glove compartment of my car. It would have his papers and some money. I was very careful to wear a hat and gloves and rather conventional, unobtrusive dress.

Then I would drive this young man back to the United States. We often talked; they would tell me a little bit about themselves and they would ask me about myself. I would come back into Detroit over the Ambassador Bridge. I was asked at the immigration window, "Are you an American citizen?" and I would say, "Yes." They would say, "How long were you in Canada?" and I would say, "Oh, I was just over for the evening. My friend and I were just over for the evening," or, "This is my nephew" or "cousin."

Then I would drive back to the tunnel and go through a different gate. At the other end of the tunnel was the immigration office. I would walk into the office and say, "This young man wishes to apply for landed immigrant status." By then I would have given him the papers and the three hundred dollars that was in my glove compartment. Then I would wait, sometimes twenty minutes, sometimes two or three hours, just sitting there in my car, waiting for this young man to come out. If he was refused, I had to take him back to the United States. If he got his immigrant status, I took him back to the house where I picked him up.

I didn't know the names of these young men. They didn't know my name. They didn't even know my first name. The safe house had to be moved several times. I must have done it twenty or thirty times over a period of a couple of years. They were very careful not to have you come too regularly. I don't know how many other women there were—I think they were mostly women.

I loved doing it for this reason: every one of those young men was a decent guy. I thought how awful it was to be taking fine young men like this with principles and skills—men who want to be teachers and doctors and health workers—and send them to another country. A lot of them never came back. I felt a very great sadness that young men had to leave their families, their lives, their jobs, their futures as Americans, and go to another country because they opposed the war.

When President Carter initiated draft registration we were down on the post office steps with placards and information about draft counseling. There were some people there saying, "Don't register." We didn't do that, but we talked to them about alternatives. We showed them a sample of the card they would have to fill out. Down at the bottom of the card was a place for you to mark if you wanted a military recruiter to come and call on you. We had tiny stickers that fit in that space that said, "I am registering under protest."

You wouldn't believe some of the men who came and talked to us on the post office steps. It was heartbreaking. Many were veterans; they would come up and thank us for what we were doing and say, "I was over there. I don't want my son to go. I don't want my brother to go. I don't want the kid down the block to go. I don't ever want anybody to have to go to war."

Margaret Stein, 1984. Photograph © by Renée Burgard.

MARGARET DAWSON STEIN

*One other thing we did was a reading of the names of
people killed in Vietnam, which went on for about eighteen hours
in a local park. We silently read the names of the Americans
killed, since they were the only names we had. There were about
fifty thousand names.*

M argaret Dawson Stein was born on the family farm in Esmont, Virginia, in 1921. Her father was a farmer and merchant who operated a store in which he sold farm machinery and other supplies. She studied mathematics in college, and her first job was at Langley Field in Virginia in a "computing" pool, doing math calculations by hand. Although she had grown up and had been educated in a conservative, racially segregated environment, Margaret soon found herself in the midst of organizing to integrate and unionize the lab facility.

She became involved in a variety of issues over the years; community housing, energy, antiwar and antinuclear protests. The sense of community and close friendships with others working for change—the sisterhood of it all—are part of what keeps her going. Occasionally there is also humor. Once during the Vietnam War, she and several other women were dressed with aprons with "PAX" (peace) written on them and large pockets for literature. They were in a local mall leafletting for a shoppers' boycott of companies that made products for the war. A police car drove up to them, and an officer jumped out and said, "Where's the riot?" An anonymous caller had called in a report of a mob of demonstrators at the mall. What the officer found were three well-dressed women. Margaret suggested the officer go home to his supper. He followed her advice.

I grew up in the South and there was certainly a lot of racism, but you know, when it's just been part of your life it doesn't hit you. You don't notice separate drinking fountains. We lived in the country. Schools were segregated, of course. There were a number of what were then called Negro families around where we lived, and we played together. We could play with the little black girls until we were about eight or nine, then no more. I remember one time I invited a black child whose father worked in the local slate quarry home to spend the night. It was just terrible. My parents found some reason to take her home. I think she did eat supper. We had a woman who helped my mother at the house from time to time, a black woman whom I was crazy about. I apparently thought there would be nothing wrong with me going to live with her; I thought it would be just terrific to live with Betty. It didn't seem strange to me. I was called "Miss" by the black people, Miss Margaret. My brothers were "Mister." That didn't seem unusual either. It's all I knew.

My mother knocked herself out trying to help look after people: making sure people had enough to eat and firewood. One of my mother's brothers had five children and during the depression they spent the entire summer at our house on the farm because things were tough. There was very little money, but on the farm there was no shortage of food, and we had a house, which is more than a lot of people had. We didn't see bread lines or soup kitchens or anything like that. My mother used to can huge quantities of what she'd call soup mix, tomatoes and corn. She'd furnish these to the school cafeteria for the free lunch tickets. There was a concern for social issues on the neighborhood level, but we weren't involved in wider issues. I can't imagine my parents getting involved in sit-ins to protest.

I went to college when I was sixteen. In my family, a very traditional southern family, for some reason it was the girls who went to college and not the boys. The college I went to was a woman's college, and I studied to be a math teacher. They had the equivalent to sororities, but they were called "literary societies." When I was a sophomore, I wrote an editorial on the discrimination in sororities. It brought on a storm. If anybody had wanted me in one of the clubs, they didn't after that.

When I was a senior, there was a protest against the strict rules, especially for upper-division students. There was a big protest rally one night, which I went to, and students cut and boycotted assemblies and classes. Unfortunately, I spent most of that protest time in the college infirmary with the mumps. But it was an exciting time; my friends would stand outside the window and give me reports. They really did change the rules. But I wasn't involved in any larger social issues.

After college I went to work at Langley Field in Virginia, which later became part of NASA. The work at Langley was for what was then called the War Department—a better name for it than the Department of Defense. At the time I didn't feel any conflict in working for the government and for the war effort. I was hired as a "computer." The pool was similar to a stenographer's pool, except we were doing mathematical calculations. During the war, they started hiring some black people. The first to be hired was a man, a black engineer. They would reserve a table for him in the cafeteria. Our supervisor led a protest; they were segregating him from the whites at his own "reserved" table. I would never have done this on my own. I mean, I never in my life had sat a table with a black person. We continued to march to that reserved table and sit at it, six or seven of us. So that was the end of the segregation in that cafeteria.

During the McCarthy era, half the people I worked with in this section were being investigated; they were members of the Federation of Architects, Engineers, Chemists and Technicians and were trying to organize the lab to improve working conditions. Many were fired. I wrote a lot of statements for their hearings, saying that I thought they were good, loyal citizens and not trying to overthrow the government. You'd have to have the statements notarized, and when I'd go to the notary public, the person would warn me I'd get in trouble writing things like that.

I did graduate work in statistics at Berkeley. My teacher was one of the leaders in the fight against the Loyalty Oath in California in the forties, although he decided to sign it and remain teaching. The only political work I did was around the Loyalty Oath, because in 1952 there was an initiative on the ballot to extend the Loyalty Oath to all state employees. I lived at the international house on campus and tried to collect a little money from people at meals. People warned me that I mustn't get mixed up with that band of Communists. I was also still writing letters for people from my work group at Langley. But it never occurred to me to be afraid. I just felt it was wrong to require people to say what organizations they belonged to.

In our family, the peace movement was very much a part of all our activities. The children were affected by what we were doing, and we were affected by their interest. When the oldest child was about three, she started looking at this copy of a book by Felix Greene called *Let There Be a World*. It had these awful pictures of victims of Hiroshima. I tried to hide the book because I didn't want her to see it. She found it and said, "Momma, what is this?" So I explained about the bomb, that we must be sure this never happened again. She said, "Well Momma, what are you doing about it?" That can really spur you on to do more.

During one of the first marches against the Vietnam War, this same child wanted to go, and we were very nervous. It was the first big march, and we didn't know what might happen. So my husband said she couldn't go. She made herself a little picket sign and went marching around the house picketing us chanting, "Take me to the march. Take me to the march." She eventually got to a march, but not that one.

Another daughter made a marvelous comment when my husband was arrested outside of the Oakland Induction Center in about 1967. He went to jail, and she said, "Momma, why did they put Daddy in jail?" I said, "Oh, well, they said he was disturbing the peace." She said, "But he wasn't, he was disturbing the war." I thought that was a marvelous comment because it certainly was what he was trying to do.

One of our daughters and a friend organized a "pedal for peace" tour during the Vietnam War and got other children involved. Another time she and a friend "adopted" a child in South America to support. They put on events to raise money. It was very satisfying to see them having a concern for people in the world.

She was in the fourth grade when we bombed North Vietnam. We were phoning everybody to call the president to protest. She heard all this. She was a rather shy child at that time, but the next day she came home and at supper she said, "I got up in my class today and asked all the students to have their parents phone the president to protest the bombing. That's what I shared today."

I was president of the WILPF branch during the Vietnam War. Almost our entire activity was centered around the war and the draft. Always marches and ads in papers. We cooperated with a lot of groups. We put on a big meeting on Vietnam at a local high school after we started bombing North Vietnam; about six hundred community people came. We had paid for an ad announcing the meeting, and the paper didn't want to publish it at first. We often set up tables on campus to get students to write postcards on issues: Vietnam, Central America, Angola, South Africa—you name it, we've been there with a table.

We had "Vietnam Summer" like other towns all over the country. The whole thing was proposed by Martin Luther King. Ours was the biggest group west of the Mississippi. Our local WILPF membership doubled just because of people opposing the war; it went from one hundred to two hundred.

One other thing we did was a reading of the names of people killed in Vietnam, which went on for about eighteen hours in a local park. We silently read the names of the Americans killed, since they were the only names we had. There were about fifty thousand names. It went on all day long with people taking turns. They marched to the park at about 7 A.M. and then started reading. It went on until two in the next morning. A group of local seminary students participated in the event by swiping some votive candles for us. They also read names.

We were very involved with antidraft work. We felt that high school students ought to know about changes in the draft law. So we made a big

Margaret Stein in the 1950s, Moffet Field, California, emerging from plane.

effort to get the school districts to give the students information on where they could get draft counseling. Some schools wouldn't agree to do anything, so we picketed them and leafletted the students. At one school the principal was so opposed to our action that he went on the loud speaker system to all the classrooms and warned the students against our group across the street. Well, during lunch the students all flocked over to see what we were doing! We also went to draft boards to leaflet about draft counseling; we had leaflets in English and Spanish. We did that all through the war.

Many of the draft resisters went to trial. Some were given community service time; some went to jail. I remember going to some of these trials. One of my friends is in many ways very proper. She would be well dressed and sit in the front row mending her husband's shirts. When the judge came in, she refused to stand. There was a lot of resistance by these very mild women. They have a mild manner, but they are determined.

The courts were jammed with draft resistance cases. The issue of the draft was approached from many angles in the trials. My husband, who is a statistician, got involved in giving testimony opposing the lottery system. Everybody was supposed to have an equal chance at being called up, but the system didn't seem to be as random as it was supposed to be. There was a local case questioning the lottery, and the lawyer got several statisticians to look at how likely it was that all these people in this one little area would have low numbers and be called first. The statisticians found it wasn't very likely. The government lawyer got up and said, "I don't care how eminent you statisticians are. President Nixon ordered a random lottery, therefore he got a random lottery." Actually it turned out not to be random.

One of the big things in the fall of '67 was the Vietnam Moratorium, which called for a halt in the war. That was organized originally by students on campuses everywhere. We had a huge meeting with about nine thousand people; they filled the auditorium, and we had to have the sound piped out to the crowds outside. For one particular action in October we set up houses in each neighborhood where students would have their headquarters; when they were leafletting they could go and get a cup of coffee and get more literature. Probably every WILPF member had students at their house that day, feeding and supporting them.

We work on arms and nuclear issues, including nuclear plants and lots of local issues: employment, housing, energy, Aid for Families with Dependent Children, etc. Very few of the things that we've worked for for many years have actually happened. There have been minor successes. But in the process of working on local issues, we have developed a very good working relationship with many groups in the county and with the two unions that represent county employees. When I first joined WILPF it was very much slanted toward international projects. I remember they were raising money for radios for farmers in India so they could get crop information. That was important, but certainly not as basic as keeping a low-cost clinic open in our community.

As a man from the local Center for the Independence of the Disabled said when we were working together on a project, "You know, if you all weren't doing this, nobody would." We were once at a social action committee at a local Unitarian church and a black man who was active in his community came over to one of us older women. She was very nicely made up with a very fluffy, nice hairdo. He said, "Where have you fluffy-headed white people been all this time?" The more we got involved, the more we learned about our community and got more diverse groups of people working together.

Some of our local projects seem a far cry from the arms race, but I think it's proper because of the stated goals of WILPF: "to work by nonviolent means for those political, social, economic and psychological conditions that can insure peace and freedom." It doesn't even say "to work for peace and freedom." It says to work for the *conditions*. It seems to me that we won't have peace and freedom anywhere until people's basic needs are satisfied. Then we all can have the opportunity to become involved in wider issues. Some of us have the luxury of being able to worry about the arms race, but if you don't know where supper is coming from, you don't worry about larger issues. We need more younger members, but if there's a working woman with a family, there's just not much time left, no matter how dedicated they are.

I work with a marvelous group of people. You knock yourself out writing leaflets, addressing envelopes, calling people, but it's not so arduous if you're doing it with people you like to be with. I'd say my best personal friends are WILPFers.

Occasionally individuals will get very discouraged and drop out a while. But you come back. I don't know, maybe you just expect to go on and you just keep going. Look at the Vietnam War. The peace movement had a great deal to do with stopping that war, putting pressure on Congress. But look how many years it took. Look how many years it took to change public opinion, to change votes. It was a very long struggle. Central America will probably be just as long. There's always going to be another thing to do, but you just keep going. Probably it's the warmth of the relationships that helps; it helps you keep going in the face of defeat. The people help sustain you; the sisterhood of it.

Work in the peace movement is very long term. It takes a long time before you see much effect from what you've done in many cases. I think it's important to choose activities that you can see some effects. We'd all like to end racism, but somehow you have to bring that down to something manageable where you can see some results. I don't think we should be discouraged that we're in it for a long time; most things worth doing take a long time.

155

5.

Vision and Action

Madeline Duckles, 1984. Photograph © by Renée Burgard.

MADELINE TAYLOR DUCKLES

Women are audacious, not afraid to go out on a limb, and they are
not afraid to dream. I think one of the things that sustains me is
the wonderful women, you know, the wonderful people in the
peace movement. We support one another and sustain one another.

Madeline Taylor Duckles was born in Loomis, California, in 1916,
where her father was a fruit rancher and her mother an elementary
school teacher. She was educated at the University of California at
Berkeley and at Teachers College at Columbia University. A supporter of public radio, she worked part time at KPFA in Berkeley,
California, in 1956. She joined WILPF in the forties and was an
organizer for Women Strike for Peace. She went to Indochina on
peace missions and helped organize a Med-Evac program with the
Committee of Responsibility to fly napalm-burned children from
Saigon to the United States for treatment during the Vietnam War.
More recently, she raised funds to equip a double-decker bus for
peace projects in her community. She says, "Working for peace and
justice issues seemed to me natural and right and proper. When
people say to me, 'How do you happen to be in the peace movement?' it always seems to me the most ridiculous question because
we've reached the point where this *should* be the normal thing for
people to do." She lives in Berkeley, California.

We've made progress in civil rights, environmental issues; we've progressed on every level except for peace. Here we were, armed to the teeth when Women Strike for Peace began protesting nuclear testing when strontium 90 was appearing in children's teeth. We wanted to do something quickly. So women all over the country called a "strike" and left their work and families to protest. At that time, we had exploded two bombs and now the world has about fifty thousand nuclear weapons. So we haven't made any progress at all! And WILPF was working hard right after women's suffrage trying to get women more involved in the political process, trying to stop war toys and get the U.S. out of Central America in 1917 and we're still there now. The problems persist.

My political education began when I went to the University of California here at Berkeley. At that time the YWCA was where the action was. There were a few remarkable women in charge of it. There were discussions of race relations, the Spanish Civil War, and labor issues. I began at the University in 1933, and this was the year of the great longshoremen's strike in San Francisco. I had never been to a union meeting before. We were gathering canned goods for the strikers. It was for me a very exciting time. All kinds of political issues were discussed.

I don't remember rejecting the values of my family, which I suppose you would call redneck, but working for peace and justice issues seemed to me natural and right and proper. When people say to me, "How do you happen to be in the peace movement?" it always seems to me the most ridiculous question because we've reached the point where this *should* be the normal thing for people to do. But still, war and preparation for war is normal, and to be in the peace movement is abnormal.

Women bring to the peace movement the best feminist qualities, which are patience, tolerance, compassion, and a hell of a lot of intelligence. We're much more loath to make judgments. We have the courage to change our minds. We're not nearly so reticent about admitting mistakes and changing course when we do wrong. Of course, there are aggressive women, but they are not the "norm" for women.

The women's movement activated a great many women, and it activated them on the issues of equality for women in jobs and the Equal Rights Amendment more than it did on the peace issues. For a long time we were trying to get to NOW to set up a peace platform. I have a speech I give on any occasion that peace is a woman's issue. My current speech, in case you would like to hear it, is that foreign policy must become a community issue, when in an administration, foreign policy is military policy. Military policy means a loss of our community services and ultimately a loss of our lives. We're in double jeopardy: if the weapons they're making are used, we'll all be dead, and meanwhile, the arms race is killing us economically. I'll stop my speech there.

In the course of antiwar work, I was involved in the Committee of Responsibility, which brought war-injured Vietnamese children into the United States for medical treatment they couldn't get in Vietnam. After treatment, they would return to Vietnam. It was very difficult to get these children out of Vietnam, and they could only come with the permission of the American government and the Saigon government. They could only come on a space available basis on a Med-Evac plane to Travis Air Base. It went on for most of the war, and altogether we got eighty-five children out of Vietnam, usually pretty severe cases requiring plastic surgery. Then the Saigon government thought it would be a good idea to send paraplegics, who were extremely difficult to care for and expensive from a hospital point of view. We had a number of those too.

At that time I was the Northern California chair of Committee of Responsibility and that involved administrative work in organizing various centers. We had centers in several San Francisco Bay area cities and also in Seattle and Portland, Oregon. We worked with local hospitals. This was an organization made up of doctors and clergymen and a lot of ordinary citizens like me.

We had to raise our own funds by contributions. We had an office in San Francisco. I met every one of those children. If you have seen a napalmed child—the worst were phosphorus bombs. You could brush off napalm; it's a jellied gasoline. But phosphorus, which was an "improvement," would burn to the bone. You couldn't brush it off. Then the government accused us of just trying to get the napalm burns to publicized them. They said there were no napalm burn victims. Most of them were dead, it's true. It was chemical warfare, there's no question about it. We used it all the time in Vietnam. I used to be an expert on this. But you know, the laws of war—it's a contradiction in terms; when you have war, you have no laws. Killing people is illegal and war is killing.

It was very, very difficult. We had two goals. One was to save as many children as we could. The other was to try to show the American people what the war was like. We had a wonderful film, which had been made by people in Los Angeles with a lot of footage that our doctors had taken in Vietnam, then film of the children having treatment here and their progress. It was extremely moving. The response was always good. It was interesting, this film of our work was primarily humanitarian, so you could get into schools and churches, and you could talk to groups of children in high school or an elementary school about other children in a way that you could not if you went in for a political discussion. But at the end of it, there was always a question period. Children would say, "Was he injured by a bomb?" "Yes, he was." "Well, what about their bombs?" You would say, "There were no bombs. They were not bombing Americans, and they were not bombing the Vietnamese people." It became a

Madeline Duckles in Hanoi with American POWs (left to right) Mark Gartney, Paul Gordon Brown, and Bill Mayhew, 1969.

political discussion. A great many people became involved initially for humanitarian reasons, for moral and ethical reasons, and many, many became politicized.

I went to Vietnam in 1969 to visit prisoners of war. After I returned, I was in every paper from San Francisco to New York. One newspaper columnist said, "You would think madam would be more concerned about her husband's career." My husband said to me, "What does he think my career would have been? I think it's an important thing to do." It was what I wanted to do with my life and time. I don't think there have been any sacrifices. If you do what you like doing, it's not a sacrifice.

The worst thing that ever happened was that I got a threat from the Minutemen, a right-wing group. This came through the mail, a small envelope, like an invitation to a cocktail party or an open house. On one side it had these crossed things. It said, "This is the sight of a rifle, which gives it accuracy. These cross hairs are on the back of your neck." I called the police about it, and they said, "Well, we heard about those." They said I could take it up with the postal commission. I said, "If this was sent by the Black Panthers, would you be up here tomorrow? or in an hour?" I was annoyed. They didn't do anything about it.

I think there can be a nonviolent revolution, and I'm committed to nonviolent social change. I think that's the only way it can come about. Now I'm involved in a project—what is a day without a project?—to try to reach that 29 percent of the people who don't vote at all. We had several community groups around here that had the same idea almost the same time—wouldn't it be great if we had a mobile peace resource unit, a vehicle. So what we have is a peace mobile. It's known as the Martin Luther King Peace Mobile because he was the first one to articulate the concept that peace and social justice are the same struggle. We've already got it equipped. It has a loud speaker. It has a public address system. Upstairs we have remodeled and refitted a playroom with beautiful multi-ethnic toys. They have a computer with global resources software, with nonviolent computer games to teach cooperation. There's a game something like chess. There's one on mountain climbing, and you can't win unless you cooperate. It has a typewriter. It has a copying machine. Downstairs is a place for people to have meetings. There is a little stove and a little refrigerator. You can make coffee. People can type up their leaflets. They can run them off. It also has a solar panel to demonstrate there are alternative sources of energy. It now needs two thousand dollars for a good coat of paint. It will cost that much to scrape off the old paint. It's a double-decker London bus.

We raised money the hard way. I think I don't have any friends left—I asked them all to contribute. I went through my address book and sent out umpteen thousand fundraising letters. We applied for grants in all directions. The peace mobile is available to the community to check out, like a library book. It has a driver, a wonderful young woman who helps with the programs we do on the bus. When we first got the bus, we thought we would use it to attract attention to an event we were having. But that's not the best use of it. The local communities get involved in planning programs using the bus.

Every group that takes the bus and uses it has to have a course of training in how to use the equipment in the bus. Their written materials have to be in at least two languages. People who use it have to make the connection between their community project and the militarism of this country. For example, there is a group that used it once a week in San Francisco. It's a group which deals with a variety of women's issues: legal support for women, wages, and other issues. The refitting of the bus was done by an Asian design group, which is a multi-ethnic group which trains young apprentices in woodworking and cabinet making. We got so many spin-off projects.

Let me tell you about one, an oral history project that eight young school kids—elementary, middle, and high school—are doing. We have a video camera on the bus and a video monitor. Their project is to hold adults accountable for their future. Most of these kids are the ones who are from what is called "disadvantaged" neighborhoods. They are marvelous because they ask questions in a very direct way that an adult would not ask. The first interview they tried to set up, they said, "What kind of drugs do you sell here?" This is something that no adult would start with. But they are very direct and uninhibited. There was one man who was going to be interviewed, quite an old black man, and he wanted to know what the questions were going to be. He wanted the questions in advance, so they gave him the questions. He prepared his answers. When the kids got to him the first thing they said to him was, "How did you get that scar on your face?" It was not on the list. This man said, "Nobody has asked me that for forty years." They said, "Well, how did you get it?" When he was a kid in the South he got it in an encounter with the KKK. This is the kind of thing that you and I would never think of asking, or we would be too inhibited to ask.

The kids have done public service announcements on commercial television around election time. Some were shown in Los Angeles just before the Olympics. They said what they wanted to be when they grew up and asked people to vote their conscience. "Vote for peace when you vote." They did these in Spanish, English, and Cantonese.

The peace mobile's first operation, before we installed all the equipment, was to get out the vote. It was not yet fully equipped, but it had a great big sign—"Martin Luther King, Jr. Peace Mobile"—and it had a "Viva Del Pace," a "Paz," and a similar slogan in Chinese. We had all kinds of signs on the bus and had the public address system going. We had the most marvelous group from Richmond, California, a lot of them from the Rainbow Coalition, and the Freedom Singers, with a swinging gospel rhythm. They started out with "We're going to change this world" in these wonderful rich voices. "Peace, jobs and justice, we're going to change this world." Then somebody would get on the speaker system and say, "You have two more days to register to vote, vote now." They stopped in a housing project in North Richmond and everybody fanned out with their clipboards and knocked on doors. The Freedom Singers were singing "Let it shine, let it shine, vote people, let it shine!" It was so exciting.

One of the things that I have thought for a long time was that we should have a national women's conference and we should do what England does. The party out of power has a "shadow government" of whomever they would put in power if they were elected. The women's conference would select a secretary of state, a president, vice president. We would write a foreign policy. We would have a budget. We would have a medical plan and educational plan. The sky would be the limit. We would create goals to aim toward; a picture of what society could be.

Women are much less concerned about making themselves ridiculous. When Women Strike for Peace first went out on strike against atmospheric nuclear testing I had never done anything like that before. Some women wouldn't participate at first because it was kind of undignified. Now, of course, everybody does it, goes out on demonstrations. This is the thing about the women's plan and the women's shadow government. Women are audacious, not afraid to go out on a limb, and they are not afraid to dream. I think one of the things that sustains me is the wonderful women, you know, the wonderful people in the peace movement. We support one another and sustain one another. You can meet somebody in the peace movement whom you haven't seen in years. When we see each other we don't talk about "old times," we begin with right where we are now, how we are continuing to work for peace and justice. One woman I know said to me, "I have a rosary of people in my life; each one is a bead and I tell these beads over and over in times of despair." Isn't that a lovely thought!

Louise Wilson, 1984. Photograph © by Renée Burgard.

LOUISE PAGE AUSTIN WILSON

The Congregational church actually made a Quaker of me because they wouldn't quite go all the way on what I considered the ethic of Christian belief—an ethic not confined to Christians—that love is the conquering force, not war, not violence.

Louise Page Austin Wilson was born in Jersey City, New Jersey, in 1910. Her father was a banker and philanthropist, and her mother was a homemaker and activist. Louise attended Vassar and the New York School of Social Work. She belonged to over fifty organizations by paying dues or making contributions to show her support. She and her husband worked in Washington, D.C., for thirteen years with the New Deal; during that time she organized for women's trade unions and was a social worker. Religious beliefs form a foundation for her peace and justice work. She believed that Christ was a "real hardheaded revolutionary, but that He taught nonviolent revolution." The sixties were an important period in her activism, in opening her up to a "zest for learning and ability to care about the *now.*" In this spirit, she continued to grow and work for peace and nonviolent social change. She died in Palo Alto, California, in 1989.

My parents were both idealists and dreamers. My father's ambition to be a sort of Horatio Alger appealed to my mother. I imagine she saw herself as a person who could be very helpful to him. My parents were conscious of their social responsibilities. Father was a board member of a settlement house in New York City. My mother was in a group called The Cause and Cure of War, which was a very important organization in the late twenties and thirties. She was also on the board of a black hospital in Newark, which was quite a forward thing for her to do. My father was a trustee of Tuskegee Institute, a black college.

They thought they were very tolerant, and tolerant is the right word because they thought that the best people in the world were white Protestant people. If you came from Boston, that would be the very best. The next best thing was to come from New York. Anything west of New York was not good. In terms of black people—Negroes, as we called them then—in theory they were fine, but in practice they certainly were one or two steps below us.

My mother and some friends started the school I went to as a child in the early twenties. It was a wonderful school based on really progressive principles for those days: teaching children when they are ready, making learning fun, and learning through experience. For example, we did our math by measuring a park that was nearby. It was quite a shock when I went to public school.

During my junior year in college, in the middle of the depression, I had a friend who asked me to go down to New York for a weekend where we visited institutions for poor, troubled people. That was the first glimpse I ever had of another way of life. I also became interested in socialist circles and joined the League for Industrial Democracy. Their point of view felt right to me. By this time my father had a very high position in the banking world, and I felt uncomfortable with that. My discomfort with his status threw me into the arms of the other side. I was troubled about institutional banking. I felt he hadn't paid enough attention to the conditions of the people working for him or their wages.

I was majoring in sociology and taking courses in the family structure in America. My vision broadened considerably. I went to the New York School of Social Work. I did my fieldwork in Newark, New Jersey, in 1933. It was a tragic situation. They were shipbuilders, and nobody was building ships. It was a large eastern European immigrant population. The state had just set up a welfare system structured to deal with a few families needing a boost; the agency was overwhelmed by the tremendous task of administering to the numbers who applied for aid. That thrust me lock, stock, and barrel into a situation where I came to know people who didn't have enough to eat and who were devastated by poverty. My work in that agency reinforced my ideas that there was something wrong with economic distribution in the country.

When I graduated from college I went to Russia with my Russian history teacher and some other women from my class. Going to Russia was my rite of passage. The part that interested me was the social experiment. I was not caught up in any Communist movement in this country or anything like that, but I was very excited about their new outlook on ways to live. We did see poverty and devastation from the war, and oppression, but we also saw hope and growth.

My husband was always a great internationalist. He had gotten his master's degree in international justice at The Hague, in the Netherlands. I learned a lot about politics from him. I accepted the New Deal as a better way for us. We went to Washington for the New Deal, thinking we'd stay for about six months. We stayed for thirteen years!

I worked for the civil rights movement through a project of the League of Women Voters to gain the vote for the District of Columbia. I also worked with League of Women Shoppers, which was a national women's consumer organization that said that women have a lot of power through their consumerism. That was where I did my first picketing and demonstrating.

There was a tremendous burst of industrial unionism during that period as well. The laundry workers were trying to unionize against terrific odds. So we marched up and down in front of the laundry saying that we wouldn't take our laundry there if they didn't support the union workers. Demonstrating outside the laundries was a bold and radical thing for me to do in terms of my experience and my family background. I also worked with a women's trade union in direct organizing for restaurant workers. I used to go to restaurants and order a cup of coffee or something and talk to the waitresses about joining the union.

Throughout my life I have belonged to a number of Protestant churches. When we came to California, we went to the Congregational church. The minister of the Congregational church was an activist. He used to coordinate peace events in the town and lead the marches. He invited speakers who were interested in exploring the theology of social action and liberation theology. It was a very important period in my life, both mystically and politically. He believed in nonviolence. I learned about pacifism from him. We began to study social issues in theological terms. The church itself would not make a commitment to nonviolence. The Congregational church actually made a Quaker of me because they wouldn't quite go all the way on what I considered the ethic of Christian belief—an ethic not confined to Christians—that love is the conquering force, not war, not violence. So I went over to the Quakers.

I was working in the Welfare Department in 1967 when I was given two students from San Francisco State. I enjoyed working with them very much. It took me up to the campus for staff meetings. It was a very yeasty experience because of the variety of people who were going to the school at that time. The chair [of the Social Work Department] was progressive and saw that social work had something to offer in social change as well as the amelioration of ills. I was happy to accept a position on the regular staff of the school as a field supervisor. A large percentage of the students were black young men and women from rather impover-ished districts in San Francisco. It was the time that the Black Panthers were forming, and the Black Student Union was very strong at San Francisco State. They were feeling out where their power was. They were challenging us, challenging the system. Some of them were very angry. It was not always an easy situation. But that was very minor compared to the excitement of it.

A group of us on the faculty wanted to withdraw Letterman Army Hospital from the list of placements for student fieldwork. This was an example of the kind of small activity that goes on when people are concerned about peace issues; you don't win the "war" but you can do some small thing. The first year that I was on campus full-time was 1968, and that was the year when we first had major strikes: against the Viet-nam War, in support of the black student program, and a faculty strike over conditions. We refused to have our classes on campus during the strikes. We met in all sorts of clubs and churches around San Francisco. A good deal of our discussions were about the strikes and the origin of the Vietnam War and the Black movement. We did a lot of standing in lines, protesting. It was my first experience, in fact my only real experi-ence, in confronting the police; they were bringing in the "attack squads." There would be a line of protesters and four feet away would be these fierce looking creatures in their helmets with all their sticks and bullets and guns. We tried to look in their eyes and talk with them, but it was just impossible. They appeared very inhuman. It was scary for me because occasionally, if there was anything disorderly, they used mace. I was afraid that I might not be able to breathe because of my bad lungs. I'm afraid I wasn't very courageous.

We were ordered to come back on campus and not to engage in the strike. We didn't do it, so we were fired. About one-third of us were active union participants in the strike. But we had good legal advice and in about a week we were reinstated. We were a good strong group, and you felt all of that mutual support. Many students were getting arrested during those days. Some of us on the faculty guaranteed their bail money.

There were some very courageous people in the university, and it was a good lesson for me. Some stood in a line when there was rioting and police were clubbing protesters. That experience taught me a good deal about the practical difficulties of protest. It was energizing.

After I left San Francisco State, I went back to the Social Services Department in San Jose where there was a lot of ethnic ferment. Many Hispanics had come into what had been a primarily black, impoverished area. I had latitude for experimentation in the section I was supervising. A great deal of what I learned at San Francisco State enabled me to do a better job there. We tried to do neighborhood organizing. It's a brand of social work that was much more satisfying to me than the earlier psychiatric work I was trained to do.

We tried to empower the people. It was nearly an impossible situation for the clients. It's hard for them to believe you are working in their best interests when you encourage them to stand up for their rights against the Social Services Department. Their livelihood depended on their getting financial support from the department. However, there were some pretty spunky people in the neighborhoods.

I'm not really an intellectual in some senses. I've done some research in the social work field, but I'm more interested in going after something enthusiastically rather than with a careful analysis. I don't think I've made any particular contributions to the peace movement in the area of new thinking. But I have encouraged a few other people to work enthusiastically in the peace movement. I also have a "stick-to-it-iveness." I've learned a tremendous amount through the years about what makes things work and how to get organizations going. I do well helping organize organizations and doing the work that needs to be done, finding donors, keeping records, publicity, and so forth. I feel that those things are important and supportive to the movement. I consider my contributions pedestrian—but I see that as important too.

One of the things that makes the political system work best is direct action. I put less priority now than I used to on the electoral system and a lot of weight on individual actions. But, by doing that, we may lose something that I think is very important: the ideal of representative democracy. So I keep one foot in and one foot out of the political process.

Our children have gotten involved in peace and justice issues. I've learned a lot from them, and they're very supportive of us. Our son resisted the draft, and our other son lives in a community that lives close to the land. Our daughter started a tax resistance movement in Washington, D.C., and was interested in selective service issues. She had very strong convictions about not only not paying taxes, but not taking interest and not having money in banks.

One year when our children and their families were here visiting we went up to San Francisco for a peace march. We joined all the hundreds of thousands of people and different groups—all the far-out ones like the Winos for Peace and the Prostitutes for Peace as well as the traditional groups. After a while we got a little tired walking so we stood on the corner with a placard that said, "Three Generations of Our Family for Peace." As people walked by they would make friendly remarks and clap. The solidarity that comes with the marching is great.

My original education in politics came entirely from my husband. He helps me to sharpen my point of view. We've learned how flexible we can be. I've been a partial tax resister, a telephone tax resister for years, and I'm working on being an open resister in increasing amounts. My ideas about constructive nonviolence do say that conscience is higher than the law. I really felt moved to do some kind of tax resistance, but he didn't want to, and we were doing joint income tax returns. We had many, many talks about it. Then he found a way that we could separate our taxes. He still doesn't agree with me, but it's not a source of contention. We live with each other's positions. Fifty years is not long enough to know the possibilities in a person. His dedication to a world of law is just absolutely firm and unshakable. He doesn't go to meetings usually, but by what he says to people and what he believes, he gives strength to the cause.

As the civil rights movement developed I began to understand the concept of the pacifist as activist. Before that I think that I thought that a pacifist was a person who just "refrained." Some of the books that particularly helped me with those issues were Erik Erikson's *Gandhi's Truth* and Martin Luther King's *Stride Toward Freedom*. They pushed me to try myself to be an active pacifist. I was very moved by *The Autobiography of Malcolm X* and James Baldwin's *The Fire Next Time* because they stretched me to begin to think about anger and nonviolence.

I think I could sum up my religion something like this: I express appreciation for the creative force in life in song and prayer. Religion means to me an appreciation of creation. I have a little trouble referring to it as God, although that's what comes easily because that's the way it's often identified. I don't see God as all-loving and powerful, however; the force of creation has created a number of different powers here on earth. One of them is the power of evil. I see that working very actively, as an almost maniacal drive toward destruction through nuclear weapons, promoting war, etc. I think that's part of creation, part of the creator. I don't try to integrate it with the force of love.

I've been reading the journal of May Sarton, *At Seventy*. She says, "Now I wear the inside person outside and am more comfortable with myself." She feels younger because she doesn't have to pretend she's something she's not. That's a direction I'm moving in. I believe Jesus was a real hardheaded revolutionary, but that he taught nonviolent revolution. My religious conviction is that we are at a point where we can't just say God is all-beautiful and all-powerful and leave it up to him. We are asked now to be cocreators, and we have that choice to align ourselves with the power of love or the power of evil.

The 1960s haven't ended for me, in the sense that they were a period of opening, a tremendous zest for learning and a tremendous ability to care about the *now*. The children were grown then and I could absorb myself in the issues. In the sense of it being a time of growth, I don't think it has ended, although it was a more explosive kind of growth. Many activists of the 1960s burned out in the 1970s. I keep plugging away at the same issues. I don't see any breaking off point.

Right now I'm at a very serious point in my life. Having taken this backward look, I now feel finished with that part of my life. I'm not quite sure now how I want to use my time. I don't have any sense of life after death although I'm certainly open and a little bit curious about what might happen. The main thing is that eternity is now.

I've been looking at the aspects of my life that have made me into an activist for peace and justice instead of a bridge player, which I might well have been. Every once in a while I do have a kind of twinge for not having done something famous, I will admit that, but I realize that I very consciously took the low road all along. Sometimes I do have a twinge that I don't live a life more perfectly in tune with what I believe, but on the other hand, life often calls for compromise. We are living today in the most horrendous of times—the bomb, militarism, the lack of freedoms and civil liberties, the erosion of the environment. We need to explore the possibilities for nonviolence.

My life has not been dramatic, but what I had to offer is persistence. Most of the people I know working for peace and justice are able to nourish a small flame and encourage others to go on. That's enough for me.

Rose Lucey, 1989. Photograph © by Renée Burgard.

ROSE MARCIANO LUCEY

We are a nation built on symbols. Everybody has a symbol or myth that they live by. We are in the midst of a military myth. We have never done research on what peace has meant in this country, so I want a Peace Academy so you can point to it and say to our kids, "Look, this is what our nation is about also."

Rose Marciano Lucey was born in 1918 in Clinton, Massachusetts, and raised in what is now a suburb of Boston. She was a daughter of Italian immigrants at the "bottom of the social ladder." Even as a young girl, she did factory piecework at home with her family to make ends meet. Because of lack of opportunity, encouragement, and resources, Rose never attended college; life's experiences and observation have been her teachers. Rose's view of peace work is a broad one, encompassing multiple human needs and concerns. Her approach is to ask, "What have you done . . . every single day for peace?" Her lifelong work to promote peace and end injustice of many kinds is based in The Christian Family Movement, an outgrowth of her interest in the Catholic Worker Movement. The CFM advocates scripture-based action for social change on a local, daily basis, with a global vision. Rose and her husband, both active in the movement most of their adult lives, were a motivating force behind the citizens' lobby to establish a U.S. Peace Academy. She has nine children, including one adopted Korean. She lives in Oakland, California, and is active in community organizing around the issues of AIDS and homelessness.

My mother and father were immigrants from Italy and worked very, very hard. My mother was always proud of the fact that she went to the fifth grade in Italy, which was a lot, in those days. But she was also a woman of innate intelligence. One of the very first things I remember growing up was that she went to night school to pass the citizenship test. But more than that, she got interested in politics and went around to try to get the Italians in our ghetto neighborhood—and we did live in a ghetto—to learn how to read and write and register to vote.

Our town is now a suburb of Boston. We were at the bottom of the social ladder. The town was only eight thousand people, and there was incredible stratification. At the top were the Episcopalians and the Methodists. On the ladder right below them were the Irish. At the bottom of the ladder were the Italians; we were the guinea-wops.

I didn't learn the history of that term until two years ago. When the slaves were brought to Massachusetts and docked in Boston, they were taken to a section of the city which was called New Guinea. When the slave period was over and the Italian immigrants started to come in, they moved into that same section of town.

When we went to school the first thing that happened to me was that my name, a beautiful name, Rosaria, was changed by the teacher, who said to my mother, "Mrs. Marciano, that's much too long. We'll call her Rose." I understand clearly what you do to a child when you take her name away. That has been part of my growing up process. Many friends have said, "Why don't you reclaim your name?" But that little girl is gone, in many ways, and I don't want to reclaim her.

I was very bright. But students were segregated into different academic groups. The Italians, mostly, and a few Polish people were put into what were called the business classes to learn typing, and the ones who were going on to college were put into a separate section. I have resented that to this day because, although I do some writing for various magazines, have written a book, and give lectures, I never did go to college. In the first place there wasn't any money to go, but in the second place, nobody ever spoke about the possibility of going to college.

I had no expectations. I remember that when I was about six or seven years old my brother and I would get up at five o'clock in the summertime. We would go down and stand in line to get boxes of tags to take home from a local company. We would get a box of five thousand tags, and I think we got five cents a thousand for stringing the tags. My mother also sewed baseballs for a small baseball factory in town. She would sew the small ones because they're very intricate. She had a special device shaped like a horse; she would put the ball in the mouth of the "horse" and then step on a lever to hold it so it wouldn't move. We soaked the leather in water to get it ready. As I got older, I could sew these more difficult balls. We did that after school, whenever we could. I remember working all the time at something. But it wasn't atypical; everybody worked except the ones who were higher up on the ladder than we were. My mother was also a seamstress and made beautiful gowns; she worked all the time at something.

By the time I graduated from high school, it was 1935 and the country was just a disaster. I got my first job at the Denison Manufacturing Company for forty hours a week for eight dollars. There was no coffee break; there was no going to the lavatory. There was always somebody on your back. You wouldn't dare say, "How were things yesterday?" to the person sitting next to you. That was not possible.

After I grew up I wanted nothing to do with Italians. I can empathize with every ethnic group where the young people don't want their parents to speak their language. I don't know a word of Italian because we would not allow our parents to speak Italian to us.

My brother wanted to start a union at the Denison Manufacturing Co. and was told that if he persisted he would lose his job. This was at the height of the depression, so he quit trying to organize a union.

I remember the Sacco-Vanzetti case. I would have been about nine years old. The memories are absolutely vivid in my mind, the absolute terror of the "good" Italian people; we were suspect just because we were Italian. The case was tried only ten miles away from our town. I can remember the whispering and the fear; the big thing I remember was the terrible fear.

I guess going to the Catholic Worker House in Boston in the thirties would be my first work to change the social structure in a nontraditional way. We worked in the ghetto areas of the North End of Boston. In 1939 our big project was to start a cooperative bookstore in Boston. It was a center for people from the whole area who were like-minded, who were thinking of justice and peace issues.

We had seminars and workshops. We had the first liturgical art exhibit in the city of Boston. The prestigious *Boston Globe* gave us two whole pages. We were using the image of Christ as a celebration of life, not as crucified and suffering. Our bookstore was a celebration of people taking control of their lives.

During World War II one of the young artists my husband and I knew was a conscientious objector. Our whole group was going to the Catholic Worker House and was involved with peace and justice issues. By that time we were married, and almost every weekend we had soldiers or sailors coming to our house, so the whole conversation was about the horrors of war. I remember my husband cried when Hiroshima happened.

After the war we moved to California and got involved in a movement that is little known, even in the Roman Catholic church, based on a kind of liberation theology. It's called the Christian Family Movement. It's not enough to read scripture. What you do is read scripture and say, "If I believe that Jesus lived and is living today, what would Jesus do in this situation? Would he be going down to the food kitchen and feeding the poor?" Yes, he would, but he would also be challenging the system. So we went through seven years of study and action, not only us, but one hundred thousand couples in this country and now in fifty-one different countries. This movement started in about 1945. We were organized in small groups. You went through introductory work to help you understand that you live one life; you don't separate church from work from school. Everything is interconnected.

The next whole year we spent on what was going on inside our families. Then we moved out to what was going on in our church, and our community, getting involved in the political structure. From that we went into studying the political questions for the nation, beyond the community. Then we studied international life. You studied the scripture, and then you went into what we called the inquiry method. You would take a situation and ask a question: "What's going on, how do you like the schools? your job?" Then you make a decision of how to act, to organize and make changes. Once you do that action you don't drop it. You try to integrate it into your life. You build a network of people.

In the fifties our whole thrust was the question of race. In one year we lost twenty-thousand couples who said race had nothing to do with them; there were no black people in their communities.

Those years were horrific years because the year that we got into politics was just about when McCarthy started his devilish stuff. Those scary times can deflect you from any interior voice that says, "You can do something," because you don't dare step out of line. We had an interdenominational conference based on a papal encyclical called *Pacem in Terris* in 1962. It was the first great paper on nuclear war. If anybody had paid attention to that we wouldn't be fighting on the lines that we are fighting today. We had the first "Pacem in Terris" conference in the country. The day after the conference, on everybody's windshield in our parish, there was a paper accusing my husband of being a Communist. The McCarthy era terrified us. If you were against McCarthy, you were Communist.

Young students who come and talk to me, they say, "You're seventy-one years old, why are you still active?" I say, "If you don't have a foundation that really trains you—we were trained for seven solid years in the Christian Family movement—it will be hard. I'm still in the movement."

The church was coming out of a time when it was completely suspect. In our town it was bad enough being Italian, but my God, to tack on being a Catholic! I've often resented the marvelous church buildings while people starved. But the church was not only a spiritual representation, it was a literal, beautiful place where you could feel welcome. It was warm, and there was always something going on that took you completely out of the terrible situation you were living in. In those days the priests were trying to keep body and soul together for these people. Today I really and truly believe that the Roman Catholic church in America has enough stature that it can in fact turn its churches into places for the homeless and be more of a social agency.

I have no college degree, but I understand a lot of things from experience. I was with a group of twenty Notre Dame students on an "urban experience" at our soup kitchen where we feed two hundred street people. They had already been to the AIDS center where I also volunteer. They were literally bug-eyed. They had never seen any of the things they had seen in the two days that they were here. I maintain that is not only a travesty of education, but it's a disservice to the nation. The future of the nation depends on educated people who understand what the true life of the nation is all about.

All of this I've been talking about is peace work. When I talk with people I try to get them to identify one thing that they have done or they believe they can do to make this a better world and to change a system.

In 1966, on our way to the University of Notre Dame for a "Pacem in Terris" conference, we stopped to see the Air Force Academy Chapel because we had seen it on the cover of *Time* magazine. It was an incredible experience, in a sense a mystical experience. I have never seen a more beautiful place. The day was magnificent, a bright blue sky. The chapel was beautiful, with those spires that look as though they are touching the sky. We happened to come out of the chapel when the cadets were marching. It was really a thrilling experience. Peter, our twelve-year-old, said, "This is where I want to go to school."

We got into the car and we were driving day and night to get to Notre Dame. Dan and I were taking turns driving. I remember it was three o'clock in the morning, and I said to Dan, "Why is it that there is such a beautiful place where kids can go and study about war and there's no place to go to study about peace?" By the time we got to the University of Notre Dame we had really latched onto this idea.

We decided that we would ask to have an ad hoc workshop on the question "Why not a National Peace Academy?" There were eight thousand people at that conference and about two hundred fifty came to our workshop. We asked the convention if they would support the proposition that as long as we had nine war colleges, we should have a National Peace Academy. That's the only time the conference has ever taken a position. We sent a telegram to President Johnson. We had people in one hundred fifty congressional districts who had promised to start asking the question of their congresspeople.

We started a little newsletter called *Campaign for a National Peace Academy*. We focused on what was going on in Vietnam and on ending the war. At that time it cost forty-eight thousand dollars to graduate one person from West Point. What if that money were used to teach peace, not war?

Every time we were in a march we always raised the question of the Peace Academy. But I thought we weren't ever going to get anyplace. It was now ten years since we started. We maybe had five thousand to seven thousand supporters all around the country. We worked through the Christian Family Movement, with groups like the American Association of Retired Persons, teachers' organizations, etc. We opened a Washington office in 1972. In about 1984 we had a majority in the Senate. The bill for a National Peace Academy went before the Congress and got all the way to committee; it never got out of committee or came up for a vote until it was attached to the Defense Appropriations Bill in 1986. They decided then to put it under the State Department—which didn't want it at all—and call it the United States Institute of Peace. So it was established at long last.

I'm still plugging for a National Peace Academy that is more like our vision, and so are thousands of other people, but it's not totally different from what we had in mind. In the bill there's a lot of what we wanted. We wanted the education of the people of this country on peace, conflict resolution, and ways of changing the system. That's going to take several lifetimes. But as a result of everything we've done, we have kindergartens teaching peace; we have peace departments or classes now in two hundred fifty colleges. That's a result of all of the work that all of these people did in all of these years.

We are a nation built on symbols. Everybody has a symbol or myth that they live by. We are in the midst of a military myth. We have never done research on what peace has meant in this country, so I want a Peace Academy so you can point to it and say to our kids, "Look, this is what our nation is about also."

In the year 1792 there was a proposition sent to George Washington from Benjamin Rush, a signer of the Declaration of Independence, and the black genius Benjamin Bannecker who printed the first almanac in this country. A year later the *Bannecker Almanac* printed the peace proposal. There is a letter from George Washington that says, "This is an idea we must pursue." I have spoken to over two hundred different groups from schoolchildren to veterans of the Second World War. I have never once had one person answer, "1792," when I ask the question, "When do you think the peace movement started in this country?"

It's not told; it's not taught in the schools. My God, can you imagine what a revolution there would be if the students knew this and learned peace? That's why I really hold the university and the church equally responsible for a lot of the inactivity in the field of justice and peace. The most prestigious universities are mouthing all these things about peace, but when it gets to the bottom line they are not doing enough.

Every person who says that they want peace has to decide what their gift is, how the system is going to be changed, and they have to devote themselves to that one thing they do best. Then they have to work with others. Nothing is going to happen without networking.

We have to change the system of the Pentagon. There was no Pentagon when I was growing up. There was no Pentagon when I was young and married. There was no Pentagon when my children were little. The Pentagon has taken over our economy, and we have allowed it.

Look at Eisenhower, all of the writings by the generals who have fought in wars and what they have told about peace. My God, General MacArthur of all people—his peace statements, who knows about them? People aren't making the connections that we have to make. We have to prove that peace has to do with the homeless, peace has to do with the people who are not working, peace has to do with the quality of education we have.

In one sense it is easier to feel great sympathy for people who live on a different continent and go and work in the villages there than it is to work in our own neighborhoods. The cathedral is our parish, but we decided to go to a very poor parish instead. That means that I really have to struggle with myself, with the person who wanted to get out of the ghetto as fast as I could. When you are in a small room where you can only feed fifty people and there are one hundred fifty people standing in the cold and somebody might have a knife and somebody might be angry and a fight might start, you have to really face the reality that you are frightened and that you don't really want to come back the next time. And then you come back, because this is for peace and justice.

When you're working at an AIDS clinic and you know that in two weeks twelve of the people you are feeding, caring for, and hugging will be dead, you have to face reality. That's what peace is all about. That's part of how I'm building a world of peace, to end the homophobia and the fear in this country—how can people drive out a family with a child with AIDS and burn their house?

So the question becomes, "What have you done where you work, every single day for peace?" That's what the Gospel, scripture, is all about.

Jesus was working with people day in and day out. Gandhi was working with people day in and day out. If your call and your gift is to be a doctor, then by God, you'd better be the best, caring, peacemaking doctor that there is.

Part of me says, "You're only a guinea-wop kid, and how come you're talking this way?" Then another part of me says, "No way. I may not have any piece of paper from a college, but I have traveled. I have seen the utmost poverty in every continent, and side by side I've seen the most obscene materialism by people who call themselves Christians or Jews or Moslems or whatever." I have learned a lot by this very simple church group that started forty-five years ago, that said you take scripture and you ask the questions "What's going on? What can I do to work for change?" You can build a world of justice and peace. You take a small step. Life is very exciting, and I look at that guinea-wop kid, being called Rose because Rosaria was too long for the teacher, who was not allowed to be in a college course. I'll stack my life up against anybody's.

Elise Hansen Boulding, 1974. Photograph by Chris Brown.

ELISE HANSEN BOULDING

The word empowerment *wasn't a word we used then, but I was
trying to empower women by showing them that what they
understood and the skills they built in the community and family
work they did were relevant to making peace in the community at
large and dealing with social problems.*

Elise Hansen Boulding was born in Oslo, Norway, in 1920. An
emerita professor who has taught at Dartmouth, the University of
Colorado, and the University of Michigan, Dr. Boulding is a re-
nowned peace and conflict studies scholar and activist and has edited
and authored several books on the subject. She and her husband
Kenneth Boulding have pioneered peace studies, conflict resolution,
and mediation in the university curriculum. She was the founding
editor of *International Peace Research Association Newsletter* and a
founder of the Consortium on Peace Research, Education and Development. She was also international chair of Women's International
League for Peace and Freedom. Elise was active in Women Strike for
Peace and researched WSP to provide a profile of the group's membership. Of her life of activism she says, "I have always assumed that
if you were a pacifist and concerned with world peace, you were
going to be in for trouble. That was just the way it was. . . . I see
conflict as basic to the human process. . . . My goal has been to initiate a dialogue between the action and research perspectives." She
lives in Boulder, Colorado.

I had a very strong feeling, from the earliest I can remember, that if there should ever be a war, I knew a way to be secure and safe, and that was to go and hide in the mountains of Norway because that was my mother's image of a place that was safe. I first became aware of the urgency of involvement in peace activities when I was a senior in college and Norway was invaded, because suddenly my dream of the safe, secure place, which I had had all those years, was shattered. I had a very profound emotional and spiritual crisis in which I came to realize that the only way to have safety and security was to have it for the whole world, and that led me to the peace movement.

We were in no way an activist-oriented household, so I didn't have any sense of appropriate action. I spent most of my time, with the kind of energy that might have gone into public affairs, playing the cello from the time I was ten through high school and college. One of the things that happened through my music playing was that I played in quartets with people who were very strong pacifists and Quakers. I was exposed to this whole business of conscientious objection and alternatives to war. I started going to Friends Meeting, which was in the basement of our college chapel, on Sunday nights. I didn't join, but it just felt like a good place to go. It seemed like they were headed in the right direction.

The end of my first year out of college I joined the Friends Meeting and that gave me all kinds of avenues into peace action. Syracuse was full of peace activists. I usually say to people that I acquired my Quakerism, the beginning of my personal social activist experience, and husband all on essentially the same day because I met Kenneth the day my application for membership in the Society of Friends was accepted. He was there with the quarterly meeting. I was also accepted by the meeting to go to the civilian training unit for women in American Friends Service Committee. We were supposed to train to go overseas. The United States wasn't yet in the war, and we were to go overseas and work in the battlefields. But it wasn't possible for me to go. By the time fall came two things intervened. One was that Kenneth and I got married. The second thing was that already it was getting very difficult to go abroad, and of course by December 1941 we were very much in the war. I didn't go overseas, but the training was wonderful. I had been taught to do things with absolutely no equipment and materials. We learned how to cook if you didn't have any cooking utensils. It was a wonderful training for an unconventional life.

I remember feeling, like many women did, that I wished I were a man so that my conscientious objection could be recorded. My mother's emotional and personal commitment to pacifism came out to reinforce my intellectual commitment. I was exposed to the people who had been in Spain during the Spanish Civil War doing relief work. I heard them talk about what it was like to work with the starving children and dying people. This became very vivid for me. All of it went to reinforce my pacifism and peace testimony.

After Pearl Harbor my husband and I drew up a letter to our friends asking them not to support the war, that war was not going to solve the problems of the world. He had to resign from his position at the League of Nations because he had made a statement on a political matter, which officials were not allowed to do. We were practically thrown out of our Friends Meeting because they were not prepared to support our action; it was seditious in a technical sense. We had a brief experience of feeling like there was no support anywhere.

At Fisk University, where Kenneth next worked, I was plunged into a very exciting intellectual world. This was before any of the civil rights movement. I discovered segregation the hard way by going into town on a bus with one of my neighbors on the campus. I got on the back of the bus where she was sitting. When I tried to get off the bus in town the bus driver slammed the door in my face. He didn't let me out right away. I began having experiences showing me what it meant for my black friends.

Later at Iowa State, where Kenneth was teaching, I worked with a sociologist doing a random sample of farm and urban women. I did most of the interviewing for that study as his research assistant and wrote my thesis on what I found. I was studying the sociology of the family. It was a fascinating experience interviewing women about how they coped while their husbands were overseas. It gave me a different perspective on war, a woman's view.

I felt absolute, unadulterated horror that I lived with for a long time after the bombing of Hiroshima and Nagasaki. I think it threw me very heavily into the Friends Meeting, dealing with the spiritual problem, but did not throw me into a state of activism. The activism came later.

McCarthyism didn't affect me personally, but I became very aware of how fearful people were. One graduate student had written a letter to the editor of a local paper about peace issues, and the FBI sent an agent to track her down. She was scared out of her wits.

I had joined WILPF during my homemaking period in the late fifties or early sixties. I became involved with a group of mothers who wanted their children to be pacifists. I had been involved in the YWCA and the League of Women Voters; neither of those organizations dealt with how you raised pacifists and WILPF did. I came in and focused on children; it was natural for me to move into chairing the childhood education committee. We did lots of fun stuff working with teachers and creating constructive relationships with schools. We had the antiwar toys campaign. I found that work very satisfying. It seemed so relevant to me.

Our children were small, and it related to the way they would be educated and how they would grow up.

Then I was on the national board of WILPF. I had been volunteering a couple of years prior to that in the Center for Conflict Resolution that Kenneth had cofounded at the University of Michigan. But I wasn't really sure I should be on the board because I didn't think I was really a political person. I didn't have a background of civic and political work in changing national legislation and local legislation. A lot of the WILPF women seemed to have lots more governmental experience than I did. All my work was either in the peace research side or with children. One of the women laughed and said, "You're political!" Nowadays we say the personal is political. I found the women on the executive committee marvelous, and I learned a lot.

I got the idea that WILPF could sponsor a newsletter that would tell scholars about peace research. The WILPF Committee thought it was a good idea. The first two years of the *International Peace Association Newsletter*, it was a WILPF project. It went to WILPF members as well as scholars. As a result of networking, we were able to hold a conference on peace research jointly sponsored by WILPF, the Quakers, and UNESCO. The association is still going strong. It was a very interesting personal transition for me from being a homemaker/volunteer to becoming a peace research professional. During the time I was volunteering at the Center for Conflict Resolution I also became active in Women Strike for Peace and helped start the WSP newsletter for the first year. My first major independent research project was on who joined WSP and why.

Although most of the peace work I had done was with mixed groups, such as Friends or the Fellowship of Reconciliation, I took very seriously the basic notion, which now looks like a very traditional notion, that women had something special to offer. I felt that women had a special responsibility for peace. That's widely debated now. I had been involved with Margaret Mead in the preparatory work for the U.N. International Cooperation Year while I was on the international executive committee of WILPF, and she and I both gave speeches saying that women have to be housekeepers not only for their families, but for the world. I wrote that kind of metaphor into my peace activities.

I don't think women are naturally more peaceful than men. They have to learn to be peaceful, just like men do, but women are in situations where they develop their peaceable capabilities, such as child rearing. You have a chance to learn things when you work with children. Men who are removed from that process of human growth, don't get the same chance to cultivate that peaceable nature. It's not inherent.

I published my dissertation at a time when people were just beginning to write on the women's movement. My concern really came from looking at the Third World and a broad spectrum of women. I always had trouble relating with a large part of the women's movement in this country because they seemed to be middle-class women worrying about their relations with their jobs, their salaries, their men, and so on, and it just didn't connect with the way I had thought about the problem. One of the reasons I wrote *The Underside of History: A View of Women through Time* was that I needed to lay it out the way I saw it. It was more complicated than the way I thought the women's movement was looking at it.

I began to appreciate WILPF members in a way that I hadn't before because WILPF members had been there all along and they never got carried away by these narrow concerns. They were always looking at a broader picture of economic and social structures and opportunities for everyone. I felt there was an enormous difference in the human style of WILPF that seemed so much better than much of the women's movement. I would hope that when the history of the women's movement is written that what WILPF stood for comes out quite clearly. I think it's very important the way WILPF has found a balance.

Our Dartmouth WILPF became an empowerment group for women to examine violence in the family and community and relate it to international violence and develop new concepts of nonviolence. These were very thoughtful women who had not belonged to any peace organization before.

I also was involved with Women Strike for Peace; that didn't lessen my WILPF activity. WSP presented itself, at that time, as a short-term movement that was reaching women who wouldn't otherwise be reached. I worked with them in that spirit. I felt that the important commitments were the long-term commitments and WSP wasn't then prepared to make long-term commitments.

I was involved in civil rights to counsel the parents of children who had gone south for the voter registration drives, because they were terrified. They couldn't understand what their children were doing. This was really a peak activity time for me. We trained them in nonviolent group work.

But Vietnam is what really pushed me into direct political activism, trying to get the United States to withdraw from Vietnam. We had some harassment, and I knew that any time there was a meeting at our house there was probably somebody writing down the license plate numbers. We knew we were being watched at every demonstration.

We wanted to get one of the candidates to take a position on American withdrawal from Vietnam. Our Democratic candidate refused to do that, so I was persuaded by WILPF and other people to run for Congress in 1966. I did a lot of educational speech making and door-to-door work. I thoroughly enjoyed it. The Republican candidate won the election, but people told me afterwards that he was so well educated by me that he turned out to be a much better congressman than anybody expected.

After the Vietnam War, when we were in Boulder, Colorado, something became clear to me that had not been clear to me before: most of the young people who came to the Vietnam movement were not pacifists. I remember having a really hard time with that set of attitudes and spending a lot of time trying to look at the world through the eyes of the students, to get a feeling for what it meant to them. The positive side of that was that I realized they were looking with fresh eyes at a government that was more oppressive and "wicked" than I had realized. I learned something from their view about oppression and victimization and the evils of the state that had not been part of my earlier view. But what saddened me was that many of them did not have a strong commitment to peacemaking and nonviolence. It was just not there. I was beginning to teach peace studies here on campus and developed a program in answer to these concerns.

The word *empowerment* wasn't a word we used then, but I was trying to empower women by showing them that what they understood and the skills they built in the community and family work they did were relevant to making peace in the community at large and dealing with social problems. They knew more than they thought they knew, and they had skills in mediation and conflict resolution which men often didn't have. They had sisters in other countries who were working on the same things, and they needed help to find the pathways and connections. They needed to learn more about their connection to the past. I always used WILPF as an example of how women worked for peace in the family, school, community, nation, and the international scene. WILPF was a model that I carried with me wherever I was.

After a conference of COPRED, the peace research consortia, in 1970 in Boulder, we got the idea to get together scholars from the peace research community and the U.N. diplomats to talk about conflict resolution, so that we could come up with something new. I wanted to get them to visualize a world without weapons, to use the imaging technique I had carried with me for many years.

Earlier, in the 1950s, I translated *The Image of the Future* from Dutch. The book dealt with the concept that the way you image the world affects your behavior and the future. I did some writing and speaking about that because it is very empowering to tell people that if they do some of the necessary work, the things they dream about can come about. They can make a difference. That became part of my whole tool kit.

My major mediation role has been between peace researchers and peace activists, each of whom think the other is failing to address the real needs of our time. Activists are impatient with looking at the long haul and evaluating implications of their actions for other parts of the social system in which they are acting. Models seem abstract to them. Peace researchers have too little respect for the understanding of humans in action, which activists have; they underestimate the value of their intuitions and the significance of emotional focusing they provide. They are not interested in providing the nitty-gritty kinds of information activists need. My goal has been to initiate a dialogue between the action and research perspectives, allowing each to be teacher-learner in relation to the other.

I see conflict as basic to the human process, and a sense of history helps me when the going gets rough; whatever is happening, humans have faced comparable struggles in the past. I feel an integrative spirit at work in human beings, a gift from our creator, which makes it possible for us to make of conflicting needs, wants, and interests new syntheses, new solutions for the human condition. The integrative spirit is also a visioning spirit, which makes it possible to visualize other and better ways for humans to live together. The envisioning spirit empowers us because we know that something other than what is, is possible. We know that it is worth our efforts to work for our visions.

Dagmar Wilson, 1989. Photograph by Michael O'Gorman.

DAGMAR SAERCHINGER WILSON

*We saw women as a vehicle for a new peace action. There were
already many peace groups and individuals, but the situation was
still grave. These groups had become part of the peace
establishment, and we didn't think they were as effective as they
once were. We were able to do things that couldn't have happened
in an already existing organization.*

Dagmar Saerchinger Wilson was born in New York City in 1916.
Her mother was a housewife, and her father was an American journalist and foreign correspondent who did one of the first weekly
broadcasts to the United States from England. Dagmar attended
schools in Berlin, England, and Belgium where her father had assign-
ments. Her mother's best friend was imprisoned and went on a hun-
ger strike for women's suffrage.

Dagmar is a graphic designer, landscape painter, stage and cos-
tume designer, and children's book illustrator. The environmental
hazards of atmospheric testing—strontium 90 turning up in babies'
teeth and the milk supply, and the madness of backyard fallout
shelters—were among the stimuli for her to begin to work against
nuclear testing. One of the founders of Women Strike for Peace, she
describes her role modestly as a "lightning conductor" for the energies of women in the peace movement.

She characterizes the worst of military planners as having a "sand-
box mentality": "This is what little kids are doing when they're fighting over the bucket—you know, 'It's mine!' I mean, in some countries
everything is shared. Native Americans have the concept of the earth
belonging to everybody and being shared, not carved up into separate parts."

Thirty years ago I was responsible for an action that resulted in a national peace movement which is still going strong, Women Strike for Peace. I'm not really a "political" person, although I was brought up as a pacifist. As a child growing up in the years following the "war to end wars"—World War I—I believed that nations would work out their conflicts rather than fight. Other wonderful things were happening too. Women had been liberated—my mother was a voter. I went to a progressive school for boys and girls, which in Europe, where I grew up, was not common. Socialism seemed like a wonderful experiment. I really believed that the world was moving forward in many areas, all favorable to mankind.

However, after World War II, I realized that there was something happening that was beyond politics and that affected all human beings. I felt that the question of survival on earth was not a matter of politics, nor a matter of power between governments, but was a matter of deeper concerns common to all humanity.

Many things moved me to become active step by step, but the last straw was the arrest of Bertrand Russell in 1961 in London's Trafalgar Square. He sat down with others to block traffic as a protest. He let it be known that having tried through normal channels to alert the world to the extreme danger that we were in, pitting ourselves against each other with these destructive new weapons, he felt it necessary to make a gesture. I was impressed by that. One night soon after his arrest, I was talking about his protest to some English friends who were visiting my husband and me here in the United States. They were turning me off with jokes and making cynical wisecracks. They were intelligent people distinguished in their professions, and I was distressed by their response. This was also the time of the Berlin Wall. The media had said it might mean war, and of course, war would mean nuclear war. Our administration was telling us to build fallout shelters to protect our families. I felt indignant, more than indignant. I felt insulted as a human being that responsible people, governments, were asking us to do anything so stupid, as ineffectual as this, instead of coming to grips with the problems that were causing the tensions we were facing. My husband, who knew me well enough to realize that I was getting quite tense, said, "Well, women are very good at getting their way when they make up their minds to do something."

That phrase stayed with me. The next day I called a friend at the Committee for a Sane Nuclear Policy in Washington, D.C., to ask if SANE was going to respond to the Committee of 100 in support of Russell's actions. I said, "I feel like chartering a plane and filling it with women to picket the jail." This guy said, "Well, that's an idea for your women's movement." I said, "Women's movement? What do you mean?"

I hadn't mentioned anything of that kind; I hadn't even thought about it. Anyway, he gave me an idea.

I stayed by the phone and thought, and thought, and thought. I said to myself, "Well, what about a women's movement?" I picked up the telephone and started calling all my women friends from my phone book and Christmas card list. I wanted to see what they thought. I have always been very telephone-shy, so this was an unusual thing for me to do. It turned out that everybody that I spoke with had been worrying about this problem. We women thought that the fallout shelter idea was an inane, insane, and an unsuitable response to the world situation and spelled disaster. The response I got was really quite enlightening. Each woman had it in the front of her mind, including a lot of women who were really not politically active.

I soon gathered together in my own living room a small group of women out of those whom I had called. Three days later we met at my house. Six days later, at a big meeting planned by SANE, we announced an "action." This marked the formation of Women Strike for Peace.

What we planned was a one-day event. The women would go on strike and leave the men "holding the baby." We said: "Now what do you think would happen if all the women went on strike?" The whole country would stand still. We thought it was a good way to demonstrate our own power and show that women were an essential part of our social structure and had a right to be heard. Six weeks from that day, there were demonstrations in sixty cities in the United States.

We were not part of the women's liberation movement. Ours was a peace movement activated by women. And there is a difference. We were women working for the good of humanity. One woman in our early group who was a very good writer wrote a statement of purpose that was powerful. One of the strengths of the movement was that it was cliché free. We were not political activists who were used to the old phrases. We were speaking much more out of our everyday experiences, but we were educated and literate. This was our statement:

We represent a resolute stand of women in the United States against the unprecedented threat to life from nuclear holocaust. We're women of all races, creeds, and political persuasions who are dedicated to the achievement of general and complete disarmament under effective international control. We cherish the right and accept the responsibility of the individual in a democratic society to act and influence the course of government. We demand of governments that nuclear weapons tests be banned forever, that the arms race end, and that the world abolish all weapons of destruction under United Nations safeguards. We urge immediate planning at local, state and national levels for a peacetime economy with freedom and justice for all. We urge our government to anticipate world tensions and conflicts through constructive nonmilitary actions and through the

United Nations. We join with women throughout the world to challenge the right of any nation or group of nations to hold the power of life or death over the world.

That really sums up my personal beliefs; I couldn't have stated it as well.

We saw women as a vehicle for a new peace action. There were already many peace groups and individuals, but the situation was still grave. These groups had become part of the peace establishment, and we didn't think they were as effective as they once were. We were able to do things that couldn't have happened in an already existing organization. I hoped that WSP would go on as long as it was effective, but I believed that in time it would be replaced by something else.

We had learned that nuclear testing was having hazardous effects on our environment, specifically on the open fields on which cows were grazing. This was contaminating the milk supply with strontium 90. This touched us very closely. We found out that strontium 90 was replacing calcium in children's bones. When we heard voices from Capitol Hill saying, "Well, well, it's too bad; this is just one of the hazards of the nuclear age," we really began to wonder about the sanity of our nation's leaders. Women Strike for Peace was an idea whose time had come. I was the lightning conductor; it just happened to be me. The time had come when either the people of the Earth would live together or die together.

In January of WSP's second year the New York women decided to come to the White House to stage a demonstration. They filled the longest train that had ever left Pennsylvania Station in the history of the railway, all with women. That day President Kennedy was scheduled for a press conference, and we thought no one would pay any attention to our demonstration. There was an enormous rain storm that soaked all the women who were coming off the train, ruining their hats—we always made a "respectable" appearance with hats and gloves. They walked through the rain to the White House and became soaked to the skin. At the president's press conference a well-known journalist representing the *New York Post* asked, "Do you think that demonstrations at this time have any influence on you and on the public and on the direction which we take in policy?" The president replied by saying that he had seen the large numbers of women out there in the rain and that we could understand that he agreed with our message and that our message had been received. We got wonderful publicity out of that, since the press conference was televised and broadcast nationally.

Soon after we began with one-day actions all over the country. We had permanent relationships with the sixty cities that had demonstrated on the first day. We had established a phone "tree" so that we could organize actions quickly. Eventually we realized that we had to have regular meetings and we had to have a national office, and so a national movement grew from our simple beginning with a one-day action. But we never had elected representatives; we preferred a movement rather than an organization. We continued to make decisions by consensus. So many people had been penalized in the past for left-wing activities. Our structure—or lack of it—meant that it would be very, very hard for anyone to be held accountable for the whole movement.

We soon had a program researching the effects of strontium 90. We took groups of people to government offices where we found everybody very willing to give us the facts. They were not reassuring. However, getting the word out was difficult. We took the press with us wherever we could. The publications that we issued were used in universities. We were respected; we weren't just a hysterical mob of women. People recognized that we had brains, and we were sensible.

We organized a delegation of one hundred women—fifty from the United States and fifty from European countries, including the Soviet Union—to visit the 1962 eighteen-nation disarmament conference in Geneva. We lobbied all the delegations and wanted to address the plenary session. We were informed that instead of addressing the plenary session, we could meet with the Soviet and United States cochairs. A young woman—she was a Quaker—volunteered to organize us for the meeting. I learned the power of Quaker silence from her. We marched through a light rain to where the sessions were held in the suburbs of Geneva. The rain seemed to be a good omen for us; we'd always succeeded in the rain. We walked in silence, which was quite a tour de force for us chatterboxes. We waited for an hour and forty-five minutes in total silence. Finally the Soviet and American cochairmen, Valaerian Zorin and Arthur Dean, came in with their translators, secretaries, and a few press. The important thing was that they walked into a room that was totally silent; the silence was palpable. Then I got up and spoke, which I did feeling rather like a schoolmistress. We wanted them to know that we held them responsible for the future of the human race and we thought it was time they got on with the business of ending the nuclear arms race. We presented them with mountains of petitions. The press coverage in Europe of our action was excellent. That was our first really international venture.

WSP played a critical role in the 1963 Partial Test Ban Treaty's passage, but our greatest triumph was our confrontation with the House Un-American Activities Committee. They pounced on us in 1962 by subpoenaing nine WSP women. We were advised by others who had a go-around with the Committee that we "should not make a big fuss." But one of our women said, "No, this is not the way we're going to do it. If they're subpoenaing Dagmar Wilson, we should all volunteer to testify." Now that was an absolutely brilliant idea. We sent telegrams through our network saying, "Volunteer to testify. Come if you can. Hospitality offered. Bring your baby." Hundreds of women volunteered to testify. This was a new twist—most people were tempted to run a mile when the Committee pointed its magic wand at them.

I was the last one to be subpoenaed. It was a great relief to me, to be able to have my say. I had the benefit of two days of hearings before my turn came. By that time I felt quite comfortable. My testimony was summed up best by someone who said that I treated the attorney for the Committee just as though he were a rather tiresome dinner partner.

Our WSP meetings were very informal, with no protocol; we ran them like we ran our carpools. Well, that was extremely baffling to these political gentlemen. And at one point one said, "I don't understand how you get anything done at all." I answered, "Well, it puzzles us sometimes too."

The Committee was trying to find out if there was Communist influence in the peace movement. WSP was concerned about war and peace; we didn't think the world was worth blowing up over political differences. We could see ourselves marching arm in arm with Soviet mothers for the sake of our children, so we were not intimidated by the Committee's strategies. I was asked at the end of my testimony whether we would examine our books to see if we had Communist women in our midst, and I said, "Certainly not"—we would not do anything of the kind. "In fact," I said, "unless the whole human race joins us in our quest for peace, God help us."

One of the funny things about our "inquisition" before the Committee was that we were asked, in a sinister tone, if we had a mimeograph machine. It's true that we were mimeographing materials to distribute among ourselves. You know, someone's baby was always around, and we kidded ourselves that the print might appear on a child's diaper. Anybody turning a baby over might find a description of where our next meeting was going to be. So much for the sinister implication of a mimeograph machine.

We got very good press. I think that everybody was thoroughly fed up with the Committee. Congress was embarrassed by it, and the press was bored with it.

People hardly ever have an opportunity to confront their attackers. So my couple of hours with the House Un-American Activities Committee was worth years of psychotherapy as far as I'm concerned. Instead of punching pillows, I was able really to unravel the misconceptions, to straighten out the record, and to put things in their proper place.

We cannot afford another world war. That's one thing that I know. In the Vietnam period, for the first time in history a whole generation of young people said, "Hell no, we won't go." This, and the presence of the peace movement, has somewhat restrained our government. Congress is aware that we can't easily round up young men to go and fight in other countries. I think it's very important to keep our voices heard and be active as long as we possibly can. It was hard on my family, no question about it. I was a freelance illustrator, and I was losing contracts. I couldn't get my work done and was always distracted, going off for talks, meetings, or demonstrations. My children wanted their mother to be like other people's mothers. After the initial demonstration, it was quite clear it was going to be an ongoing movement. It began to wear on my husband too. The first five years were very intense.

I have distanced myself these days from the peace movement, and this is not because I'm any less concerned. I simply can't keep it up. It's not my natural life-style. I just have to go back into my studio and get in touch with nature every so often or I go nuts. But there are others to take my place. There are people for whom the peace movement is the equivalent of the art studio for me. That is where they find their creativity and their satisfaction. These are the ones who carry on. I get up in a hurry and make a lot of noise and stomp around for a while. Then I have to go back to my own thing. That's where I am at the moment. But I can't say I'll never be active again.

Mary Duffield, 1989. Photograph © by Renée Burgard.

MARY BUELL DUFFIELD

The most powerful new "commodity" is information; it's a renewable resource. We can all enrich each other. It seemed to me that having electronic access for children all over the world would be a really fantastic thing . . . because the secret of radio is that it works the way the universe works, harmonizing forces, positive and negative.

Mary Buell Duffield was born in 1916 in South Bend, Indiana, to a conservative Southern Baptist minister's family. She studied journalism at Berkeley, California, and went to Germany on scholarship in 1940 where she experienced Hitler's powerful mob psychology and anti-Semitic violence firsthand. She returned to picket Nazi ships in Oakland, California.

A public school teacher, she was frequently fired for challenging authority and standing up for her beliefs. She now teaches youngsters about peace and global politics on her boat, anchored in Santa Cruz, California, through a program she founded called Satellite Sailors. The program involves U.S. children as "peace pirates"; they sail the Caribbean, to Nicaragua, or to the coast of South America and communicate with children in the countries they will visit via ham radio.

I came from a radically conservative background. My father was a Southern Baptist minister who felt that the more Communists you could kill before lunch, the safer we would all be. I'm exaggerating only a little bit. I gave up on all religion. I thought if that was what it meant to believe in God, then let me run away from that.

I think my first positive political action was back in Berkeley. I graduated in 1940, and that was right when Hitler was really riding high. I was offered a scholarship to go to Germany, which was a really appealing thing to me. I was to write a regular column for the *San Francisco Examiner* about how marvelous things were in Germany. The German embassy would pay my expenses. The railroads were on time, etc., but I saw what was really happening. You can't imagine what an impact it had on me, to listen to Hitler ranting with thousands and hundreds of thousands of people packed into plazas listening to him. It was typical to be swept up in that enthusiasm; I could understand that because I have an empathy for people. I quickly came back from Germany.

We picketed Nazi ships in the Oakland estuary. People don't have any idea how strong the Nazi movement was in America before we went to war. That's probably the first time I decided it was time to take action and do something. Of course, I got a lot of threatening letters. I pride myself on how active I've been and how effective by how many radical letters I get threatening me and telling me I should never teach in the schools, and so forth.

In Berkeley I was also caught up in the Spanish Civil War, sending in our lunch money to help the Lincoln Brigade. I had some very good friends in the Brigade; some of the most talented people I knew in Berkeley, who could have become great leaders, went over and lost their lives when World War II was being rehearsed in Spain.

I had heard Hitler speak and had seen his effect, even on myself, but I was still not a practicing pacifist. I believed a lot of the wartime propaganda about the atrocities—all the devils were on their side and all the saints were on our side. I wanted to be a pacifist, but having a husband and two brothers in the war, I was primarily interested in getting them home alive, getting all the boys home alive. It was a torment for me.

During the war my husband and I went to the relocation camp in Manzanar, California, and saw what was happening with the Japanese Americans who had been interned there. Most of us went there because we thought we could teach or use our clerical abilities to try to relieve the load. It wasn't much help. Their life was "put your hands up you yellow bastards." The spirit they had was beautiful. Manzanar was in the desert and was a very, very bad place to be. There used to be fields and pastures years before, but the state water authorities decided to reroute the water to the Los Angeles aqueduct. All the farmers went broke. The dust storms were so bad that I had to go to the hospital for a while. The dust was so thick that you couldn't even breathe through your nose.

The Japanese there were a revelation to me. And I learned about myself. I had been raised by this really conservative family that felt that the only right people were in the middle class and white Americans of a certain religion. My husband and I both felt that what was being done to the Japanese was wrong, but yet we still had that funny feeling about the Japanese and their slanted eyes. How's that for generous, wonderful, white middle-class me? One day I was sitting there watching a Japanese father swing his child on the swing out in the desert. I thought, "My God, that man loves his children the same way we do. Those people have feelings." It was a revelation. *Those* people. I was overcome with this feeling because I had been a "liberal," but it was primarily a response to my father's conservatism, to oppose him. I really got some kind of heart for the whole thing at Manzanar.

After the war we went to Alaska and homesteaded and didn't get much into politics there because of raising a child and surviving in the homestead. But I saw things happening there with some of the natives that duplicated exactly, almost as if they had taken a TV script from the Wild West, what had happened to the Indians—just change the names and locales, it was the same thing. I saw them take the Eskimo fishing rights away and the mineral rights. They didn't do it blatantly; they never do. They would pass a law saying that unless you were at your fishing trap on June 19 at noon, you lost it. Of course, it had been in the families for generations. I saw that; I was there watching it happen.

We wanted to do something about it, so my husband ran for office as state senator, but he was killed in an airplane accident. I stayed in Alaska until 1947 when a terrible storm smashed our home. I had to wrap my son up in a coat and get rescued from pyramids of snow; he was very ill. I brought him down to the United States. Since then I've lived primarily in Santa Cruz, California, and have become part of the peace movement here.

For a while I had a very static period, politically speaking, while I taught and cared for both my terminally ill parents who lived with me. My son had his lungs frozen in that accident in Alaska, so I had a very sick child and parents too. I also adopted a daughter. I taught journalism and mass media. I went to some peace meetings on the loyalty oath issue. Because I took a definite stand on it I was fired from three teaching jobs. That was hard because I was the breadwinner for four people, some of them ill. I just could not sign the Loyalty Oath saying I would be faithful to my country when I wasn't sure that my country was going to do right. I had worked up the salary scale and just begun to pay off all the bills, and then, wham, I went down to the bottom of the scale. I went back to teach at the high school I attended as a kid and was very pleased at that because I loved that school. I stood up in a faculty meeting when they first proposed a loyalty oath there and said, "Of course we can't accept this," and looked around. All the teachers were nodding their heads, like, "You're so right Mary," but it turned out that I was the only one who voted that way. They all said, "We sympathize, you're right, but . . . ." So I was notorious because I was the only "obvious commie" in the lot. When I lost my job I had to move and uproot my family again.

As a journalism teacher, I believe in freedom of the press for kids. We would always try to balance the viewpoints to give the kids a real sounding board. The local school boards had a fit because they thought the school paper should only write about cheerleader tryouts and all that. Our little paper won honors, but they didn't know what to do with me.

The next thing I got fired about was the UNESCO clubs. I would organize them during lunchtime. One of the school board members brought up that everybody knows what a commie outfit the U.N. is, so I was forbidden even to put up a notice on the school bulletin board that we were going to have a meeting. I put a notice up and was fired.

At another school I taught mass media, and the Lion's Club gave me a movie camera. We started making films and videotapes. They let me have the kids who were maladjusted in school. These kids were very creative, and we started winning awards. There was a company polluting the ocean. The students went down at low tide in their skin diving suits and plugged up the pipe from the company that was buried under the water. They had a kid at the plant to watch the reaction. They knew that the minute that stuff began to spill back up into the factory they would run down and unplug it. So they had a movie camera down there too. They filmed them running down to the beach; they didn't even see us filming it.

We used to put on film shows that the whole town came to. We put on a show that night, and somebody got wind of the pollution exposé we planned and called the principal and said, "Do you realize what that commie teacher is doing down there? You better call off that film show." We were just setting up all the cameras, and the principal walks down the aisle and says, "Mary, what are you going to show tonight?" I say, "Well, we have one about the sun, and a love story, and we have film about a local manufacturing plant." He says, "That's the one. Let's not show that." I said, "We just can't start censoring. We made our own money for this outside of school. I'm not going to shut the kids down. It happens to be true; there's a company polluting." He said, "Well, I have to shut you down." I said, "Yes, you could, but you're going to look funny taking this gray-haired lady out, hauling her out the aisle kicking and screaming." He looked at me like "goddamn it" and walked out of there. We showed that film, and it made headlines in the local paper. We weren't very popular with businessmen after that.

The thing the Quakers taught me was not to hate. Up to then I'd been "damn the other side," like my father, only taking the opposite viewpoint. I suddenly realized you can't go around judging who are the bad and good guys. You have to start with how we help each other get out of this mess we've gotten into.

When my children left for college, I moved on a boat to get away from all the memories of my husband's death, my son's illness, caring for my ill parents—all that. I lived on the boat until a couple of years ago. Then a wonderful thing happened. I discovered a marvelous thing to share, to "team teach" with the ocean. The thing I wanted to teach is simply to empower youngsters to develop their full potential. I discovered the magical impact of sailing, and sailing not just to pursue geographical horizons. Now, it's a wonderful thing to see landfall in early morning on a sailboat, but I wanted to see if we couldn't use the boat to push back cultural horizons and explore new cultural territory. I took some high school kids in the summertime on cruisers to explore friendships—we call them Peace Pirates.

We'd sail into different ports and tape-record discussions in the schools. We would let them know by ham radio that we were coming, and the teacher would get the kids thinking about the world's major problems and what kinds of action they plan to take, collectively and individually to try to solve them. We would go in and tape-record their interactions. We didn't go in saying, "Hey, we've got the answers and are going to convert you to our viewpoint." We said, "Let's see how we can communicate and cooperate to help solve some of these problems." The kids liked it because we were calling on them: "This is your time to be alive in the world. Get with it! Help us and see what we can do together."

The idea is to form networks of young people to communicate—and the young at heart qualify. I get to talk on these networks—about pollution problems, resources going to weapons of destruction, etc. I found out everywhere we went that youngsters are much more sophisticated than we think. I get tired of people who dismiss youngsters. Many people don't even bother to pay attention. They should be given more voice in politics and listened to by decision-making bodies.

The most powerful new "commodity" is information; it's a renewable resource. We can all enrich each other. It seemed to me that having electronic access for children all over the world would be a really fantastic thing. I had a dream. When you open up a radio you see all these transistors, and they look beautiful. I dreamt that there were these beautiful circuit boards floating around on the clouds and all the capacitors were faces of children, different colors, making this marvelous reso-

205

nance, because the secret of radio is that it works the way the universe works, harmonizing forces, positive and negative. Resonance on the radio is what enables you to tune in and get music by blending and harmonizing these different frequencies. When I found out that the same forces in radio were keeping the stars apart and holding people together, it just was terrific. So I wanted to empower young people with those skills to communicate information.

My goal was to get youngsters to put their highest powers to their highest uses. Kids with artistic abilities design the cards we send to people we contact; kids with musical abilities design background music for our tapes. They participate in what I call Planetary Citizenship through our Satellite Sailing program—we talk through satellites. This wasn't an idea unique to me. I was just able to articulate it in certain ways and make it visible; that dream made it so powerful. You'll never get the kids who have been on this boat with other kids to hate each other.

We also put a tape recording in a bottle and put it in the water; their little contribution to the ocean of human hopes. They're made so passive by our culture; they sit and watch the TV or listen to the radio. They sit in the classroom, and the teacher says, "Turn to page 33." They have to realize that the world is like a gigantic picture puzzle, and each of them has a piece of the solution. They have to figure out how that piece fits in.

We change sea charts—being peace pirates, we realize we're creating a new world. You know, Indians had names for places, but Columbus renamed them on behalf of his country. We're renaming them on behalf of the future. We send a copy of that part of the chart they played a role in naming home with them, so they realize that the world changes and they play a role in it. They are very powerful symbols, the bottle and the charts.

One of the peace sailors on one trip, an Italian kid, went back to Milan and at a school assembly had a long parchment and asked the kids to sign a statement that she or he would never take a job which would bring harm to another human being on the planet. Every single kid in the school signed it.

Once a TV station interviewer asked one of my younger crew members what difference fifteen kids could make. He answered, "Fifteen kids here, fifteen there." That guy stayed and filmed us and we were on the six o'clock and eleven o'clock news that night for half an hour all over southern California.

The inspiration for my using the boat for peace was that I read a little article in a San Francisco paper about a man named Earl Reynolds who had taken his boat and gone on many peace missions. One was to the Marshall Islands; we had told them we wanted to test the atom bomb and we didn't want to test it in our backyard. He knew what that meant to the people, and he felt if we were going to test atom bombs we should not do it in somebody else's backyard. So he took his boat out there and sailed right where they were going to test the bombs. They arrested him, of course, and towed him out of there. But that was a tremendous influence on me. There's a man who obviously loves sailing but uses it as a symbol of the planet, spaceship earth.

Many times friends would go up to Livermore Labs in California, where nuclear weapons research is done, and make their stand and get arrested, and I'd feel very badly that I wasn't doing that. They said, "What you're doing is absolutely unique, and you ought to do it." I have a hard time doing protest work because I could be taking kids out sailing. I chose to do what I do. There are many who support my sailing program, educators and school board members, who know I occasionally take part in protests. The wonderful thing about this program is that I'm no longer "it," if I ever was it—the kids are it. There's no way they can kill it.

I used the same communication technique in Nicaragua when I went there with the Peace Brigade. The Peace Brigade never takes sides, and we don't go anywhere with people with guns. The idea appealed to me because I really feel the crucial confrontation between forces of violence and international cooperation is so close. The balance of the world is so delicate; we will tumble off if we don't restore it. All my spare time I spent in a school, tape-recording; I told them that American kids were waiting to hear the tapes, and I had translated tapes for them from American kids. We had the questions up on the blackboard on what were the problems confronting their generation and what can young people around the world do about them. One young girl said, "Before we can transform the future and before we can work on our neighborhoods and our families, schools, cities, our nation, and world, we have to transform our hearts. We have to learn to love everybody and to work for peace." Here's a kid who lives in a bomb shelter. I spent all my time trying to teach them ham radio skills so when the day comes they can put up a small radio and antenna there so they could talk to the world and tell what they experienced in Nicaragua.

I would love to see women sweep into political office on a large scale because I think that because we nurture kids it makes us more nurturing. I'm a feminist in many ways, but I prefer to be a humanist. Buckminster Fuller said that the world is in such bad shape that there's no room for anything but utopia, and I really feel that.

My vision of the future is to take advantage of the creative capacities of whole chunks of the human race that we totally ignore or suppress. As I explore the younger generation, I am amazed at their creative capacities and innate sense for electronic communication. Someone said to me at a planning meeting for a teleconference, "I feel as if we are stitching together the nervous system of the future."

CONCLUSION

Women and Peace: A Historical Context

EARLY DISSENT

The peace movement in the United States did not begin in the 1960s, that most visible period of contemporary history which catapulted many unlikely partners into the movement—radical students and housewives, veterans and hippies. Nonviolent dissent, religious and secular pacifism have a long tradition in this country. An appeal for a department of peace within the federal government was made as early as 1793 when Dr. Benjamin Rush, a signer of the Declaration of Independence, and Benjamin Bannecker, a black mathematician, architect, and designer, published in Banneker's *Almanac* a proposal for a U.S. peace office equivalent to the War Department.[1]

Early dissident leadership arose out of the colonial peace churches—the Amish, Brethren, Mennonites, and Society of Friends, who to this day maintain their commitment to pacifism, and early secular peace organizations such as the New York Peace Society, Massachusetts Peace Society, and the American Peace Society. Among other activities, these groups lobbied for a world court, which was established at The Hague, Netherlands, in 1899.

Radical secular pacifists led the abolition movement and developed many of the techniques and tools of nonviolent protest, including "civil disobedience, tax refusal, public disturbances, boycotts, and direct actions such as sit-ins."[2]

Although not themselves subject to the military draft, women were active in these early religious and secular peace groups. They also pioneered many social reform organizations. Because women were rarely allowed leadership positions in mixed groups and were often denied the

209

right to speak at mixed gatherings, they founded independent groups for social change.

SUFFRAGE AND WOMEN'S PEACE CAMPAIGNS

It was in the suffrage movement that feminists honed their skills for further participation in the larger sphere of national and eventually international politics—even before they gained the vote. The more radical feminists became disillusioned when their suffrage cause was ignored by the politicians who had once courted their support for abolition. They resolved to maintain separate women's organizations where they could develop leadership potential and build momentum for advances in women's rights and other issues, including peace.

Different strategies emerged among feminists working for the vote, and yet all worked for the common goal of ratification of the Nineteenth Amendment. The suffrage movement also addressed such related concerns as the protection of women workers and general social reform, drawing connections between issues to broaden the base of support for their primary cause, women's rights. Soon, however, the war in Europe began to draw the focus of many feminists away from suffrage (as abolition had earlier) toward the cause of maintaining U.S. neutrality and promoting mediation between the belligerents.

By 1914 most women's organizations in America, where much of this new impetus for peace making now took place, had resolutions on their books committing them to peace and arbitration. Three weeks after war had been declared in Europe a prominent suffragette called Fanny Garrison Villard [daughter of William Lloyd Garrison, the abolitionist] had had no difficulty at all in finding 3,000 women to lead down Fifth Avenue in a march against the war. . . . In January, 1915, a vast convention of women packed the Grand Ballroom of the New Willard Hotel in Washington to proclaim a "programme for constructive peace" under the aegis of a new Women's Peace Party of whom Jane Addams was the chair.[3]

Jane Addams founded Hull House in 1899, one of the first settlement houses in the United States, to address the problems of the immigrant population. She saw the relationship between forces of social and economic oppression and discontent and the causes of war. Addams's writing on war countered the views expressed in William James's influential essay "The Moral Equivalent of War." He proposed mandatory male service to foster values of manliness and discipline—the stirring characteristics of men at war. In her "Moral Substitute for War" Addams advocated in place of these warlike "virtues," selflessness, comradeship in peace, altruism, humanitarianism and nurture.[4]

Many people, reflecting the male values of the time, considered her view idealistic, unrealistic and "womanly"—the ultimate pejorative in the double standard that placed women on the pedestal of the "separate sphere" as guardians of virtue, while denying them opportunity to apply those values in active, public life. But Addams defied the norm; her public life involved her in direct pragmatic negotiations with the harsh realities of war and economic violence.

That women formed their own peace organizations was a natural outgrowth of their experience and cultural expectations. Although most women remained isolated from mainstream political action in their "separate sphere," politically concerned women were building their skills and confidence, gaining political savvy, and preparing to confront the male-dominated, violent world with female experience and promote an "ethic of care" to temper men's "ethic of justice."[5] While infused with idealism and vision, feminist peacemakers were also pragmatic, well-educated, motivated women experienced with the techniques and challenges of the long abolition and suffrage campaigns. They understood that lasting peace required equal rights, national and international justice, and personal freedom. The women of the Women's Peace Party (WPP) turned a good deal of their energies, in the midst of the suffrage campaign—which they did not abandon—to address the causes and cures of war. Lacking the vote in their own country, American women proposed universal suffrage to enable women to enter the public sphere. There they could work to bring peace to the warring states and ameliorate economic and social conditions.

INTERNATIONAL CONGRESS OF WOMEN

At the urging of its European members, the WPP called an International Congress of Women to meet in The Hague in 1915. Over a thousand women came from twelve countries, both neutral and belligerent, to find common ground on which they could unite their energies and resources toward mediating the war. This was to be the birthplace of WILPF.

The press was condescending and insulting about their efforts: What were these women doing? It was bad enough that they were clamoring for suffrage; now they were meddling in international issues. One paper said of their enterprise: "The sitting . . . was remarkable for its extreme dullness. . . . The most noteworthy feature of the first day's proceedings was the enthusiasm displayed by the delegates at the promise which was made to treat them to an excursion to the tulip fields at Haarlem." The *New York Times* called Addams "a silly, vain, impertinent old maid."[6]

Criticism came from within the movement as well. Carrie Chapman Catt, one of the cofounders of WPP, disagreed with the concept of the international women's peace congress, likening the effort to "throwing a violet at a stone wall."[7]

In their strenuous sessions—relieved by a trip to see the flowers, no doubt—they adopted twenty resolutions under six headings to lead to mediation and peace: Women and War, Action towards Peace, Principles of a Permanent Peace, International Co-Operation, Education of Children, and Action to be Taken.[8] They asked neutral countries to form a conference for mediation to develop peace proposals. They resolved to serve as envoys to the leaders of both neutral and belligerent nations and the president of the United States. They planned another women's peace conference to be held in the same place as the formal peace conference ending the war in order to be present to contribute their ideas to the peacemaking process.

Although their attempt at "citizen diplomacy" and reconciliation failed to slow the progress of the war, their efforts were brave and unprecedented.

The WPP continued to work for conciliation and had the support of nearly twenty-five thousand women in 1917, when the United States entered the war. As the country mobilized for war, Catt abandoned the WPP and pledged the full support of her National Women's Suffrage Association to the war effort. (Catt was to rejoin the women's peace movement after the passage of the suffrage amendment, however, and form a coalition of eleven women's organizations called the National Conference on the Cause and Cure of War.)[9] Though the defection of Catt's suffragists cost the WPP members, the party carried on with its plans for a postwar international women's congress. The congress was held in 1919 in Zurich because the Central Power delegates were denied entry to France. They got down to business by cabling President Wilson to raise the blockade and institute immediate relief, soften the terms of the treaty, demand disarmament of all nations, and support the League of Nations. Representatives were sent to Versailles to meet with the treaty delegates and returned to their own countries to build support for the League of Nations proposal.

It would have been surprising and even revolutionary had the aims of the 1915 women's peace congress been adopted by the major powers, given women's status at that time and the escalation of the war, but in fact several of the points in Wilson's Fourteen Point Peace Plan were drawn from the resolutions of the women's congress. WPP members went on after the war to forge an organization—the Women's International

League for Peace and Freedom—which was born at the 1919 congress and continues to provide a forum for women to work toward peace and freedom. The Women's Peace party became the U.S. section of WILPF.

WOMEN AND THE POLITICAL PROCESS AFTER SUFFRAGE

Division over goals and strategies within the women's movement continued to trouble WILPF and other women's organizations. But the obstacles to women becoming a unified political force came not only from within the women's movement in its failure to coalesce women voters into an effective voting bloc. The political process remained entrenched in the male power structure, which continued to obstruct women's political growth and progress. Also, overall voter turnout declined in the twenties and thirties as both women and men were disillusioned with the political process.

Just what did women suffrage and peace activists do after suffrage was won? Did they go back to their kitchens and nurseries, failing to fulfill the promise of an enlightened electorate that the feminists had sought? Did they abandon efforts to ensure continuing peace? Many politically enlightened women did what women have always done; they took care of their families, schools, churches, and communities. They promoted culture and worked for clean streets, child protection, improved conditions in the workplace, and domestic and international peace. The passage of the Nineteenth Amendment in 1920 is often cited as a political benchmark after which feminist efforts became quiescent. Women may not have had the predicted "civilizing" impact on electoral politics, but they did not reduce their efforts in voluntary groups and social reform measures. "Striking continuities tend to be overlooked if 1920 is supposed to be the great divide and only electoral politics its sequel."[10] Women remained active in voluntary associations largely outside the political process. They continued to engage in the same kinds of lobbying efforts and organizing as in earlier reform efforts, using skills they refined during the suffrage campaign. Their lobby represented a more powerful "engine than ever before, because it drew behind it the train of women's votes."[11]

During the suffrage campaign and the antiwar campaigns, women faced charges of being unwomanly or unpatriotic because of their involvement in political reform. During World War I this was especially so. The Espionage Act of 1917 and the Sedition Act of 1918 prohibited actions construed to aid the enemy or obstruct recruitment to the military. It prohibited the mailing of any antigovernment propaganda; acts that discouraged the purchase of war bonds; and criticism of the U.S. Constitution, the government, or the armed forces. Although WPP wasn't prosecuted, its publication the *Four Lights* was suppressed.[12]

In 1919, anti-Communist campaigns began that were to persist for decades. Brigadier General Amos Fries, chief of the Army Chemical Warfare Services, permitted his librarian, Lucia Maxwell, to construct and distribute a chart called the "Spider Web" conspiracy chart, which linked women activists and reformers with Communist organizations. Some of the charts were printed with Maxwell's poem: "Miss Bolshevicki has come to town, / With a Russian cap and a German Gown, / in Women's clubs she's sure to be found, / For she's come to disarm AMERICA." John Weeks, the secretary of the War Department (whose Massachusetts senatorial campaign was defeated by suffragists), eventually ordered the charts destroyed, but they had already been widely distributed. Some versions of the charts had men's names added with color coding: red for radicals, pink for progressives, and yellow for pacifists.[13]

Despite political setbacks and red-baiting, the women of WILPF remained active and hopeful. Groups like WILPF continued to nurture women's organizational and lobbying skills. They kept the issue of peace before the public, and they made the connection between peace and other issues, as Addams had. Although peace was WILPF's primary goal, it addressed racial discrimination, labor's right to organize, and a host of other issues. This multi-issue approach to peace—the belief that there can be no peace without freedom and justice—and the strong organizational structure it developed in the United States and internationally were to serve WILPF well through the years. Through continuing effort, WILPF healed some of the splits between pacifists and suffragists and moved away from the separate spheres theory. Women brought a fresh perspective and energy to issues of world politics; having been excluded from power and political hierarchies, they could be said to have a more objective view of how politics could operate. Whatever naiveté this new view may have had, could be offset by the women's dedication and vigor.

WILPF continued work toward establishing a noncoercive League of Nations, outlawing war, and accomplishing disarmament. In 1929 the Kellogg-Briand pact was signed. It renounced war as an instrument of national policy and was described as a "high water mark of American international cooperation . . . and a unique triumph for peace activism."[14] The administration continued naval buildup, however, and it "valued the treaty chiefly as a visible means of solidifying the world's will to peace behind the untrammeled leadership of independent America."[15]

During the years between the world wars, WILPF worked to build alliances with farmers and with labor. Efforts were directed toward convincing both sides in labor disputes to forgo violence. WILPF spoke out increasingly against racism and anti-Semitism in the thirties. WILPF's executive secretary, Dorothy Detzer, was the moving spirit behind the 1934 Nye Congressional hearings on graft and stimulation of the arms race by the munitions industry. WILPF members circulated the Oxford Pledge for Peace and helped defeat a proposal to conscript women.[16]

Several peace organizations, including WILPF, sponsored a constitutional amendment to restrict the government's warmaking powers by requiring a national referendum to declare war. Senator Lynn Frazier of North Dakota worked with the Women's Peace Union to propose such an amendment to Congress every year between 1926 and 1937.[17] Many WILPF members became individually involved in antifascist organizations and Spanish Civil War relief. There wasn't a cause for peace and justice that WILPF overlooked in the United States or internationally in the years between its founding and the outbreak of World War II.

WORLD WAR II AND WILPF

With war once more brewing in Europe, WILPF advocated U.S. neutrality and mediation, again to no effect. During World War II the U.S. section of WILPF lost half its membership; some women thought WILPF was too pacifist, and others thought WILPF's position was not pacifist enough. Once the United States was involved in the war, WILPF members did what they could to ameliorate the effects of the war and became involved in war relief efforts. Members also supported conscientious objectors.

European branches of WILPF engaged in remarkable instances of nonviolent action during the war. The Polish section was dissolved, but its members joined the Resistance. On one occasion several Polish WILPF members removed Jewish children from a deportation train. Many women took Jewish children into their own families.[18]

The Danish WILPF section kept an active membership of twenty-five thousand women who did education and relief projects. They sold "peace flowers" to German soldiers, who reportedly wore them inside their tunics.[19]

During the war the Dutch branch argued that women were proving their worth and equality in the peace movement and no longer needed a special women's peace organization. There was spirited debate, and at the end, the case for continuing WILPF won the day. Members felt that WILPF was an influential organization with an excellent program and to dissolve it might weaken the peace movement at a critical time.[20]

WILPF leadership did, however, admit the failure of nonviolent resistance and post–World War I peace activism to prevent or to counteract the spread of war. International WILPF President Emily Greene Balch communicated to the World Jewish Congress in 1942: "We are all answerable in part for the development of a state of things where the moral insanity of Hitler [sic] Germany was possible, and for a state of things where the civilized world can find no better way out than competition in reciprocal slaughter and destruction. We were not ready in time with any other method than this slow and cruel one."[21]

After World War II the U.S. section of WILPF redoubled its efforts to ensure future peace. WILPF became active as a nongovernmental organization in the United Nations. Members were active in protesting the Korean War and in the early civil rights movement. WILPF supported women's rights and the Equal Rights Amendment and greatly increased its membership during the Vietnam War. It was vigilant in publicizing the danger of nuclear proliferation.

Over the years, WILPF has maintained its dedication to peace and freedom and has remained a multi-issue organization with an effective international and national hierarchy and strong educational and lobbying programs. It remains active in the United Nations. But ironically the very strengths that made WILPF an active survivor in the long struggle for peace worked against it in the early sixties. A new generation of women awakened to political issues and especially the dangers of atmospheric testing and looked for organizations with more flexible structures and grass-roots character. Just as in the World War II period, in the sixties WILPF was caught in the dilemma of being too radical for some and not radical enough for others. Women formed new organizations without the historical ties and formal structure of long-established organizations; they developed less hierarchical, more direct-action-oriented groups.

WOMEN STRIKE FOR PEACE: A FRESH PERSPECTIVE ON ORGANIZING

In the fall of 1961 a group of self-described housewives in Washington, D.C., formed Women Strike for Peace and galvanized over fifty thousand women all across the country in one-day actions protesting Russian and American nuclear policies. The five founding members of WSP first met as members of SANE (Committee for a Sane Nuclear Policy). They were dissatisfied with the failure of SANE's leadership to take seriously issues such as the contamination of milk by strontium 90 from above-ground nuclear tests. The women were looking for a more flexible organizational structure than they found in SANE, one more responsive to their concerns and quicker to act.[22]

The one-day actions ranged from simple individual acts to mass visits to legislative offices and citywide forums. WSP never intended to be an organization at all, just a nationwide series of one-day strike actions. It strove to be and remain leaderless. Many women never before active in peace issues were attracted to the idea of a one-day, creative strike, to leave their jobs and families and be part of a local action against the dangers of atmospheric testing. Each community planned autonomous actions that were part of a loosely knit whole. Women who were part of traditional peace organizations such as WILPF were attracted to the fresh approach and nonorganizational philosophy of WSP. WSP was not founded as a feminist organization; it developed a style its leaders characterized as "feminine" (even ladylike), antihierarchical, spontaneous, given to direct action. They were, by and large, "middle-class, middle-aged peace mothers wearing white gloves."[23]

They did not choose the word *strike* to identify with radical labor (although women were asked to leave their work and homes and participate in the actions). In fact, some groups joining the movement called their groups "Women for Peace" rather than use the word *strike*. The Los Angeles WSP newsletter, "LA WISP," published a peace dictionary to counter the left-wing image of the word *strike:* "We construe our name to mean 'putting forth the roots of peace, causing Peace to be the root' in our land."[24] Members maintained a ladylike image. One issue of the newsletter stated, "We are Women. We are Ladies, even. We voice a Mother's protective View for the whole world. . . . Stay as lovely as you are, girls."[25]

"Housewifely" tactics, familiar to the women from the PTA, League of Women Voters, and other groups, became the hallmark of early WSP actions. New York WSP members constructed a block-long petition against the arms race out of hundreds of feet of dish toweling. At other demonstrations the women wore photographs of their children on their hats as they marched.

The one-day strike actions generated widespread interest among their participants in continuing the action and keeping in touch with the different WSP groups that were formed. Eventually, groups organized strike actions on the first day of each month. One Berkeley, California, WSP member carried a white sash in her purse, "at all times ready to be a member of a silent public demonstration for peace."[26] Other groups picketed or formed study groups to learn how to get media publicity and visibility for their actions.

WSP members had not, for the most part, been politically active before their involvement in WSP. WILPF members also participated in creative direct-action efforts, as did women in other groups, but WSP's direct action, without massive coordination and bureaucratic structure, was attractive both to women who were inexperienced in political protest and to those who were frustrated by organizational bureaucracy in established groups.

Eventually WSP set up a Washington office, but made it very clear that this office was to provide only coordination, not leadership. Leadership remained on the local level. A periodic newsletter informing members about various local actions was issued, and membership lists were gradually compiled. WSP held several national conferences to debate issues such as whether it should be more than a single-issue group. Members resolved through consensus to continue WSP's efforts and not disband after the nuclear test ban treaty—one of their major goals—was passed in 1963. Members were active during the time of the Cuban missile crisis, protested the presence of U.S. military advisors in Vietnam, organized civil rights actions, and mobilized around other related issues. WSP's reliance on direct action as a fundamental protest technique continued as the organization broadened its focus beyond the one-day action and single-issue approach.

For the most part, WSP members lacked historical feminist consciousness. Although not intentionally nor in principle a feminist organization, WSP members were protofeminists; their nonhierarchical, consensus-based organizational style contributed to the developing feminist process and structure of the 1960s. They challenged the "feminine mystique" Betty Friedan so ably described by becoming involved in political issues outside the domestic sphere. Without the feminist terminology of consciousness raising, they raised women's awareness and self-esteem.[27]

WSP's shining hour was during the 1962 House Un-American Activities Committee hearings. Despite its mild image, WSP's actions in the political arena eventually subjected it to the red-baiting that WILPF had encountered since the 1920s. Some groups purged suspected members. WSP did not.[28] Instead, the women offered voluntary testimony to demonstrate their pride in their peace work and to overload the hearing chambers. They started the first day of the hearings by trying to lay a wreath at the suffragist monument in the Capitol Rotunda, but were prevented from doing so by guards.[29] Supporters and members crowded the hearings, gave flowers to the women testifying, and spontaneously stood when their members were called to testify. The crowd laughed appreciatively when the WSP was accused of having a hierarchical structure controlled by the Communist party, since WSP so assiduously avoided formal leadership structures. When charged with having Communists in their membership, the women pointedly indicated they would accept anyone who was dedicated to peace. A Herblock cartoon in the 11 December 1962 *Washington Post* showed two senators talking at the hearings. One leans to the other and says, "I came in late; which was it that was un-American—women or peace?"

TAKING STOCK

Women in the organized U.S. peace movement joined with other women to form separate women's peace organizations, such as the WPP,

WILPF, and WSP, to build their own leadership skills, to bring the feminine/feminist stamp to peace issues, and to speak with voices steeped in an "ethic of care." WILPF is steadfast, well organized, and lively in its maturity. It has forged a strong identity and earned respect among other peace groups, in the United Nations, and among nations. WSP, formed out of the outrage and protest of "housewives" against harmful nuclear testing in the sixties, tried alternative organizational structures and forums for protest. It still has an active membership devoted to many of the same issues as WILPF. Both groups, in their distinctive ways, continue to provide an inspiring, supportive training ground for women peace activists.

A critical question remains: What have been the fruits of women's labors for peace? It is unlikely that even the most idealistic of WILPF and WSP members believe that universal peace and disarmament is possible in their own lives, or even in the lifetimes of their grandchildren. This is as true today as it was when WILPF was founded in 1915. For most of the women involved in the struggle for peace and justice, it is a lifelong and long-term process, enjoying only short-term successes. They see no other choice. To surrender to disillusionment and despair or to surrender freedom to the "protection" of armed camps poised for attack are not acceptable options in their view. For those who left the active struggle for periods of their lives or those who have left the struggle for others to carry on, there is firm conviction that women working for peace will eventually carry the day.

These women show the world and other activists the value of their perspective and the power of communities of women working for peace and freedom. They demonstrate women's substantial energy, strength, and perseverance.

"When I think about the future," said WILPF and WSP member Alice Richards, "I'm torn between hope and despair. There are so many dangers, and in many ways, they are increasing all the time. I think of what H. G. Wells said, that civilization is a race between education and catastrophe. Our job is cut out for us. I guess the thing that keeps one going in the peace movement is that to drop out completely is to give in to despair. Taking part in it is what keeps you hopeful, to make sure that education wins."[30]

Notes

1. Charles Duryea Smith, ed., *The Hundred Percent Challenge: Building a National Institute of Peace* (Washington, D.C.: Seven Locks Press, 1985), 158.
2. Robert Cooney and Helen Michalowski, eds., *The Power of the People:*

Active Nonviolence in the United States (Philadelphia: New Society Publishers, 1987), 14.

3. Caroline Moorehead, *Troublesome People: Enemies of War, 1916–1986* (London: Hamish Hamilton, 1987), 23–24.

4. Linda Kay Schott, "Women against War: Pacifism, Feminism and Social Justice in the U.S., 1915–1941" (Ph.D. diss., Department of History, Stanford University, Stanford, California, 1985), 240.

5. Carol Gilligan, *In a Different Voice: Psychological Theory and Women's Development* (Cambridge: Harvard University Press, 1982), 173.

6. London *Daily Press* and *New York Times* quoted in Moorehead, *Troublesome People*, 26–27.

7. Schott, "Women against War, " 26, from a letter to Addams from Catt, 12 November 1915.

8. Gertrude Bussey and Margaret Tims, eds., *Pioneers for Peace: Women's International League for Peace and Freedom, 1915–1965* (Oxford: Alden Press, 1980), 20.

9. Nancy F. Cott, *The Grounding of Modern Feminism* (New Haven: Yale University Press, 1987), 87, 94–99.

10. Ibid., 85.

11. Ibid., 87, 94–99.

12. Schott, *Women against War*, 240.

13. Cott, *The Grounding of Modern Feminism*, 246.

14. Charles De Benedetti, *Origins of the Modern American Peace Movement, 1915–1929* (Milwood N.Y.: KTO Press, 1978), 185.

15. Ibid., 209–10.

16. Bussey and Tims, *Pioneers for Peace*, 186.

17. Charles Chatfield, *For Peace and Justice: Pacifism in America, 1914–41* (Boston: Beacon Press, 1971), 112.

18. Bussey and Tims, *Pioneers for Peace*, 181.

19. Ibid., 182–83.

20. Ibid., 187–88.

21. Ibid., 173.

22. Amy Swerdlow, "The Politics of Motherhood: The Case of Women's Strike for Peace and the Test Ban Treaty" (Ph.D. diss., Department of History, Rutgers University, State University of New Jersey, New Brunswick, New Jersey, 1984), 122.

23. Ibid., ii.

24. The Los Angeles WISP newsletter for 7 April 1961, quoted in ibid., 176.

25. Ibid., 500–1.

26. Ibid., 188.

27. Ibid., 515–16.

28. Ibid., 305.

29. Ibid., 162.

30. Alice Richards, videotaped interview in Atherton, California, for Women's Peace Oral History Project, 1989. Videotape and all audio tapes of the project will be given to the Swarthmore College Peace Library Collection.

Bibliography

Addams, Jane. *New Ideals of Peace.* New York: Macmillan Co., 1907.

———. *Peace and Bread in Time of War.* New York: King's Crown Press, 1945.

Boulding, Elise. "Who Are These Women?: A Progress Report on a Study of Women Strike for Peace," Council for Research on Conflict Resolution, Ann Arbor, Mich., March 1963.

———. "Perspectives of Women Researchers in Disarmament, National Security and World Order," *Women's Studies International Quarterly* 4, no. 1 (1981): 27–40.

Bussey, Gertrude and Margaret Tims, eds. *Pioneers for Peace: Women's International League for Peace and Freedom, 1915–1965.* Oxford: Alden Press, 1980.

Chatfield, Charles. *For Peace and Justice: Pacifism in America 1914–41.* Boston: Beacon Press, 1971.

———, ed. *Peace Movements in America.* New York: Schocken Books, 1974.

Conway, Jill. "Women Reformers and American Culture." *Journal of Social History* 5 (Winter 1971–72): 166–69.

Cook, Blanche, ed. *Jane Addams on Peace and Freedom 1914–1935.* New York: Garland, 1971.

Cooney, Robert and Helen Michalowski, eds. *The Power of the People: Active Nonviolence in the United States.* Philadelphia: New Society Publishers, 1987.

Cott, Nancy F. *The Grounding of Modern Feminism.* New Haven: Yale University Press, 1987.

De Benedetti, Charles. *Origins of the Modern American Peace Movement, 1915–1929.* Milwood, N.Y.: KTO Press, 1978.

———, ed. *Peace Heroes in Twentieth Century America.* Bloomington: Indiana University Press, 1986.

———. *The Peace Reform in American History.* Bloomington: Indiana University Press, 1980.

Brittain, Vera. *Rebel Passion: A Short History of Some Pioneer Peace Makers.* Nyack, N.Y.: Fellowship, 1964.

Detzer, Dorothy. *Appointment on the Hill.* New York: Henry Holt and Co., 1948.

Deming, Barbara. *Prison Notes.* New York: Grossman Publishers, 1966.

Elshtain, Jean Bethke. *Women and War.* New York: Basic Books, 1987.

Foster, Cate. *Women for All Seasons: The Story of the Women's International League for Peace and Freedom.* Athens, Ga.: University of Georgia Press, 1989.

Gilligan, Carol. *In a Different Voice: Psychological Theory and Women's Development.* Cambridge: Harvard University Press, 1982.

Jensen, Joan. "All Pink Sisters: The War Department and the Feminist Movement of the 1920's." Fourth Berkshire Conference on the History of Women, Mount Holyoke College, South Hadley, Mass., 1978.

Josephson, Hannah. *Jeannette Rankin, First Lady in Congress: A Biography.* Indianapolis: Bobbs-Merrill, 1974.

Kline, Ethel. *Gender Politics.* New York: Harvard University Press, 1984.

McAllister, Pam., ed. *Reweaving the Web of Life: Feminism and Non-Violence.* Philadelphia: New Society Publishers, 1982.

Moorehead, Caroline. *Troublesome People: Enemies of War, 1916–1986.* London: Hamish Hamilton, 1987.

Randall, Mercedes M. *High Lights in W.I.L.P.F. History: From The Hague to Luxembourg, 1915–1946.* Philadelphia: Women's International League for Peace and Freedom, 1946.

Reardon, Betty A. *Sexism and the War System.* New York: Teachers College Press, 1985.

Schott, Linda Kay. "Women Against War: Pacifism, Feminism and Social Justice in the U.S., 1915–1941." Ph.D. diss., Stanford University, 1985.

Smith, Charles Duryea. *The Hundred Percent Challenge: Building a National Institute of Peace.* Washington, D.C.: Seven Locks Press, 1985.

Swerdlow, Amy G. "The Politics of Motherhood: The Case of Women Strike for Peace and the Test Ban Treaty." Ph.D. diss., Rutgers University, The State University of New Jersey (New Brunswick), 1984.

Terkel, Studs. *The "Good War": An Oral History of World War Two.* New York: Ballantine Books, 1984.

Wittner, Lawrence S. *Rebels Against War: The American Peace Movement, 1933–1983.* Philadelphia: Temple University Press, 1984.

Zinn, Howard. *A People's History of the United States.* New York: Harper Colophon Books, 1980.

WILPF and WSP Papers

The Norlin Library, Western Historical Collection at the University of Colorado, Boulder has published a *Guide to the Women's International League for Peace and Freedom Papers* (1982). The collection dates from 1915 to 1978.

The *Guide to the Swarthmore College Peace Collection* (1981) contains records for WILPF from 1914–80, including records of the Women's Peace Party (1914–20), WILPF international records (1915–80), WILPF U.S. section records (1919–80), and records of the Jane Addams Peace Association (1941–74). The collection also includes records for Women's Strike for Peace (1961–80), notably the Los Angeles WSP papers.

The Eleanor Garst collection at the State Historical Society of Wisconsin contains WSP papers from 1961–65.

Index

Abolition, 209, 210
Addams, Jane, 4, 48, 210–11, 212
AIDS, 179, 181
Air Force Academy, 179
American Association of Scientific Workers, 119–20; *see also* union organizing
American Civil Liberties Union (ACLU), 122–23
American Committee to Aid Victims of German Fascism, 32
American Friends Service Committee, 129, 186, 187
anti-draft. *See* draft resistance, conscription
anti-fascist: Spanish Civil War, 32–33; WWII, 215
anti-Semitic, 32, 38, 60–62, 71–72, 138
arms race, education, 44; *see also* Riverside Church
Arnett, Peter, 44; *see also* POW
atmospheric atomic testing, 134; *see also* Strontium-90
atomic bomb, 7, 24, 73; *see also* Hiroshima, Nagasaki

Balch, Emily Greene, 4, 215
Bannecker, Benjamin (Bannecker Almanac, 1793), 180, 209
Birch Society, John, 16
birth control, 39
Black Panthers, 112
black students, political organizing, 170
Black Student Union (San Francisco State), 170

Cambodia, 41
Canada, 135, 145; *see also* draft resistance

Carter, Jimmy, 17–18
Catholic Church, 27; discrimination, 178–79
Catholic Interracial Council, 25, 26
Catholic Worker Movement, 24, 25, 177
Catt, Carrie Chapman, 212
Central Intelligence Agency (CIA), 14
Center for Conflict Resolution, 188
childcare, 27, 143–44
Christian Family Movement, 177–78
civil disobedience, 7, 12, 34–35, 41–42, 52–53, 110, 152
civil rights, 16, 26, 52–53, 64, 112, 189; Civil Service Commission, 120; March on Washington, 42; Monroe Civil Rights Act of California, 122; *see also* discrimination, integration, racism
Coffin, Rev. William Sloan, 44
cold war, 44, 90
Committee for a Sane Nuclear Policy (SANE), 4, 194, 216
Committee of Liaison with Families of Prisoners of War, 43–44; *see also* POW
Committee of Responsibility, 161–62; *see also* Vietnam
communists: red-baiting, 7, 14, 51, 87, 91, 97, 98, 151, 178, 198, 214; *see also* Daily Worker, Dorothy Day, HUAC, McCarthy
concentration camps, 32–33, 70–71
conflict, 191
conflict resolution, non-violent, 28, 190–91
Congressional candidate, 51–52, 189–90
Congress of Industrial Organizations, 143; *see also* union
Congress of Racial Equality (CORE), 98

224

conscientious objectors, 28, 130; *see also* draft
conscription (National Training and Service Act), 103–4
consensus, 197
Consortium on Peace Research, Education and Development (COPRED), 190

Daily Worker, 97; *see also* communist
Day, Dorothy, 24, 25; *see also* communist
Dellinger, David, 44; *see also* POW
department of peace, 209
depression (1920s, 30s), 78, 96, 108, 150, 168
Detzer, Dorothy, 214; *see also* Nye Hearings
disarmament conference (Geneva, 1962), 197
disarmament education, 34, 41, 44; *see also* Riverside Church
discrimination: in sororities, 150; against women, 118–19
dissent, 34
draft (Vietnam): 123, 130, 135–36, 144–46, 152, 153

Eisenhower, Dwight, 74, 181
Einstein, Albert, 73
Equal Rights Amendment, 216
Espionage Act of 1917, 213
Evers, Medgar, 113
Executive Order 9066, 79

Fair Employment Practices Commission, 120; *see also* civil rights
Falk, Richard, 44; *see also* POW
farmworkers, 22, 26–27, 131; *see also* union
FBI: Japanese Americans, 78–79, 88, 187; Vietnam, 15–16
Federation of Architects, Engineers, Chemists and Technicians, 151; *see also* union
Fellowship of Reconciliation (FOR), 25, 188
feminist, feminism, 4, 28, 38, 41, 98, 217–18
Fisk University, 187
Ford, Gerald, 14
Four Lights, 213
Fourteen Point Peace Plan, 212; *see also* Woodrow Wilson

Frazier, Senator Lynn, 215
Free Speech Movement, 135
Friedan, Betty, 218
Friends. *See* Quakers, Religious Society of Friends
Fries, Gen. Amos, 214
Fuller, Buckminster, 207; *see also* utopia

Gandhi, Mahatma, 102
gays, 112
Geneva Accords (1954), 144
Geneva Disarmament Conference (1962), 197
Gestapo, 60, 61
Gore, Leroy, 38; *see* McCarthy
Gray Panthers, 134, 170
Gregory, Dick, 52–53

Hague, The, 211
Haight Ashbury, 110
Hanoi, 14, 44; *see also* Vietnam
Hiroshima, Nagasaki, 12, 82, 90, 134, 151, 187; *see also* Japan
Hiroshima (John Hersey), 134
Hispanics, 112, 171
Hitler, 32, 60, 70, 98, 202, 215; German opposition to, 70; Mein Kampf, 60
House Un-American Activities Committee (HUAC): 1950s, 86, 98; 1960s, 6, 13, 14, 197–98, 218; *see also* communist, McCarthy, Women's International League for Peace and Freedom, Women Strike for Peace
Hull House, 210; *see also* Jane Addams
Hunter College School of Social Work (Louis M. Rabinowitz School of Social Work), 39; *see also* social work, welfare, birth control

Indiana University, 97; *see also* integration
integration, 27, 98, 120–21, 151; *see also* civil rights, racism
International Congress of Women (1915, The Hague, Netherlands), 211; *see also* WILPF
International Peace Association Newsletter, 188
internment camps (Japanese American): Manzanar, 202–3; Puyallup, 79–80; Tanforan, Topaz, 87–89

invasion (World War II): of Holland, 60, 62–64; of Norway, 116

Japan: Army of Occupation, 82; invasion of China, 87; *see also* Hiroshima
Jewish Committee, Amsterdam, 61; *see also* Resistance, Holland
Jobs for Older Women, 134
Johnson, Lyndon, 25
Johnson, Mordecai, 98, 99

Kansas Journal, 103
Kellogg-Briand Act (1929), 69–70, 214
Kennedy, John F., 196
King Jr., Martin Luther, 26, 52, 65, 109, 110, 112, 113, 152
Korean War, 82–83
Kristallnacht, 62
Ku Klux Klan, 97–98, 164

Langley Aeronautical Laboratory (Langley, VA—later NASA), 118–20, 150–51; *see also* integration, union
Lawrence Livermore National Labs, 34–35, 129, 207; *see also* nuclear weapons research
League for Industrial Democracy, 168; *see also* socialism
League of Nations, 187, 212, 214
League of Women Shoppers, 169
League of Women Voters, 169, 187
Lenin (*State and Revolution*), 48
Letterman Army Hospital, 170
liberation theology, 24, 169, 178
Lincoln, Abraham, 136
Lincoln Brigade, 202; *see also* Spanish Civil War
loyalty oath (California, 1950), 48, 120, 151, 203–4

MacArthur, General Douglas, 181
McCarthy era (Senator Joseph), 14, 23, 38, 52, 64, 86, 104, 151, 178, 187; *see also* communist, HUAC
McNamara, Robert, Secretary of Defense, 40; *see also* Pentagon
Marx, Karl, 24
Mead, Margaret, 188
media, 41, 54, 134, 204–5
Minutemen (reactionary group), 162

Mobilization for Survival (1969), 42; *see also* Vietnam
"Moral Equivalent of War, The," William James, 210
"Moral Substitute for War, The," Jane Addams, 210–11
Movement for a New Society, 130–31
Muste, A. J., 28

napalm, 28, 68–70, 161; *see also* civil disobedience, Vietnam
National Association for the Advancement of Colored People (NAACP), 98, 99, 108, 123
National Conference on the Cause and Cure of War, 168, 212
National Organization for Women, 160
National Peace Academy; *see* United States Institute of Peace
National Training and Service Act, 103–4
Nazi, 61, 70, 202
New Deal, 169
New York School of Social Work, 168
Nicaragua, 207; *see also* Peace Brigade
Nisei Young Democratic Club, 87; *see also* communist/"red"-baiting
Nobel Peace Prize, 4
non-violence, 26, 28, 35, 169; non-violent revolution/social change, 163, 172–73
nuclear holocaust, 60, 73
Nuclear Test Ban Treaty, 128–29
nuclear weapons research, 42–43; *see also* Lawrence Livermore Labs
Nuremberg trials, 70, 71
Nye Congressional Hearings (1934), 214

oral history, 163–64
Oxford Pledge for Peace (1931), 215

Pacem in Terris (Papal Encyclical, 1962), 178; Conference, 178
pacifist, 25–26, 28, 54, 97, 202, 215; as activist, 172
Partial Test Ban Treaty (1963), 197
Paul, Alice, 142
peace atom, 104
Peace Brigade, 207; *see also* Nicaragua
peace churches, 209
Peace Mobile (Martin Luther King, Jr.), 163–64
peace movement: children, response to

mothers' activism, 13, 17, 40, 41, 42, 152, 171–72, 199; constituency, 73, 135; education for peace, 123–24, 138, 187–88; organization/organizing, 4–5, 13, 41, 171; solidarity, 35; unity, 138, 154–55, 160, 171, 181; women of color, 3, 40; women, middle-class women, 3, 12, 14, 40, 217; women, attitudes/characteristics of, 16, 17; women's empowerment, 16; women's movement, 13, 16, 188–89, 194–95; women's role in peace movement, 5–7, 12, 17, 28, 40–42, 45, 112, 114, 160, 165, 188, 209–10, 214, 219
peacenik, 68
Peace Pirates, 205–6; see also Planetary Citizens, Satellite Sailors
peace researchers and activists, 190–91
Pearl Harbor, 78, 87, 187; see also Japanese Americans, World War II
Pentagon, 40, 181
Planetary Citizenship, 206; see also Peace Pirates, Satellite Sailors
populist, progressive tradition (Wisconsin), 38
Potrero Neighborhood House (San Francisco), 111–12
prisoners of war (POWs), Vietnam, 14–15, 162; see also Committee of Liaison with Families of Prisoners of War
PTA, 128

Quaker, 48–49, 169, 186, 188, 197, 205; see also Friends, Religious Society of Friends)

racism: black, 39, 65, 97, 99, 108–9, 111, 121, 150, 178; Japanese-American, 83, 86–90, 202–3
Rankin, Jeanette, Jeanette Rankin Brigade, 40; see also Vietnam
religion (and peace), 172
Religious Society of Friends; see Friend, Quaker
representative democracy, 171
Resistance movement, World War II: general European, 215; in Germany, 61; in Holland, 60–64
revolution, 48, 54; Russian, 142, 169
Riverside Church, New York City, 41, 44; see also disarmament education

Rush, Benjamin, 180, 209
Russell, Bertrand, 194

Sacco and Vanzetti, 32, 143, 177
Saint Joseph Order, 22
SANE. See Committee for a Sane Nuclear Policy
San Francisco State, 170–71; see social work
Sarton, May (At Seventy), 172
Satellite Sailing, 206; see also Peace Pirates, Planetary Citizen
Sedition Act of 1918, 213
Seeger, Pete, 38, 72
segregation, 102–3, 121–22, 151, 187; see also civil rights
separate spheres theory, 5, 211, 214
socialism, 97, 168, 294; see also League for Industrial Democracy
social work, 39, 90, 272; see also Hunter College School of Social Work, welfare
Spanish Civil War, 32, 97, 186–87, 202; see also anti-fascist
Steffens, Lincoln, 142
Sterns, Marshall, 99
strontium-90, 13, 33, 40, 160, 196–97, 216; see also atmospheric testing
student movement (U.S.), 144; see also black students, draft, Vietnam
Student Non-Violent Coordinating Committee (SNCC), 39
Student Relocation Committee, 90
suffrage (Nineteenth Amendment, 1920), 142, 173, 210–11, 213

tax resistance, 172; see also civil disobedience
test ban treaty, 34; see also disarmament
Thomas, Norman, 28
Tokyo Rose (American equivalent), 89–90
Tuskegee Institute, 168

union organizing, 91, 119–20, 131, 143, 160, 169, 177
United Nations, 128; U.N. International Year of the Woman, 17; UNESCO, 188, 204; U.N. International Cooperation Year, 188
United States Institute of Peace, 179–81
utopia, 207; see Buckminster Fuller

Vietnam: 6–7, 14–16, 25, 83, 110, 130, 135–37, 144, 151–53, 161, 170, 189–90, 198–99, 216; Spring Offensive, 144; Vietnam Moratorium (1967), 153; Vietnam summer, 152; Vietnamese women, 43; Vietnamese Women's Union, 144; *see also* draft, non-violence, WILPF, WSP

voter registration, 102, 176

Walter-McKerron Act, 86, 151

war resister, 130; *see also* conscientious objection

welfare: department, San Francisco State, 170–171; system, 39, 90, 108, 168–69, 171; *see also* social work, depression

Wells, H. G., 219

Wilson, Dagmar, 14

Wilson, Woodrow, 212; *see also* Fourteen Point Peace Plan

Women's Action for Nuclear Disarmament (WAND), 4

Women's International League for Peace and Freedom (WILPF), 4–5, 34, 39, 83, 34, 90, 91, 104, 110, 129–30, 152, 153, 154, 160, 187, 188, 189; issues,
214–16; during the 20s and 30s, 214–15; during Korean War, 216; during World War II, 215–16; during Vietnam War, 216; founding meeting at the Hague, 211–12; post Vietnam, 216, 218–19; U. N. Non Governmental Organization (NG), 4

Women's Party, 142

Women's Peace Party (WPP), 210, 211–12; *see also* Four Lights

Women's Peace Union, 215

women's "shadow government," 164–65

Women Strike for Peace, 4–5, 12, 13, 14, 33, 40, 42, 43, 110, 134, 137, 160, 165, 188, 189, 194–98; founding and development, 216–19; (*see also* CIA)

World Jewish Congress (1942), 215

World Peace Council (1949, 1952), 49–50

World War I, 213; *see also* Espionage Act of 1917 and Sedition Act of 1918

World War II, 7, 136, 187, 215–16

World War III Memorial Wall, 91–92

Young People's Socialist League, 97; *see also* socialism

YWCA, 86, 160, 187; *see also* racism

The Editor

Judith Porter Adams lives in Menlo Park, California, and has a Ph.D. in English from Miami University, Oxford, Ohio. She is the director of the Stanford University Oral History Project and has been an affiliate scholar at the Institute for Research on Women and Gender at Stanford. She has served on the boards of the peace center and battered women's shelter in her community and is part of a volunteer video project that produces programming for local public-access cable TV, focusing on peace, justice, environmental, health, and other issues. A peace activist since the Vietnam War, she has directed the Women's Peace Oral History Project since 1979.